Pastoral Companion to the Roman Missal

PAUL TURNER

Pastoral Companion to the Roman Missal

PAUL TURNER

WLP 003240

ISBN 978-1-58459-514-4

Associate Publisher and Editor: Jerry Galipeau

Director of Publications: Mary Beth Kunde-Anderson

Copy Editor: Marcia T. Lucey

Design and Layout: Denise C. Durand

REGINALDO FOSTER
QVI AVCTOREM DOCVIT
NON MODO DE GRAMMATICA VERBISQVE
SED ETIAM PVLCHRITVDINE ARTEQVE
LINGVÆ LATINÆ
AVGENDO AMOREM EIVS RITVS ROMANI
ET MAGISTRIS

26 3.36
TwP

I wish to thank

Jerry Galipeau and Steve Janco,
   who brainstormed;
Mary Beth Kunde-Anderson, Michael Novak, Jennifer Odegard, and Alan Hommerding,
   who contributed;
Bruce Harbert,
   who included;
the people of Saint Munchin and Saint Aloysius,
   who endure;
God, who hears the prayers of the Church.

P.T.

Table of Contents

Ordinary Time 92

Foreword

The new English translation of the third Latin edition of *The Roman Missal* is about to be published, a work achieved after several years of close consultation between the English-speaking Episcopal Conferences of the world and the Holy See. During this time the process has been facilitated by the International Commission on English in the Liturgy (ICEL), whose eleven bishop members[1] have had the privilege of discovering anew some of the many hidden riches of the Church's liturgical and theological tradition.

Originally, of course, all these riches were preserved by the Church, and handed on from generation to generation in the Latin language. Today, the most widely spoken language in the Church is Spanish. However, English is the most widely spoken language in the world. And it was in the light of that growing phenomenon that, already at the time of the Second Vatican Council, a number of English-speaking bishops began to take account, with regard to the question of language, of the enormity of the task confronting them. In time, and in part because of their encouragement, a major change would come about in Church life, namely the celebrated shift from 1600 years of daily Latin usage to a vernacular liturgy. In this task, the great challenge, of course, was to preserve the beauty of previous liturgical texts and to maintain and ensure their catechetical effectiveness in transmitting the faith.

There is an ancient and important Latin tag that is often quoted in liturgical circles: *lex orandi, lex credendi!* In other words the way we pray gives shape to the things we believe. The bishops knew that, if the transition from Latin to English was to be brought about effectively, they would need to involve qualified people who would take all the care necessary to complete the task. And so it was that during the morning's coffee break at a coffee bar in the south transept of St Peter's basilica, near to St Josephat's altar, a small group of English-speaking bishops from several countries met to discuss how they could best do this. (Incidentally, the coffee bar was known as 'Bar Jona'!) The bishops held a meeting at the Venerable English College several days later, on 17 October 1963, where the International Commission on English in the Liturgy (ICEL) was born.

The result of that decision, all those years ago in 1963, has undoubtedly been something precious for the Church because, by creating a single English-speaking text for the celebration of Mass, we have been able to express, in the English-speaking world, our unity in faith around the one Eucharistic Altar of Sacrifice. English has become the new Latin. Today, English plays the role of an international language, the same role that Latin played in Europe a thousand years ago. And what's more, there are many scholars from non-English–speaking countries who use our English texts as the basis from which to prepare their own translations of the Missal. What is produced in English not only serves a wide constituency throughout the world but, more importantly, also serves the work of unity, of communion. Therefore it requires that the work be undertaken with the utmost care so that what is handed on is nothing other than the tradition of the Church which has been placed, in trust, into our keeping.

Soon after I had been elected the chairman of ICEL in 2002, I began to appreciate in a new way a text in St Paul's letters that I have cited ever since at every meeting of the Commission. This text is the earliest account we have in Sacred Scripture of the celebration of the Eucharist:

> I received from the Lord what I also delivered to you, that the Lord Jesus

on the night when he was betrayed took bread, and when he had given thanks, he broke it, and said, "This is my body which is for you. Do this in remembrance of me." In the same way also the cup, after supper, saying, "This cup is the new covenant in my blood. Do this, as often as you drink it, in remembrance of me." For as often as you eat this bread and drink the cup, you proclaim the Lord's death until he comes.[2]

I am struck by the care with which the Apostle recounts what happened at the Last Supper and the care with which he faithfully hands on this account as a great and precious treasure to the Church. This narrative gives witness to the motivation and pattern for what we do, week by week, and day by day in the Church—the celebration of the Mass following our Lord's own example and command. In the translation I have used, the Revised Standard Version, Saint Paul says that he 'delivered' this account to the Church at Corinth. Other versions say that he 'passed [it] on'[3] or 'handed [it] on'.[4] The Latin Bible uses here the word *tradidi*, a form of the word that has given us the English word 'tradition'. Saint Paul hands on a tradition that has continued across nearly two thousand years to this very day.

The last sixty years, since the end of the Second World War, have seen a massive questioning of tradition in the Western world. This is apparent, for example, in education, which has seen old disciplines and skills, what we might call received wisdom, give way to new methods and models. The questioning and even rejection of tradition is very visible in the decline of family life and the rise of new patterns of relationship. It can be seen in the arts with their constant exploration of new forms. It can be seen in the design of our buildings and our cities. And, not surprisingly, it can be seen in the ways in which we believe in and worship God, if we do so at all. Of course 'new' can mean better, but just because something is new does not necessarily mean that it is better.

Today, we are part of that process of absorption and appropriation. The Council articulated its response to the contemporary world most fully in its constitution *Gaudium et Spes*, but many of the themes of that document were also present, at least implicitly, in the first Constitution issued by the Council, *Sacrosanctum Concilium*, on the Sacred Liturgy.

It is often said that Pope John XXIII wanted to open the windows and let fresh air into the life of the Church. It is certainly true that the desire of the Council Fathers at Vatican II was to enable the Church to engage more effectively with the world and the world to engage with the Church. And the gift, first and last, which the Church has to pass on to the world is, of course, nothing other than Christ Jesus. We owe it to our Lord to make the gospel available to the people of our time. We need to preserve its unutterable mystery but, at the same time, to show that it makes sense: to reveal how much it has to offer. Pope Benedict XVI is giving us a lead in this. It is his view, often repeated, that the crisis at present besetting the Church in the West is fundamentally a crisis of worship, and that getting the liturgy right is the Church's most urgent task.

There are some people who think otherwise. They argue that, with all the other serious issues facing the Church in our time, to bother about tiny changes in the wording of the Mass is like rearranging the deckchairs on the *Titanic* or, if it's not too inappropriate an analogy, fiddling while Rome burns! But let us consider another view, namely, that the Church's central task is to worship God and to bring others to do the same, especially in the form of worship that Christ himself handed down to us. To put the same thought in another way, as did the Second Vatican Council, the Eucharist is the source and summit of the Church's life. This teaching was echoed by Pope John Paul II in his last encyclical, *Ecclesia de Eucharistia*, and it clearly follows that if there is something defective with our liturgy, then to varying degrees, damage will result.

Amongst the many things the bishops began to discuss at the Second Vatican Council, one thing became clear very early on: many of the Council Fathers wanted to see a much greater use of vernacular languages in the liturgy. Interestingly enough, the most persuasive voices in this regard came from those bishops who themselves were from the persecuted Churches of the world—the so-called Church of Silence. Not least among them were those bishops who were ministering from behind the Iron Curtain, the former Soviet Bloc. Their argument centred upon the fact that many priests were not allowed to teach or catechise publicly and therefore the only way of instructing their flocks would be through the use of their own language for the celebration of the sacraments. This is not an unimportant point and, indeed, is most relevant to our own day. It is not only what you say but also the way in which you say it that is important.

Liturgy and catechesis have more than a loose connection. They are, in fact, intertwined and interdependent. Their essential relationship was outlined by Pope John Paul II in his 1979 Apostolic Exhortation *Catechesi Tradendae*, referred to in English as Catechesis in Our Time. There he states:

> Catechesis is intrinsically linked with the whole of liturgical and sacramental activity, for it is in the sacraments, especially in the Eucharist, that Christ Jesus works in fullness for the transformation of human beings.[5]

The mutual service of liturgy to catechesis and catechesis to liturgy is fundamental to the Church's faith and life, as demonstrated in the *Catechism of the Catholic Church* and *The General Directory for Catechesis*.

Catechesis, of course, is about educating and instructing in the truths and ways of faith. Drawing upon *Catechesi Tradendae*, the *Catechism* tells us that:

> Quite early on, the name catechesis was given to the totality of the Church's efforts to make disciples, to help men and women believe that Jesus is the Son of God so that believing they might have life in his name, and to educate and instruct them in this life, thus building up the body of Christ.[6]

Or, in the words of Our Lord presented by Mark the Evangelist: "Go out to the whole world; and proclaim the Good News to the whole of creation!" [7]

Clearly, there is more to 'making disciples' than liturgical texts, but as the Second Vatican Council taught: "[…] the liturgy is the summit towards which the activity of the Church is directed; it is also the fount from which all her power flows."[8] Therefore, the liturgy quite clearly has a privileged place in the work of catechesis. And catechising requires language. When considering the much rehearsed phrase "the fully conscious and active participation in the liturgy,"[9] one question worth asking is this: Does this imply bringing the liturgy closer to the people or the people closer to the liturgy? It is not an unimportant question if somewhat enigmatic.

It is my belief that in the new translation of *The Roman Missal*, much has been achieved in opening up the liturgical treasury of the Church to the people of our time. Also achieved is a greater fidelity to the Scriptural allusions which have inspired these texts. A good example of this is the fuller translation of the *Domine non sum dignus* as: "Lord, I am not worthy that you should enter under my roof," with its reminiscence of the centurion who asked Jesus to heal his servant.

It is impossible to exaggerate the importance of the link between liturgy and Sacred Scripture, that link on which, of course, *Liturgiam authenticam* lays such emphasis. It was said of St Bernard of Clairveaux that he knew the Sacred Scriptures so well that his language was biblical — or, as our young people would say today, he began to 'speak Bible.' It is my belief that in using a translation that is more faithful to Sacred Scripture we are also teaching ourselves to speak Bible!

Father Paul Turner's book, *Pastoral Companion to The Roman Missal*, is not only timely, but will also provide us with a scholarly tool of major importance. It will help us to discover and understand better the riches that are contained in these wonderful texts which are now being handed on to us in fidelity for our nourishment and for the faith-filled vitality of the Church.

✝ Arthur Roche
Bishop of Leeds
24 July 2010
Feast of St Sharbel Makhluf

---

1. The Bishops representing the Episcopal Conferences of America, Australia, Canada, England and Wales, India, New Zealand, Pakistan, the Philippines, Scotland, and South Africa.

2. 1 Corinthians 11:23–26. Scripture text from *The Catholic Edition of the Revised Standard Version of the Bible*, copyright © 1965, 1966 by the Division of Christian Education of the National Council of the Churches of Christ in the United States of America. Used by permission. All rights reserved.

3. Jerusalem Bible

4. New English Bible

5. Excerpt from paragraph 23 of *Catechesi Tradendae* © 1979, *Libreria Editrice Vaticana*. Used with permission.

6. Excerpt from the English translation of the *Catechism of the Catholic Church* for use in the United States of America, copyright © 1994, United States Catholic Conference, Inc.—*Libreria Editrice Vaticana*. Used with permission.

7. Mark 16:15

8. Excerpts from *Vatican Council II, Volume I: The Conciliar and Post Conciliar Documents*, edited by Rev. Austin Flannery, O.P., copyright © 2007, Costello Publishing Company, Inc., Northport, NY, are used by permission of the publisher, all rights reserved. No part of these excerpts may be reproduced, stored in a retrieval system, or transmitted in any form or by any means—electronic, mechanical, photocopying, recording or otherwise—without express permission of Costello Publishing Company, Inc.

9. Ibid.

Introduction

The Roman Missal is the prayer book we use for the Roman Catholic Mass. This companion book will help you get the most out of the missal on Sundays.

The Roman Missal gathers all the predetermined words we say and actions we perform. Its scope is universal. Every Roman Catholic Mass in every country on earth uses the same book, though translated into a variety of languages.

Some words are not predetermined: the songs we may sing, the homily, the Prayer of the Faithful, and some commentaries, for example. But everything else comes from someplace, and that someplace is *The Roman Missal.*

Here are some highlights:

The Order of Mass: the script we follow at every celebration from the sign of the cross to the dismissal

The General Instruction of The Roman Missal: an explanation of the details—what to do, where to go, how to get there, and what to say

The presidential prayers: the prayers the priest says when he speaks to God on behalf of everyone else

The missal also contains the readings, although you would never know by consulting it. The readings are found in the *Lectionary for Mass*, published in four separate volumes. But if you look inside any of them, at the top of the title page, you'll find these words: "*The Roman Missal.*" The missal has two main divisions; one of them is the Lectionary. The other is the book that we used to call the Sacramentary, but which always bore the Latin title *Missale Romanum*. Today it is called *The Roman Missal.*

The Lectionary used to be combined with the rest of the missal into a single volume. The first book to bear the title *Missale Romanum* dates to 1474. It was revised after the Council of Trent in 1570. It underwent several updates in the succeeding centuries—always having the readings and prayers in the same volume. The most recent version of Trent's missal was published in 1962. After the Second Vatican Council this missal was revised and its contents divided in two. This had the practical advantage of putting the readings in a book to be used entirely at the ambo, and the other parts in a book for the presider's chair and the altar.

The division into two books also separated the contents in a more respectful manner. After all, the Bible is the word of God. The rest of the contents evolved as a fruit of the Church at prayer over the word of God. It is special to us, but it is not the same as scripture.

After the Second Vatican Council, the revised *Missale Romanum* was published in 1970, and the complete Sacramentary in English was published in 1974. The following year, the Vatican published a second Latin edition of the *Missale Romanum*, bringing its contents up to date with developing legislation. The revised Sacramentary was published in English in 1985. The first translation was a heroic effort to give English-speakers their own texts for the very first time. Within a few years, though, improvements were being sought. In 1998 the International Commission on English in the Liturgy (ICEL), which had prepared the first translation, completed a lengthy process of revision. But the Vatican did not approve that work for two reasons: It released new rules for translation in 2001, and it published the third Latin edition of the missal in 2002. Those factors caused ICEL to start again the monumental task of translating everything from Latin into English. In 2008 the Vatican reprinted the Latin missal with a few more corrections and additions, and the results were finally published in English in 2011.

Theory of Translation

The most obvious changes pertain to the translation. The first English version was freer than the revised one. A closer adherence to the Latin original reveals a deeper meaning, a wider reliance on scriptural allusions, and a closer connection with contemporary Christians who speak other languages, as well as the generations of believers who have gone before us.

The English-language *Roman Missal* of 2011 looks very different from the English-language Sacramentary of 1985 that it replaces. The reason has to do with the theory of translation that resulted in the two books. Just consider the first memorial acclamation as an example. "Christ has died, Christ is risen, Christ will come again" in the Sacramentary is based on the same Latin sentence as "We proclaim your Death, O Lord, and profess your Resurrection until you come again" in the revised missal. The Latin has not changed, but the difference in English is vast because of the new rules requiring a closer adherence to the Latin original.

The original Latin texts for the missal span the entire history of Christianity. Some are direct quotes from the Bible, such as the Lord's Prayer and all of the greetings. Some come from the third or fourth century, such as the preface dialogue. Most of the presidential prayers come from the Hadrian Sacramentary in the eighth century, the Gelasian Sacramentary in the seventh century, and the Verona Sacramentary in the sixth century—and many of those prayers are thought to be much older, but preserved in those volumes because of their continued use, poetic structure, and spiritual meaning. Some parts of the Mass come from the late Middle Ages, such as the private prayers of the priest. Some elements of the penitential rite came with the 1570 missal. Other enhancements came with the Second Vatican Council, such as an expansion of the Eucharistic Prayers. The post-Vatican II missal reached back into this long tradition and restored quite a number of prayers that had not been in use for centuries. Now with the 2002 missal, even more of these ancient prayers were added to the repertoire. Some new composi-tions appeared for the first time as well, such as a few of the prayers over the people. Among the additions in 2008 were additional formulas for the dismissal that concludes the Mass. These are being heard in English for the very first time.

The revised translation has us going back to the work that was done after Vatican II. It has re-examined the ancient and modern texts that scholars of the time included in the Mass. The reason they sound different to us has to do with the principles of translation, but not with their content. Almost everything you hear in the revised translation is identical to what has been in existence since the post-Vatican II missal first appeared in 1970. There are relatively small changes to the contents.

Contents

The contents of the 2002 *Roman Missal* slightly revise the first post-Vatican II missal. The basic outline has not changed, but the parts have been enhanced. The work is so vast that few people take advantage of its many parts. It takes a careful eye to see these changes, but they are worth noting.

Introductory Material

The introductory material is in ten parts. These sections lay the groundwork for what follows.

The Decree of the Sacred Congregation for Divine Worship. This is the original short decree authorizing the use of the revised missal after the Second Vatican Council. The decree is dated Holy Thursday, 1970.

Decree Concerning the Second Typical Edition. Another decree from the same congregation, this one introduced the changes in the second edition of the missal. The responsibilities of some ministers had evolved, some new formulas appeared, and some other parts received a light retouching. The decree is dated Holy Thursday, 1975.

Decree Concerning the Third Typical Edition. By this time, the group responsible for the decree had been renamed the Congregation for Divine Worship and the Discipline of the Sacraments, but it is essentially the same group of the pope's liturgical advisors. This decree summarizes the changes in the third edition of the missal: a revised *General Instruction*, the coherence of this book with other recently published liturgical books, the expanded calendar of saints, and additional Eucharistic Prayers, for example. The decree is dated Holy Thursday of the Jubilee Year, 2000.

United States of America. This is the text of the *recognitio* by which the Congregation for Divine Worship and the Discipline of the Sacraments in Rome approves the translation of the revised missal for the United States. It is dated March 26, 2010, even though the text was not finalized for another nine months. That is the date on which the *recognitio* was granted, and the text as it stood was presented to Pope Benedict XVI the following months, but further corrections were required before the missal was able to be published in the United States with corrections to the text, local adaptations to the *General Instruction of the Roman Missal*, and the inclusion of local saints in the general calendar.

Decree of Publication. This is the decree by which the United States Conference of Catholic Bishops affirms that the book is the one duly approved by the respective authorities and processes. It establishes the First Sunday of Advent 2011 as the implementation date. This decree was dated August 15, 2010, several months before the final texts became available.

Apostolic Constitution. Earlier than the preceding documents of this section, this decree by Pope Paul VI authorized the use of the revised missal. It is dated Holy Thursday, 1969.

The General Instruction of The Roman Missal. Of all the introductory sections of the missal, this is the one most often consulted. It is the how-to document, explaining who does what, when, where, and how at Mass in the Roman Catholic Church. It is so important that when the missal was published in Latin in 2002, a provisional English translation was released immediately so that parishes would know what it contains. The version that appears in the revised English missal has polished the translation, but the contents have not been altered since 2002.

Norms for the Distribution and Reception of Holy Communion Under Both Kinds in the Dioceses of the United States of America. These norms, which include more decrees from the Congregation for Divine Worship and the Discipline of the Sacraments in Rome and the United States Conference of Catholic Bishops, were established in 2002. There is nothing new here, except that now they are more accessible, published not in a separate document, but within the missal.

Universal Norms of the Liturgical Year and Calendar. Here is the way to figure out what days fall where, and which days have rank over others. It opens with a letter by which Pope Paul VI introduced the new calendar of feasts and saints in 1969. Among other changes, he discontinued days like Septuagesima Sunday (three Sundays before Ash Wednesday) and moved the date for observing the Solemnity of Our Lord Jesus Christ, the King of the Universe.

General Roman Calendar. Arranged chronologically through the year, these are the days that appear on the universal calendar. The dates have been adjusted to include the adaptations and expansions pertaining to the United States of America; for example, the date for the Epiphany of the Lord and the inclusion of St. Elizabeth Ann Seton. This section concludes with a paragraph describing the Special Day of Prayer approved for the United States. This day is similar in intent to the ember days and rogation days of the pre-Vatican II calendar. Every diocese within the United States may expand this with its own special days of prayer.

Table of Days. This chart shows you at a glance when Advent begins, when Ash Wednesday falls, the date for Easter, and a selection of other useful occasions. It is a table of moveable feasts. The column marked "Dominical Letter" tells you what day of the week January 1 will be that year, and hence the day of the week for the rest of the dates that year. Whenever the red capital letter A appears, you know that January 1 is a Sunday. Lower-case b means it will be a Monday, and so on. Leap years require two letters because the system of parallel calendars adjusts after each February 29 for the remainder of that year. The column marked "Sunday Cycle" gives you two letters because the new letter comes into force on the First Sunday of Advent before that year is out. This concludes the missal's introductory material.

Proper of Time

Here you find the prayers and antiphons that change from day to day according to the liturgical year. You will also find instructions concerning the Gloria and the Creed. The material is arranged by seasons, so you have to know what Sunday it is in order to find the right place. The pages appear exactly as they did in the 1985 Sacramentary, but there is a little more information here, and the texts on each page are arranged in better sense lines. You may notice the elimination of introductory lines such as "Pray, brothers and sisters" before the prayer over the offerings, and "Let us pray" before the prayer after Communion. The font size for the antiphons used to be smaller than the ones for the prayers, but they were always the same size in the Latin editions of the missal after Vatican II. This perhaps indicates the significance of all the texts on the page, even though the antiphons may be exchanged with more popular hymnody.

Advent, Christmas, Lent, Easter, and Ordinary Time are all here, followed by the solemnities that appear during Ordinary Time. In practice, Lent interrupts Ordinary Time, which resumes after the Easter season. But all the Ordinary Time Sundays are grouped together, as they were in the Sacramentary. Sometimes a week of Ordinary Time disappears because the calendar has to adjust for the movement of Christmas and Easter. The solemnities of Ordinary Time are still gathered in the back of this section, where they are notoriously hard to find. Unfortunately the *Lectionary for Mass* arranges these solemnities in a different way. Just because you can find the Solemnity of Our Lord Jesus Christ, the King of the Universe in one book doesn't mean you can find it in the same place in the other. But everything you need is all there.

The celebration of Pentecost now has an optional extended form for the Vigil Mass. These prayers were found in the supplement to the missal in Latin, but they have been helpfully integrated here. These prayers are not obligatory, but you may extend the Saturday night Mass on Pentecost weekend with additional scripture readings and these prayers. This will not be feasible in most parishes, but it is an option worth remembering.

Most of the prayers in this section are over a thousand years old—many are fifteen hundred years old. Some people objected to a seemingly obsessive conviction that the new translation should faithfully represent the Latin originals. They also lament the loss of the alternative opening prayers, which freely paraphrased the originals. Well, imagine having a letter from a foreign relative even a hundred years old. Wouldn't you want it translated as accurately as possible? The names of the authors of the original prayers are lost to the passage of time, but their work was so artfully composed that succeeding generations have all passed down these gems. We are receiving them now all polished up, in order to hear the echo of how they sounded to earlier generations of Christians.

The alternative opening prayers were composed by ICEL for the English-language Sacramentary. They had a younger history and a narrower use than the other prayers in the missal. Although many communities have prayed them effectively, they have been discontinued in favor of the classic prayers being offered by other countries around the world.

The Order of Mass

It starts with the assembly of the people and it ends in their dismissal. The Order of Mass contains the words and actions assigned to a variety of ministers and the faithful for the proper execution of the Eucharist on any day of the year. The heart of the missal, it fittingly appears right in the middle of the book. It is one of the few places you find tabs. You need them to work your way quickly to certain parts of the Mass.

Most priests, deacons, and people have had their lines memorized, and have not needed to read everything from the book. But the revised translation inaugurated a period of confusion. Familiarity will increase, but for now some presiders do not trust their memory and rely on the Order of Mass to help them through. Better to have the book in front than to improvise something that does not belong here.

The revised missal includes a more thorough array of musical chants. *The General Instruction of The Roman Missal* promotes the singing of dialogues in the Mass, and the third edition provides more generous musical notation. It is hoped that these chants will be shared by English-speaking Catholics around the world.

The Eucharistic Prayer

The Order of Mass is interrupted after the preparation of the gifts to present a special section on the Eucharistic Prayer. Here is where you will find the four main Eucharistic Prayers, exactly where they appeared in the 1985 Sacramentary.

This section is introduced with the parts of the Eucharistic Prayer that stay the same: the preface dialogue and the *Sanctus*. It was quite an innovation for the Mass of the Second Vatican Council to put the heading "Eucharistic Prayer" on top of these pages. In the former missal, the "canon" of the Mass began after the *Sanctus*. But our understanding is that the entire prayer is Eucharistic. It begins with the preface dialogue and it concludes with an amen.

The variable prefaces are all arranged here. They follow the same logical sequence of the 1985 Sacramentary. They start with the seasons of the year. They continue with Sundays in Ordinary Time. The Sacramentary followed this with "weekday" prefaces, because they are used on weekdays in Ordinary Time. Actually, the original Latin edition called them "common prefaces," which was a subheading in the pre-Vatican II missal. They appeared near the end of the prefaces, just before the ones assigned to Masses for the Dead. That is where they are today. They are still used for weekdays in

Ordinary Time, but they carry the traditional generic title.

Following the prefaces for Sundays in Ordinary Time, you find two for the Most Holy Eucharist, and then those appropriate for saints. These are arranged in a kind of hierarchy, starting with Mary and the apostles. Then come two prefaces intended for solemnities and feasts of saints, such as the day that your parish church celebrates its titular feast. If your patron is observed elsewhere as a memorial or an optional memorial, the day is treated as a solemnity in your community, and you use the appropriate preface on that day. There are now not one, but two options for the prefaces of holy martyrs, and these are followed by one of holy pastors and another of virgins and religious. After that come the common prefaces, followed by those for the dead.

The prefaces for certain feast days are available on the same page where you find the other presidential prayers for that feast. Many of the Lenten prefaces, the ones for the Immaculate Conception, Christmas, the Baptism of the Lord, the Presentation of the Lord, Pentecost, Holy Trinity, the Sacred Heart, John the Baptist, Peter and Paul, the Transfiguration, the Assumption, the Exaltation of the Holy Cross, Angels, and Christ the King are all found on the same page where you find the collect, the prayer over the offerings, and the prayer after Communion for the same day. This is a more sensible arrangement of the material for that day.

After the prefaces you find the four main Eucharistic Prayers. The first is the one with the longest pedigree in the Roman Rite: the Roman Canon. Its earliest appearance is in the writings of Saint Ambrose of Milan in the fourth century, though it has evolved quite a bit since then. In Latin the first word following the *Sanctus* is *Te*, and medieval sacramentaries usually carried a striking illumination of Jesus on the cross to decorate the first letter of that word. The custom is revived because the revised English translation now starts after the *Sanctus* with the word "To." The difference is that the Vatican II missal places the preface dialogue and the

Sanctus on the same page, which breaks the connection between the iconography and the text. The group preparing the Vatican II missal did not want people to think that the Eucharistic Prayer begins after the *Sanctus*. It starts with the dialogue.

Eucharistic Prayers II, III, and IV follow in order, just as they did in the Sacramentary. We take these for granted. The inclusion of these prayers in the Roman Rite was one of the great contributions of the Council. For hundreds of years prior to that time the Canon was the only Eucharistic Prayer that Roman Catholics used. The variety available today is generous.

Communion Rite and Rite of Conclusion

The next sections carry different titles, but they are simply the continuation of the Order of Mass. The arrangement of material is exactly as it appeared in the 1985 Sacramentary. A careful reader will note the inclusion of more musical notation to promote the singing of some of the dialogues of the Mass.

You will notice at the very end some new formulas for the dismissal. We have always had a selection of these in the United States, but there is now a selection in Latin being translated more uniformly into the vernacular throughout the world. These appeared here and again in a supplement in the Latin edition, but they appear only here in the English translation.

Blessings at the End of Mass and Prayers over the People

Solemn blessings and prayers over the people may replace the simple blessing the priest gives at the end of Mass. The deacon or the priest asks all present to bow their heads. The priest extends his hands over the people and pronounces the blessing.

Solemn blessings are almost all in three parts. The people respond "Amen" to each section of the prayer. The choices are arranged by season of the year, then by saints, and finally by occasion.

Of the twenty-eight prayers over the people, only two are designated for saints' days. The others may be used at any time. Throughout the season of Lent, a prayer over the people is recommended for each day's Mass. We have a record of that practice as early as the seventh century. The Church now restores it in the twenty-first century.

Chants for the Eucharistic Prayer

All four of the main Eucharistic Prayers appear a second time here, now with musical notation. This entire section promotes having the priest sing these prayers on occasion. In the Sacramentary, these settings appeared in the back of the book. Now they take a place right after the Order of Mass, which suggests their importance.

The main difference in these settings concerns Eucharistic Prayer I. In the 1985 Sacramentary, the length of this prayer apparently worried those who prepared the musical setting, so only a portion of it was set to music. The rest of it was to be recited. Now all of Eucharistic Prayer I is set to music in a simple tone, which affirms the integrity of the entire prayer as it encourages singing. The middle section of Eucharistic Prayer I is set to music a second time using the solemn tone.

The Order of Mass with the Participation of a Single Minister

If the priest is saying Mass with only one other person present, he uses this section of the missal. Obviously, a normal Mass is designed for the participation of an entire assembly. But circumstances may exist in which the priest has only one other person present. This section addresses that need.

Appendix to the Order of Mass

After the first publication of the Sacramentary in 1974, the Vatican approved additional Eucharistic Prayers. The ones bearing the theme of reconciliation were eventually incorporated into an appendix in the back of the 1985 Sacramentary, together with those for Masses with Children. The one for Masses for Various Needs and Occasions—in its four different forms—was published separately. Now the Eucharistic Prayers for reconciliation and for various needs have been inserted as an appendix to the Order of Mass, earlier in the book.

You may still use the Eucharistic Prayers for Masses with Children, but these will be re-translated and published separately. They were removed from the Latin edition of the missal because you would never use those prayers in Latin—no group of children on earth would understand them. There are circumstances when the Vatican II Mass is celebrated in Latin, and any of the other Eucharistic Prayers may be used in that language. The *Missale Romanum* is a practical altar book, not a repository of interesting texts. Although the children's Eucharistic Prayers exist in Latin, they were published for the purposes of study and translation into other languages—not for the purpose of usage. Because they will be published separately in Latin, they will be published separately in English.

Proper of Saints

The calendar of saints is arranged here month by month. All the prayers and antiphons that pertain to each saint's day in the universal calendar are here. Episcopal conferences add to this section those saints celebrated in their own region. The patron saints of your diocese and parish may not be listed among those in the general or national calendar. You draw those texts from the next section, the commons, unless the Vatican has approved other texts that your bishop has prepared for local usage.

Commons

The commons are used when no other texts are available for the particular celebration at hand. The first set is to be used on the anniversary of the dedication of a church. If this is the anniversary of the church where you are worshiping, the first option is chosen, and the day is treated as a solemnity on the calendar. If it is the anniversary of some other church, such as the cathedral of your diocese, then you use the second option.

The complete list of saints recognized by the Catholic Church is published in the *Roman Martyrology*. If your patron saint is not on the general calendar, you will surely find the date

in the *Martyrology*. When the missal offers no proper texts for any saint you wish to celebrate on any given day, you turn to the Common of Saints for help. These are arranged in hierarchical order: Mary, the martyrs, pastors, doctors of the Church, virgins, and other men and women saints. Subcategories group these prayers according to the season of the year or the ministry of the saint. If the day for your patron saint falls during Ordinary Time, you may observe it with these texts on the nearest Sunday.

Ritual Masses

Here you find the texts for the Masses when you are celebrating something else—the rites of Christian initiation, anointing of the sick, viaticum, ordination, marriage, blessing abbots and abbesses, consecrating virgins, professing religious life, instituting lectors and acolytes, or dedicating a church and an altar. Most of this material was in the 1985 Sacramentary, but there are a couple of changes. The Mass for anointing the sick was in an appendix in the Sacramentary because it did not appear in the *Missale Romanum*. Now it has been brought forward, and the sequence of rites has been lightly rearranged. You used to find the texts for viaticum (giving Communion to the dying) right after the ones for ordination! Now viaticum follows the anointing of the sick, and ordination precedes marriage and Masses for religious orders. There seems to be a hierarchy here too, proceeding from sacraments to sacramentals: bishop, priest, deacon, marriage, religious life, lectors and acolytes.

Masses and Prayers for Various Needs or Circumstances

This heading is self-explanatory, and all the material from the 1985 Sacramentary is still here, though it is arranged differently. Two categories (civil needs and various public needs) have been combined. Whether you have a wedding anniversary, bad weather, or just a need for more self-restraint, you'll find Masses and prayers here.

The collects in this section may be used outside of Mass for some other occasion that calls for a prayer relative to its theme. You may start a meeting, a class, or a meal with one of these. Not every heading carries a complete suite of presidential prayers for the Mass. If you are celebrating Mass with one of these solo collects, you supply the other presidential prayers from somewhere else.

Votive Masses

Some Mass texts are set aside for devotional purposes. They commemorate certain saints, titles of Jesus, or mysteries of the Church. New to this section is the set of texts for Divine Mercy. These, however, are not to be used on Divine Mercy Sunday, when the texts for the Second Sunday of Easter take precedence.

Masses for the Dead

Here are collected the prayers we say at Masses for the Dead. First among them are funeral Masses. The texts in the *Order of Christian Funerals* may still be used, but these options are also offered.

Special prayers exist for the anniversary of someone's death, as well as various other circumstances. There are also prayers for deceased ministers of diverse categories, as well as relatives and those who died after a long illness or together as spouses.

Appendices

The chant announcing the birth of Jesus Christ has been added to the missal in the United States from the Roman Martyrology, where it is traditionally found. The first appendix gives a variety of musical tones for chanting parts of the Mass. This is where you find the formulas for singing dialogues, prayers, and readings from scripture. The music for announcing the movable feasts of the liturgical year is also here. This may be sung on Epiphany, which falls during the first week of the new calendar year.

The Rite for the Blessing and Sprinkling of Water is the second appendix. Users of the 1985 Sacramentary saw this among the options for the penitential rite much earlier in the book among the texts for the Order of Mass. In the Latin missal, this blessing has always appeared here—even before the Second Vatican Council. Its location in the appendix is the return of an earlier custom, not an innovation.

The Rite of Deputing a Minister to Distribute Holy Commnion on a Single Occasion is the third appendix. It is to be used on occasions when you have too few Communion ministers and too many communicants. A priest may appoint a minister on the spot for that one occasion.

The fourth appendix is the Rite of Blessing a Chalice and a Paten within Mass. Theoretically, you could bless a chalice and paten outside of Mass, but *The Roman Missal* is designed for use at Mass, so it does not include other such texts. If you have a new chalice and paten, blessing them at Mass in the presence of the community who will share Communion from them is a good idea.

The fifth appendix is a collection of sample formularies for the Universal Prayer, or the Prayer of the Faithful.

The sixth appendix has been added to the missal in the United States. It contains the sample invocations for the penitential act that used to appear in the Order of Mass in the Sacramentary. These are virtually the same; only the location is different.

The last appendix is a collection of sample formulas for the Prayer of the Faithful. They are just samples, but you may find them handy when someone has not prepared special intentions for the day.

Preparation for Mass, Thanksgiving after Mass

In the very back of the missal is a selection of prayers that the priest may say before or after Mass. These traditional devotional prayers may be used or omitted. Some of them—such as the *Anima Christi* and the Hail Mary—enjoy wide usage in the prayer life of Catholics.

The missal concludes with several indices. The first lists the celebrations of the liturgical year in alphabetical order. If you need a prayer for St. Aloysius, for example, and you don't remember where it is, you can find a reference to it here. The second is an index of prefaces. This is more necessary now than in the past because the prefaces are spread throughout the missal; they are not all gathered in one place. The final index is a general one for the entire book.

The contents of the missal are extensive, and they represent only part of the prayer tradition of the Roman Catholic Church. More texts are found in other books from the liturgical library: the Liturgy of the Hours, the rites of the sacraments, and the *Book of Blessings*, for example.

How to Use This Companion

The purpose of the book you are now reading is to help you get the most out of *The Roman Missal* on Sundays. In writing this book, I have presumed that you will be consulting the missal throughout. It will be hard to make sense of many comments here unless you are also looking there.

Each section begins with a seasonal overview. It will give you a few tips about celebrating these liturgies in your parishes—some announcements to consider, some practices to think over. It may steer you to other helpful places in the liturgical library of the Roman Catholic Church.

I have laid out the material according to the liturgical year, just as the missal has. You will find for each Sunday a commentary that should open your eyes to the contents of the missal for that day.

For example, I'm telling you about the origins of the antiphons and prayers. You may not be able to tell a Verona from a Gelasian, but that really doesn't matter. I mostly want you to know that the texts we use at Mass did not just fall out of the sky, nor were they conjured up helter-skelter by a seminarian looking for a summer job. They have a rich history. They

have been handed down to us through generations of our ancestors. I want you to value the prayers for their antiquity as well as for their meaning.

I'm giving you lots of scriptural citations. Many of the prayers and prefaces were inspired by passages from the Bible. I'd like you to know where they come from. I hope this will enhance your work whether you are preaching, catechizing, planning a liturgy, or praying at home with the prayers of the Church. You can deepen your appreciation of these texts by looking up their biblical background.

I have included a section on the Lectionary. I'm using that to make connections between the readings of a particular Sunday with sections of the missal. In some cases, this may help a presider decide which preface and blessing to use on a particular weekend. It may help catechists explain the biblical roots of the parts of the Mass, for example when they see in the second reading a line that one of the Eucharistic Prayers includes. I decided not to force these connections. I'm including only the ones that are very clear. You will see more—for example, thematic relationships between certain prayers over the people and the readings of a particular day. I have not done that kind of work because you have the freedom to choose and the duty to apply your insights to our weekly prayer.

I've also written a suggested introduction and conclusion to the Prayer of the Faithful for each Sunday of the three-year cycle of readings. These imitate the style of the presidential prayers in the missal, and are meant as aids to the presider. You don't have to use these, but they are here if you are interested in them. Just a little gift.

The book you are holding now is only a guide, a pastoral companion to help you out Sunday by Sunday. The book you want to know best is the other one: *The Roman Missal*.

ADVENT

The new liturgical year begins with the season of Advent, a time when we await the second coming of Christ by recalling events leading up to his first coming at Bethlehem. Special readings and prayers, music and vesture, art and environment express this purpose.

The playing of musical instruments and the use of Advent decorations "should be marked by a moderation that reflects the character of this season" (*Ceremonial of Bishops*, 236). Less is more. Christmas decorations will look all the more spectacular.

Choose vesture for priests and deacons that will help set this season apart. If you have more than one set of violet vestments, you may wish to choose one that you can repeat throughout this season, and then use a different one when Lent gets here.

The Gloria is omitted throughout Advent. Exceptions are made for solemnities and feasts, such as the Immaculate Conception.

A sample formulary for the Prayer of the Faithful can be found in the missal's fifth appendix. It may be used on any Sunday as is, or it may inspire you to compose your own prayers.

Eucharistic Prayer IV is not to be used during Advent because its preface should not be replaced by a seasonal one. Any of the other Eucharistic Prayers may be used. Eucharistic Prayer II has an advantage if you want this season to feel pared down and simple, as a contrast to the coming celebration of Christmas. If you want to highlight the penitential nature of the season, you may use one of the Eucharistic Prayers for Masses for reconciliation. You are permitted to use an Advent preface with one of those prayers.

The solemn blessing for Advent may be prayed throughout the season. It asks that we might be made holy by the radiance of Christ's advent; granted faith, hope and charity; and enriched with eternal life when he comes again. This was composed from two different Advent blessings in the Hadrian Supplement. Unused for many centuries, it was added to the missal after the Second Vatican Council.

There is an alternative solemn blessing for Advent in the *Collection of Masses of the Blessed Virgin Mary*, p. 181. It may be used at any time, but it would probably be most appropriate on the Fourth Sunday, which always mentions Mary in the Gospel.

First Sunday of Advent

Overview

The blessing of the Advent wreath may take place after the general intercessions. See the *Book of Blessings* (1517–1520). It gives an introduction, responses for the people, and sample petitions. There are two options for the blessing prayer. Neither calls for the use of holy water. The first candle is lighted after the prayer. Any purple candle is fine. Anyone may light this candle; it need not be the priest. If you bless the wreath at the first weekend Mass, you really don't have to bless it again at the other Masses. You may simply light the first candle before the liturgy begins.

Ideally the music today should emphasize our expectation for the second coming of Christ. Hymns about John the Baptist are more appropriate the next two Sundays. "O Come, O Come, Emmanuel" and other songs based on the O Antiphons—ideally—should be reserved for the last week of this season.

If the Solemnity of the Immaculate Conception (December 8) falls this week, be sure to announce the times for Masses this weekend.

Parishioners are going to want to know the schedule of Christmas Masses and confessions. Include it in the parish bulletin and on the Web site. Send it out in a Christmas card. Get an e-mail ready to send out several times during the next few weeks.

Entrance Antiphon

This is the same antiphon that has continuously opened the First Sunday of Advent since at least the eighth century. The key word is "hope," which appears in the last line. On the lips of Christians, this antiphon asks God to fulfill the expectations of those who hope for the coming of Christ.

Collect

The post-Vatican II missal replaced the collect from the 1962 missal with this one. The earliest extant version of this prayer comes from the Gelasian Sacramentary. It began as a prayer after Communion for use at any time during Advent. A few small changes were made for the 1970 missal. For example, where the present prayer refers to "your faithful," the original prayer had "all your family." Making this prayer the collect for the First Sunday of Advent was a happy innovation. It contains two clear allusions to passages from Matthew 25: the parable of the wise virgins, and the separation of sheep and goats—right and left—at the final judgment.

LECTIONARY

In the Gospel of Year A, the expression "the Son of Man will come" is echoed in the Collect: "your Christ . . . at his coming."

In Year B, the first words of the second reading are one of the options the priest may use when he greets the people at the opening of any Mass (Order of Mass, 2). This same greeting is repeated many times throughout the New Testament.

In Year C's Gospel, the words "your redemption is at hand" are echoed in today's Prayer over the Offerings: "the prize of your eternal redemption." The phrase "coming in a cloud with power and great glory" is repeated in the preface: "when he comes again in glory and majesty."

Prayer over the Offerings

Today's prayer first appeared in the Verona Sacramentary as an option for use during the month of July. The words have remained unchanged since the sixth century.

Preface

The first preface of Advent was newly composed for the 1970 missal. Previous *Roman Missals* had no special preface for Advent. Both Advent prefaces in today's missal are new, and you use the first today because it sets the tone for the season by mentioning the two comings of Christ. The preface uses a vocabulary inspired by many passages in the New Testament. The majesty of Christ is noted in Matthew 19:28, 24:30, and 25:31, as well as in Luke 9:26 and 21:27. The second coming is also presaged in Luke 12:35–36, Acts 1:10–11, and Revelation 1:5–7. The watchfulness of the Church appears in Romans 8:19–21 and 2 Peter 3:13. God's manifest work appears in Colossians 1:26–27.

Communion Antiphon

This antiphon has been in use on this Sunday since at least the eighth century. There is a parallelism in Latin that is difficult to render exactly in English. The verbs in the two clauses are identical. "The Lord will bestow his bounty, and our earth shall yield its increase."

Prayer after Communion

This is a new composition for the 1970 missal, but it conflates two prayers that appeared in the Verona Sacramentary, one for the Ascension and another on the anniversary of a bishop's consecration. Somehow they work for the themes of this day.

Blessing

You may use the solemn blessing for Advent. *See p. 1* above.

PRAYER OF THE FAITHFUL

Year A

We have come rejoicing to the house of the Lord. With thankful hearts we present our needs.

— *Intercessions* —

O God,
who judge works of darkness
and offer the armor of light,
come to the rescue of your people.
Through Christ our Lord.

Year B

Let us turn to the face of the Lord, and we shall be saved.

— *Intercessions* —

O God,
whose time of coming we do not know,
make us watchful and grant our prayers.
Through Christ our Lord.

Year C

We lift up our souls to the Lord, who is good and upright.

— *Intercessions* —

Make us vigilant, O God;
hear our prayers
and give us strength to stand
    before the Son of Man.
Who lives with you for ever and ever.

Second Sunday of Advent

Overview

You do not need to conduct any special ceremony around lighting the second candle of the Advent wreath. It is sufficient to have two purple candles burning before Mass begins.

This is a good Sunday to sing hymns about John the Baptist. He appears in the Gospel each year on this day.

You may want to do something to draw attention to images of John the Baptist today and next Sunday. If you have a statue or a stained glass window, try to do something with lighting or decoration to draw attention to the saint who will figure into the Gospels this week and next.

The missal includes several prayers to say privately in preparation for Mass. The first is the prayer of Saint Ambrose, whose memorial is observed on December 7.

If the Solemnity of the Immaculate Conception (December 8) falls this week, be sure to announce the times for Masses this weekend.

Entrance Antiphon

This antiphon is the same one that has been in use since at least the eighth century. It promises that "the Lord will come."

Collect

The earliest extant version of this prayer appeared in the Gelasian Sacramentary among those assigned to Advent. It refers to the worshipers as those who "set out in haste to meet your son."

Prayer over the Offerings

The earliest version of this prayer is from the same Advent section of the Gelasian Sacramentary that gives us today's collect. After the Council of Trent, it was assigned to this position on this day. Today we still use it on the Second Sunday, but also on every Tuesday and Friday of Advent before December 17.

Preface

Use the first Advent preface again today.

Communion Antiphon

This antiphon was in place already in the eighth century. It is chosen for Advent because the singer of these lines has seen that joy that "comes" from God.

Prayer after Communion

As with the other presidential prayers, this one originally comes from the Advent section of the Gelasian Sacramentary. The Hadrian Sacramentary had assigned it to the Second

LECTIONARY

In Year B the second reading includes the phrase "since you await these things," which is echoed in the preface: "the great promise in which now we dare to hope." The Communion antiphon is taken from the first reading in Year C.

Sunday of Advent, where it has remained ever since. We also use it on every Tuesday and Friday of Advent before December 17.

Blessing

You may use the solemn blessing for Advent.

PRAYER OF THE FAITHFUL

Year A

To God, in whom justice shall flourish and from whom peace is full, we present our needs.

— Intercessions —

Send us hope, O God of encouragement, and may our harmony bring you glory. Through Christ our Lord.

Year B

We offer our prayers to the God who is patient with us.

— Intercessions —

Let us see your kindness, O Lord, by granting our prayers for salvation. Through Christ our Lord.

Year C

Let us pray always with joy because of our partnership for the Gospel.

— Intercessions —

O God,
who have done great things
    for your people,
fill us with joy by granting these prayers.
Through Christ our Lord.

Third Sunday of Advent

Overview

Once again, no special ceremony needs to attend the lighting of the Advent wreath. Just be sure you set two purple and one pink aglow.

You may be taking up a second collection for the Retirement Fund for Religious. It has little to do with the liturgy of the day, but it is a noble cause.

This is a good Sunday to sing hymns about John the Baptist. He appears in the Gospel each year on this day. You may also wish to draw attention to any of his images in your church.

The priest and deacon may wear rose-colored vestments today. It is not required. Violet vestments may still be worn.

If today is December 12, the texts for the Third Sunday of Advent replace those for the Feast of Our Lady of Guadalupe. However, Our Lady may still be remembered in the music, the homily, the Prayer of the Faithful, the decorations, the hospitality, and the festivity of this day.

Entrance Antiphon

This is an abbreviated version of the classic antiphon that opened this liturgy since at least the eighth century. The first word is "Rejoice"—or in Latin, *Gaudete*. Years ago all the Sundays were probably known by the first word of the entrance antiphon. *The General Instruction of the Roman Missal*, 346 f., still refers to this Sunday by its historic name, *Gaudete*.

Collect

This collect picks up the theme of rejoicing, introduced in the entrance antiphon. The earliest version we have comes from the fifth

---

LECTIONARY

In the rare cases when December 17 falls on a Sunday, the Gospel each year relates to the preface of the day.

In Year A, the antiphon for the responsorial psalm may be replaced with "Alleluia." Practically speaking, this may confuse people into thinking that the Gospel acclamation has arrived early today, but the alternative gives a chance to catechize about the word "Alleluia," which serves as a Gospel acclamation (Order of Mass, 13) partly because it is biblical, as this psalm gives evidence. The Communion antiphon is taken from the first reading of Year A.

In Year B, the opening verses of the first reading proclaim that God's servant was sent to heal the brokenhearted. This line inspired the first invocation of the third form of the penitential rite (Order of Mass, 6), and reference is made to other verses in Eucharistic Prayer IV (Order of Mass, 117: "To the poor he proclaimed the good news of salvation, to prisoners, freedom, and to the sorrowful of heart, joy.")

The entrance antiphon is taken from the second reading of Year C. This is the classic text that gives this Sunday its name: *Gaudete!* The collect uses the same word. The second Advent preface also refers to those rejoicing, but it should only be used if today is December 17.

to sixth-century *Rotulus of Ravenna*. This collection of prayers had long been lost but was rediscovered in the nineteenth century. The post-Vatican II missal restored this collect as a fitting contribution to today's liturgy.

Prayer over the Offerings

Making its first appearance in the Verona Sacramentary, where it is assigned to prayers for fasting in September, this text first appeared on this day in the 1570 missal of the Council of Trent, and it has remained in place through the reforms of Vatican II. However, the compilers of the Vatican II missal had access to better sources, so today's version of the prayer is even older than the one first used after Trent.

This prayer is offered at Mass every Wednesday and Saturday of Advent before December 17.

Preface

You use the first Advent preface again today unless this is December 17. In that case, you use the second one. These prefaces are not completely interchangeable as other seasonal prefaces are. They are meant to be used successively for the two parts of Advent. For comments on the second Advent preface, see next Sunday, *p. 9.*

Communion Antiphon

This antiphon is the same one that has been here since at least the eighth century.

Prayer after Communion

The earliest version of this prayer comes from the Gelasian Sacramentary, where it appeared on Tuesday of the Second Week of Lent. The "divine sustenance" alleviated the fast. Today the word for "fasting" has been removed from the Lenten prayer, and it has been moved to Advent. Even so, you can still sense the penitential feel of this prayer.

PRAYER OF THE FAITHFUL

Year A

Be strong. Fear not. Our God comes to save
   those who cry for mercy.

— Intercessions —

O God,
through whom the blind see,
the lame walk, and the dead are raised,
show your power
   by granting these prayers.
Through Christ our Lord.

Year B

We rejoice always. We pray without ceasing.
   God is faithful and will grant our prayers.

— Intercessions —

O God,
who come to the help of your servants,
remember your promise of mercy
and hear these prayers.
Through Christ our Lord.

Year C

The great and holy one of Israel is among us.
   Through him we offer our prayers.

— Intercessions —

Hear, O God, the requests we make
   by prayer and petition,
and make us rejoice in your kindness.
Through Christ our Lord.

It is repeated during Advent every Wednesday and Saturday before December 17.

Blessing

You may again use the solemn blessing for Advent.

Fourth Sunday of Advent

Overview

Light all four candles of the wreath. Try to hold off singing Christmas carols just a few more days.

The O Antiphons were composed for the Magnificat at evening prayer during the final week of Advent. They have been given a place in the Eucharist for each day as the versicle for the Gospel acclamation. This is the best week to sing hymns based on the antiphons, such as "O Come, O Come, Emmanuel." The homily could draw attention to the antiphon of the day.

You may wish to highlight the images of Mary in your church. She figures prominently in the Gospel this weekend, and she is an important Advent figure. As Christmas draws near, Mary moves to center stage.

If you have a text or e-mail distribution list for the parish, let people know the Christmas Mass schedule today. If your office staff is printing up a participation aid for Christmas Mass, be sure to include the contact information for your parish, so visitors have a way of getting in touch later on.

Entrance Antiphon

The current missal adopted the same antiphon that has been here since at least the eighth century. The chant for this day, *Rorate caeli*, still appears in some hymnals. The words ask the heavens to rain justice down on the earth—or to rain "the Just One" down on the earth. On the Sunday closest to Christmas Day, the antiphon commands the heavens to give us a Savior.

Collect

This is the same prayer that concludes the recitation of the Angelus. Many Catholics know it by heart.

LECTIONARY

Year A's second reading helped inspire the line in the preface about the prophets who foresaw the birth of Jesus. The last line of this reading has been adopted as the second option for the greeting at the beginning of Mass (Order of Mass, 2). In the Gospel, Matthew quotes the passage from Isaiah found in the first reading and cited in the Communion antiphon. A reference also appears in the prayer over the offerings. The meaning of the word Emmanuel, "God is with us," is related to the greeting, "The Lord be with you" (Order of Mass, 2, 15, 31, 143).

Year B's responsorial psalm refers to God's covenant with David in its second strophe. When Eucharistic Prayer IV says of God, "Time and again you offered them covenants," it implies the inclusion of this one. Both the collect and the prayer over the offerings refer to today's Gospel. Gabriel's greeting to Mary is related to the liturgical greeting, "The Lord be with you" (Order of Mass, 2, 15, 31, 143). When the fourth Eucharistic Prayer says that Jesus was "incarnate by the Holy Spirit" (Order of Mass, 117), it refers to Luke 1:35. The Creeds (Order of Mass, 18, 19) make the same point.

When Eucharistic Prayer IV refers to the Body and Blood of Christ as "the sacrifice acceptable to you which brings salvation to the whole world," it alludes to the passage from Hebrews that serves as the second reading in Year C.

The earliest version comes from the Hadrian Sacramentary, where it was assigned to the Feast of the Annunciation on March 25. That was also the date some people calculated for the original Good Friday, and the Annunciation may have settled on that day when Good Friday became a moveable celebration. There are still some years when the two fall on the same day. It happened during the lifetime of John Donne, whose poem "The Annunciation and the Passion" includes this line: "Th' abridgement of Christ's story, which makes one—/As in plain maps, the furthest west is east—/Of th' angels *Ave*, and *Consummatum est*." This prayer captures the same mystery. On the Sunday before Christmas, we recall the Passion.

Prayer over the Offerings

Some prayers in the missal come from sources outside the Roman Rite, and this is an example. It has appeared for many centuries in the Ambrosian Rite—still part of the Catholic Church, but centered in Milan, not Rome. Its members observe a six-week Advent, and this prayer comes on the Sunday before Christmas. It has previously been used in the Roman Rite for the Feast of the Annunciation, as the collect for today's Mass was. Its placement in today's liturgy helps unite the prayers of the global Catholic Church.

Preface

Today you use the Second Advent Preface. This was a new composition for the 1970 missal because the Mass before the reforms of the Second Vatican Council had no special Advent prefaces. The Old Testament prophets, Mary, and John the Baptist all appear here, giving a more historical thrust to this particular preface. The Gospels during the last week of Advent tell the story leading up to the birth of Christ, and this preface accents their message. In most years, this is the first Sunday that you use Advent Preface II. Several biblical passages inspired this text. John the Baptist proclaimed the coming of Christ in Matthew 3:11–12, Mark 1:7, and John 1:29 and 36. The testimony of the prophets is summarized in Matthew 11:13, Romans 1:3, and Hebrews 1:1–2. The

---

PRAYER OF THE FAITHFUL

Year A

The Lord provides signs of mercy even for those who do not request them. Let us make known our needs.

— *Intercessions* —

O God,
who showed your mighty power
when a virgin conceived and bore a son,
mercifully grant our needs.
Through Christ our Lord.

Year B

To God who has revealed the mystery kept secret for long ages, we lift our voice in prayer.

— *Intercessions* —

O God of the covenant,
who promised to maintain
your kindness forever,
be close to your people in all our needs.
Through Christ our Lord.

Year C

Jesus Christ came among us to do the will of God. Through him we present our prayers on high.

— *Intercessions* —

O God,
who spoke promises to your people,
fulfill your word and grant our prayers.
Through Christ our Lord.

---

community's watchfulness in prayer appears in Luke 2:8, 12:37, 21:36; Philippians 4:6; and 1 Peter 4:7.

Communion Antiphon

As with all the other antiphons of the season, this one was in place at least by the eighth century. Isaiah's prophecy sets the stage for the coming birth of Jesus.

Prayer after Communion

This prayer—new to the 1970 missal—was fashioned from two unlikely sources. The first part comes from a sixth-century prayer for the Feast of Saint Lawrence the martyr, and the rest is adapted from an eighth-century preface for the Fourth Sunday of Lent. The words for "paschal mystery" were changed to "the mystery of your Son's Nativity." This prayer replaces a more generic one from the pre-Vatican II missal. Together with the other prayers for this day, it sets the tone for the coming of Christmas.

Blessing

You may use the solemn blessing for Advent as provided in the missal. But take a look at the one in *Collection of Masses for the Blessed Virgin Mary* on p. 201. It will probably fit the readings and prayers a little better.

CHRISTMAS

Many people regard Christmas as the highlight of the spiritual year. They invest a great deal of time and resources in preparing and celebrating the feast. Although the liturgy and the decorations of Christmas Day focus on the historical birth of Christ, the meaning of the feast is more complex, showing how Jesus fulfilled past prophecies, and how his incarnation dignifies all of humanity.

If you exercised restraint in music and decoration during Advent, you can let loose for Christmas. Musical instruments should sound again, even in playing solos. If your parish is setting up a manger scene or crèche for this Christmas, situate it apart from the sanctuary, so that people can have access to it for private devotions and it will not detract from the rites of the Mass.

The vesture for priests and deacons should look celebratory and dignified. This is a perfect season for singing the Gloria since the opening line comes from Luke's account of Jesus' birth.

A sample formulary for the Prayer of the Faithful can be found in the missal's fifth appendix. It may be used on any Sunday as is, or it may inspire you as you compose your own prayers.

As in Advent, Eucharistic Prayer IV is not be used because its preface is not supposed to be replaced with another one. The seasonal prefaces for Christmas pair up best with Eucharistic Prayers I, II, and III. If you used Prayer II frequently during Advent to lend an air of simplicity, one of the others might now make this central prayer feel more grand.

You have three choices for prefaces throughout the Christmas season. Unlike Advent, these are completely interchangeable.

I. The first one comes from the Hadrian Sacramentary, where it was preserved for the Christmas Mass celebrated by the pope at the Basilica of Saint Mary Major in Rome (see below, *p. 12*). This was the only Christmas preface available in the 1570 missal. Because of its long history, it appears today as the first option. The reference to "light" may refer to the way Luke describes the brightness of God surrounding the angels who visited the shepherds (2:8). There may also be a reference to John 17:3, where Jesus prays for the disciples to know the only true God and the one whom God sent: Jesus Christ. The preface hopes that we who know the visible God in Jesus will be caught up in the mystery of invisible love.

II. This preface was newly composed for the post-Vatican II missal. It is based on a passage from Sermon 22 of Pope Leo the Great, one of the champions of Christmas preaching. Elements of it are found in an eighth-century preface for an afternoon Mass on Christmas Eve. The text is a study in contrasts: the invisible God made visible, the One begotten before all ages born in time, raising up what had been cast down. There may be references to God raising up the poor in Psalm 113:7 and Luke 1:52.

III. This preface was also added to the post-Vatican II missal, but it is based on one from the Verona Sacramentary. It praises God that Jesus took on humanity while allowing us to share in eternity. Second Peter 1:3–4 sounds this same theme.

The solemn blessing for Christmas is based on one from the Hadrian Supplement. It may be used at any of the principal Masses of the first part of this season. You can find an alternative in the Sacramentary from the *Collection of Masses of the Blessed Virgin Mary* on p. 201–202. It might be fitting if your church is dedicated to Mary, for example.

The Nativity of the Lord, at the Vigil Mass

Overview

The celebration of this Mass was developed at the Basilica of Saint Mary Major in Rome because that church claims to possess the relics of the crib. Beneath the main altar, slats of wood, said to be from the manger in which Jesus lay, are encased in a reliquary. The Church is dedicated to Mary under the title of Mother of God.

This Mass may be celebrated before or after first vespers. However, the texts in both the missal and the Lectionary lead you to think that Christmas is still coming. In parishes, the Vigil Masses for Christmas are much better attended than those of Christmas Day. You may use these texts, but you might find the ones for At the Mass during the Night more appropriate, even for more than one Mass on Christmas Eve.

The Gloria reappears for the first time in this Mass after an absence on Sundays for the past four weeks. Sing it, if at all possible.

Normally when you hear a reading from the Acts of the Apostles, you assume that it's Easter, and that you're listening to the first reading. This is a rare instance when Acts is proclaimed at a completely different season of the year and as the second reading. This passage includes Paul's testimony that Jesus came from the line of David. The theme is repeated in the Gospel and even in the psalm—which normally makes you think of a theme in the first reading, but at this Mass looks forward to the second.

When you recite the Creed at this Mass, you genuflect during the lines concerning the Incarnation. Normally, when people recite the Creed on Sundays, they are supposed to make a low bow toward the altar. It is one of the most ignored rubrics in the missal. Prior to the Second Vatican Council, people genuflected every Sunday at this point in the Creed, but that custom was retained only for the Annunciation on March 25 and the Christmas Masses nine months later. Someone might make an announcement such as this just before starting the Creed: "During the Creed tonight (today), we genuflect at the words that express our belief in the Incarnation." Even so, be sure the cantor, lector, or priest is looking at the complete text of the Creed, so that after everyone stands up, someone can get people started again. It's not uncommon to forget what words come next.

If you are offering Eucharistic Prayer I, you use the first of the special forms of the *Communicantes*—that is, the section that begins "In communion with those whose memory we venerate." This part of Prayer I may have originated as a purely seasonal section similar to the preface. It gives a reason why we are praising God today. You have the choice of using the words "night" or "day." Just look outside to determine which option is apt.

The *Book of Blessings* includes an Order for the Blessing of a Christmas Manger or Nativity Scene (1562–1564). It could be done during the Prayer of the Faithful at the first Christmas Mass. There is also an Order for the Blessing of a Christmas Tree (1570–1596). Elements of it could be incorporated into one of the Christmas Masses.

Entrance Antiphon

This antiphon has been in use for the Vigil Mass since at least the eighth century. It starts with the word "Today"—but note that the tense is future. The Vigil Mass presumes that the full celebration of Christmas is coming later. Participation at this Mass suffices, but the texts are not the best for those coming to just one Mass on Christmas Day.

Collect

This was an Advent prayer when it first appeared in the Gelasian Sacramentary; hence the expression "wait in hope." The prayer avoids a direct reference to the birth of Jesus in Bethlehem, which will be celebrated at At the Mass during the Night. Instead it focuses on our reception of him as our redeemer in the present and our anticipation of seeing him again at the end of time as our judge. The pre-Vatican II missal used this collect for this Mass as well.

Prayer over the Offerings

This prayer is lifted word for word from the Verona Sacramentary, where it is one of the options for a Christmas Mass. It prays that the meaning of this season will help us serve more eagerly.

Preface

You may choose from any of the three options for the preface of the Christmas season. See above, *p. 11*.

Communion Antiphon

As with the entrance antiphon, this one was also part of this Mass from the eighth century.

PRAYER OF THE FAITHFUL

Years A, B, C

God promised to confirm the prosperity of David and to establish his throne for all generations. As followers of the Son of David, we ask for God's mercy again.

— *Intercessions* —

O God of every age,
who reveal your plan to your people
from one generation to the next,
be with us and grant our prayers.
Through Christ our Lord.

Note the future tense. Again, the texts for this Mass presume that the main celebration of Christmas is still coming.

Prayer after Communion

The earliest version of this prayer comes from the Verona Sacramentary, and it was in place for this Mass already in the pre-Vatican II missal. Note here and in the collect the use of "Only Begotten Son" in reference to Jesus. The same designation occurs in the *Communicantes* of Eucharistic Prayer I (see below). This being Christmas, it is an especially fitting title for Jesus, and it is used again and again.

Blessing

You may use the solemn blessing for Christmas. It fits better with the texts of the other Masses for Christmas, but it is still appropriate at this one.

LECTIONARY

When Eucharistic Prayer I (Order of Mass, 93) asks God to look upon the gifts "with a serene and kindly countenance," it may be a reference to the second strophe of today's responsorial psalm, which blesses the people who walk "in the light of your countenance, O Lord." When Eucharistic Prayer IV refers to the "covenants" God has offered (Order of Mass, 117), it probably means to include the one with David mentioned in this psalm.

The word Emmanuel, which appears in the Gospel of this Mass, means "God is with us," and this is one of the passages behind the liturgical greeting, "The Lord be with you" (Order of Mass, 2, 15, 31, and 143).

At the Mass during the Night

Overview

This is another Mass that originated at Saint Mary Major in Rome *(see p. 11 above)*. The missal calls this the Mass "during the Night." It is colloquially called Midnight Mass, but it does not have to take place at midnight. If it's night, you may use these texts. If you have large crowds coming to a Mass in the evening, you may prefer these texts over the ones for the Vigil, which are still anticipating Christmas. People coming to church tonight are not anticipating Christmas; they want to celebrate it.

The *Lectionary for Mass* makes the same point in a comment just before the readings of 13ABC. Any set of Christmas readings may be proclaimed at any time in light of the pastoral need of the faithful. The *Ceremonial of Bishops* (239) says there are three Christmas Masses, and the Vigil is not included among them. It regards the Vigil as a pre-Christmas Mass, even though it fulfills a canonical obligation to participate on this holy day. You may wish to use the night texts for a Mass earlier in the evening.

If you have a very special set of white or silver or gold vestments for priest and deacon, this is the occasion for them. Perhaps they will wear these vestments only once a year.

The Liturgy of the Hours tells you how to celebrate the Office of Vigils just before Mass during the Night. This is optional, but if you would like some structure for the music that precedes this Mass, see Volume I of *The Liturgy of the Hours*, p. 399 and pp. 1622–1626. The procession of ministers enters accompanied by the invitatory psalm. The priest greets the people and they respond. All sing a hymn, pray the psalms, and hear the readings from the Office of Readings, including the important passage from Leo the Great. Canticles from the office of vigils are sung. The Gospel of the Resurrection—yes, of the Resurrection—may be proclaimed. Then comes the Gospel of the Christmas Vigil Mass. Then the Proclamation of the Birth of Christ is chanted from the ambo, accompanied by a procession with candles. All stand, but they kneel during the words of the birth of Jesus, and rise for the final sentence. If the choir is visible to the assembly, they can lead the way here. Then Mass begins with the Gloria. See also the *Ceremonial of Bishops*, 238.

The Proclamation of the Birth of Christ may be sung at at the Mass during the Night even if Vigils is not celebrated. The text comes from the *Roman Martyrology*, a complete listing of all the saints, arranged day by day. This proclamation now appears in the Roman Missal. Normally the priest gives the introduction after his greeting. A sample introduction is given, but he may use his own words. A deacon or another minister then sings the Proclamation, and the Gloria follows immediately.

Sing the Gloria if at all possible. The opening lines quote the Gospel for this Mass. On *p. 12* above, see the notes regarding the genuflection during the Creed and the insertion of the *Communicantes* into Eucharistic Prayer I. The entrance and Communion antiphons are lovely texts, as you will see, but there's a very simple rule for successful music at the Mass during the Night: sing carols.

Entrance Antiphon

Two options for the entrance antiphon are proposed. The first is the traditional one, quoting Psalm 2. It stands as a prophecy for Christmas Day: "It is I who have begotten you this day." It has been recorded as the antiphon for the Mass during the Night since at least the eighth century. The second does not come from the Bible. It was newly added to the missal after the Second Vatican Council.

Collect

This prayer has been offered at the Mass during the Night since the Gelasian Sacramentary. It has remained unchanged until the post-Vatican II missal, which lightly altered the word order of the Latin. The prayer asks that we who have known Christ may also delight in his gladness in heaven. There will be plenty of feasting on earth this Christmas Day, but none to compare with what awaits the faithful.

Prayer over the Offerings

Appearing first in the Verona Sacramentary as one of the options for Christmas prayer, this text was used in the pre-Vatican II missal in exactly the place where it still falls today. The word "oblation" may sound a little unusual, but it is part of a wide vocabulary of words the missal uses to describe the sacrifice of the Mass. Of more significance is the word "exchange," which appears in some patristic literature to capture the way that the Word of God became flesh so that humans could participate in divinity. The same word appears in the third Christmas preface.

PRAYER OF THE FAITHFUL

Years A, B, C

The grace of God has appeared. Rejoicing in our salvation, we bring our prayers.

— Intercessions —

O God,
whose only Son entered the world
to the song of the angels
and the amazement of shepherds,
make us sing of your wonders
by granting our petitions.
Through Christ our Lord.

Preface

You have the same options as in the Vigil Mass. There is a slight preference for the first preface on Christmas Day because it was associated with this feast for so much of its history, but it's really up to you.

Communion Antiphon

This antiphon was new to the post-Vatican II missal. It quotes the prologue of John's Gospel.

Prayer after Communion

The earliest version of this is among the Christmas prayers in the Verona Sacramentary. It remained unchanged until the post-Vatican II missal, which replaced the words "Lord Jesus Christ" with "Redeemer." We pray that our honorable lives will make us worthy of union with Christ.

Blessing

The solemn blessing for Christmas may be used. See above, *p. 11.*

LECTIONARY

The theme of light in the first reading is echoed in the collect. This passage is quoted in the entrance antiphon for the Mass at Dawn and the Mass during the Day (see below, *p. 16*).

There may be allusions to the second reading in the second preface and the prayer after Communion. At every Mass, the embolism that follows the Lord's Prayer cites this passage: "we await the blessed hope, the coming of our Savior Jesus Christ" (Order of Mass, 125).

The light accompanying the angels in the Gospel probably inspired the collect and the prefaces. See also the collect for the Mass at Dawn (below, *p. 16*). The opening line of the Gloria (Order of Mass, 8) also comes from this Gospel.

At the Mass at Dawn

Overview

This is sometimes called the Mass of the shepherds because of the Gospel reading. Although the Lectionary permits you to use other readings, these make a good choice for this hour on Christmas Day.

Even though it's dawn, try to sing the Gloria. This solemnity calls for it more than any other.

See the notes for the Vigil Mass *(p. 12)* for comments on the genuflection during the Creed and the insertion of the *Communicantes* in Eucharistic Prayer I.

Entrance Antiphon

Although this is the same antiphon that has appeared since the eighth century, the new missal now notes that it quotes not just Isaiah but also Luke. The last phrase is from the words the angel Gabriel spoke to Mary. The word "today" appears in the first line, as it does in nearly all the Christmas entrance antiphons.

Collect

Appearing first in the Hadrian Sacramentary, this collect was used throughout the life of the pre-Vatican II missal, and it remains in place today, with only a slight retouching. According to the Hadrian, this prayer was used in Rome for this Mass at the Church of Saint Anastasia, a lovely ancient building named for a martyr whose feast day, December 25, was supplanted by Christmas. In the old days the pope still said the Christmas Mass at Dawn there, perhaps as a consolation to those relying on the patronage of Anastasia. Celebrating the dawn of Christmas Day, the text asks that the light illuminating our minds will shine forth in our deeds.

Prayer over the Offerings

A version of this first appeared in the Gelasian Sacramentary, and with minor alterations, remained in place throughout the life of the missal ever since. The pre-Vatican II missal included a petition for peace in this prayer, which is noble, but it was dropped from the revised missal because it was not part of the earliest evidence for the text. The original prayer calls the dawn of day a birth, and the Incarnation a shining.

Preface

You have the same options for the preface *(p. 11)*. Choose any of the three you prefer.

Communion Antiphon

This missal repeats the Communion antiphon that has been traditional since the eighth century for the Mass at Dawn. We also associate this prophecy of Zechariah with Palm Sunday.

LECTIONARY YEARS A, B, C

The fifth appendix has a sample formulary for the Prayer of the Faithful in the Christmas season. The introduction quotes the second reading of this Mass. The theme of the "honorable way of life" in the prayer after Communion for the Mass during the Night *(p. 15)* also connects with this passage.

The final petition in the Christmas blessing from the *Collection of Masses of Blessed Virgin Mary* (pp. 201–202) cites the Gospel of this Mass.

Prayer after Communion

New to the post-Vatican II missal, this prayer replaced two previous options. It is constructed from a prayer for a feast of the Blessed Virgin Mary from the Mozarabic tradition. It bears some connection to the theme of Colossians 1:26—the manifestation of a hidden mystery.

Blessing

The solemn blessing for Christmas Day may be used. *See p. 11.*

PRAYER OF THE FAITHFUL

Years A, B, C

Light dawns for the just, and gladness for the upright of heart. Let us pray to the God whose light has come into the world.

— Intercessions —

O God,
who revealed your glory to the shepherds,
let us hear and see your mighty works,
that we may bring you praise.
Through Christ our Lord.

At the Mass during the Day

Overview

The Gospel for this Mass is the prologue to John. It is dense, but lovely; theologically rich, but potentially disappointing to those expecting to hear about a manger.

See the notes for the Vigil Mass for comments on the genuflection during the Creed and the insertion for the *Communicantes* in Eucharistic Prayer I.

Entrance Antiphon

As with the antiphon for the Mass at Dawn, this one is drawn from Isaiah 9. This missal retains this antiphon, which has been in use continuously since the eighth century. The prophecy could not be clearer: "A child is born for us."

Collect

This prayer replaces one that used to be offered at this Mass. It is new to the Vatican II missal, but the earliest version of it goes back to at least the sixth century, and may have been written by Leo the Great himself. Defying the Manichean heresy, which held that all physical matter was sinful, this prayer speaks of the dignity of human nature, which God even more wondrously restored through the Incarnation. Every day at Mass, when the priest or deacon adds water to the wine, he says a prayer that shares the same source as this one. The mixture of those liquids reminds us every day of the Christmas mystery.

Prayer over the Offerings

Also coming from a sixth-century Christmas Mass, this prayer was new to the post-Vatican II missal. It acknowledges that the Incarnation has made us pleasing in God's eyes. The concept of our reconciliation in Christ can be found in 2 Corinthians 5:18–19.

Preface

You have the same choices for the preface *(p. 11)*. Choose any of the three for Christmas.

Communion Antiphon

This antiphon repeats the one in use since at least the eighth century. It cites a line from the psalms: all the ends of the earth have seen the salvation of God. The name Jesus means "God saves," so the antiphon essentially says that all have seen Jesus.

Prayer after Communion

The Vatican II missal slightly edited this prayer to make it more like its earliest version, found among the Christmas Mass texts in the

LECTIONARY YEARS A, B, C

The Communion antiphon is virtually the same as the people's antiphon in today's responsorial psalm.

The second reading shares a theme with the prayer after Communion from the Mass at Dawn. The "hidden depths" of the mystery may relate to the partial way God spoke through the prophets in the past. This passage says that Christ "took his seat at the right hand of the Majesty on high," a reference found in the final invocation of the third form of the penitential act (Order of Mass, 6).

The Communion antiphon from the Mass during the Night (above) comes from the Gospel of this Mass. The collects for the Mass during the Night and the Mass at Dawn also refer to this passage. So do all three prefaces.

Verona Sacramentary. It hails Jesus as the author of our divine birth and the giver of immortality.

Blessing

You may use the solemn blessing for Christmas *(p. 11).*

PRAYER OF THE FAITHFUL

Years A, B, C

All the ends of the earth have seen the Savior.
Let us pray to the Lord, who is kind and faithful.

— Intercessions —

O God,
whose Word was present
    from the beginning,
reveal your glory by granting our prayers.
Through Christ our Lord.

The Holy Family of Jesus, Mary, and Joseph

Overview

When Christmas falls on a Sunday, this feast moves to December 30, a weekday. In that case, the texts are the same, but you do not recite the Creed. You also choose just one reading before the Gospel. On Sunday, though, you do it all.

The Lectionary options are hopelessly complex. You may use the first two Year A readings every year if you want, changing just the Gospel. Or you can swap out the first two readings and the psalm with the options for Years B and C. If you take the latter choice, people will hear a broader range of passages from year to year. You also dodge the dilemma posed by the second reading in Year A, which sounds sexist to many a listener. The Lectionary in the United States permits a shorter version of that reading, which also eliminates the problem.

If you use Eucharistic Prayer I, the priest includes the special *Communicantes* for the Octave of Christmas. It's a good idea to let people hear this sometime this week.

The *Book of Blessings* includes an Order for the Blessing of a Family or Household (206–210). You may find some of these prayers useful.

Entrance Antiphon

This replaces the antiphon in the pre-Vatican II missal, taken from Proverbs, when the feast was celebrated on the Sunday within the Octave of Epiphany. Now the antiphon goes right to the point of the feast: The shepherds discover the Holy Family.

Collect

This was a new composition for the post-Vatican II missal. Prior to the Council, the collect for this Mass was addressed to Jesus Christ. This one prays that we who imitate the Holy Family delight one day in the joy of God's house.

Prayer over the Offerings

This is basically the same prayer used before the Council, slightly edited. It is a prayer for our families. The prayer asks God to establish our families in grace and peace through the intercession of Mary and Joseph. The Latin original means something more like "asking with the intercession of Mary and Joseph." The Latin implies that Mary and Joseph are praying along with us; it does not tell God how to grant what we want.

Preface

You may choose any of the three prefaces for the Christmas season *(p. 11)*.

LECTIONARY

When the fourth Eucharistic Prayer prays for "those who have died in the peace of your Christ" (Order of Mass, 122), it probably alludes to Colossians 3:15: "let the peace of Christ control your hearts." The line is found in the second reading that may be used at this Mass any year.

In Masses for the Dead, when Eucharistic Prayer III is offered, the conclusion of the special insert refers to 1 John 3:2: "for seeing you, our God, as you are, we shall be like you for all the ages" (Order of Mass, 115). That text is found in the second reading of Year C.

Communion Antiphon

Although this antiphon comes from Baruch, it resembles the Prologue of John's Gospel. The antiphon was new to the post-Vatican II missal.

Prayer after Communion

As with the collect, the original version of this prayer was addressed to Jesus Christ. The post-Vatican II missal redesigned this to conform to its other prayers after Communion. The expression "the trials of this world" seems to refer to Mark 4:18–19, where the same trials impede the growth of the word of God in the parable of the sower.

Blessing

You may use the solemn blessing for Christmas *(p. 11)*, but this would be an especially good day to choose the set from the *Collection of Masses of the Blessed Virgin Mary* on pp. 201–202.

PRAYER OF THE FAITHFUL

Year A

The word of Christ dwells in us richly. In love and gratitude we present our prayers.

— Intercessions —

O God,
who protected the Holy Family
    from every threat,
guard us in our times of need.
Through Christ our Lord.

Year B

To the Lord who remembers his covenant for a thousand generations, we present our prayers.

— Intercessions —

O God,
who revealed Christ the Lord
    to Simeon and Anna,
show us your marvels and grant these
    prayers.
Through Christ our Lord.

Year C

The Father bestows love on us by letting us be called the children of God. In faith we bring our prayers.

— Intercessions —

O God,
whose Son revealed great wisdom
    in the temple,
hear our prayers
    and make your wisdom known to us.
Through Christ our Lord.

Solemnity of Mary, the Holy Mother of God

Overview

This is the octave day of Christmas, the day on which Jesus received his name, hence the choice of today's Gospel.

Among the Masses for Various Needs and Occasions is one for the beginning of the civil year, and others appropriate for the World Day of Prayer for Peace and Justice. If your bishop wishes, he may permit the use of those texts over the ones assigned for the solemnity, but most parishes will want to observe the solemnity anyway. Because of the new year, this would be a fitting time to sing the *Te Deum*, either the chant from the *Liber cantualis* or a hymn setting such as "Holy God, We Praise Thy Name."

The proper title of this day in Latin is exactly the way it is translated into English: "Solemnity of Mary, the Holy Mother of God." It sounds unusual because "solemnity" is the way we designate the biggest days on our church calendar. Christmas is a solemnity. So is the Epiphany. But for some reason, this designation appeared in the title of the day, rather than in the subheading. Perhaps it was put there by mistake because this is a new observance in the liturgical year. As it is, it seems to say that this is a solemnity about the solemnity of Mary.

Entrance Antiphon

Two choices are given. This feast was new to the post-Vatican II missal, and so are its antiphons. The first is a nonbiblical greeting of Mary, which praises her Son as King. The second edition of *The Roman Missal* properly credited the fifth-century Roman poet Sedulius as the author; the text appears in his *Carmen Paschale* 2:63–64. His name is missing from the 2002 missal, perhaps because the first three words are actually inspired by Virgil's *Aeneid* V:80, and the ending of this antiphon slightly alters Sedulius's text. Sedulius also wrote words for the hymn *A solis ortus cardine*, an alphabetical poem about the life of Jesus. Each strophe begins with a subsequent letter of the Latin alphabet. The opening strophes still appear in the Latin edition of *The Liturgy of the Hours* as the hymn for morning prayer throughout the Christmas season. The other entrance antiphon replicates the one for the Christmas Mass at Dawn.

Collect

Because this solemnity was new to the post-Vatican II missal, the collect was also, but it started as a seventh-century prayer to open the celebration of the Assumption of Mary. She is our intercessor because she lives with God forever in heaven.

LECTIONARY YEARS A, B, C

Like the Communion antiphon, the first reading probably has more to do with New Year's than with Mary or the naming of Jesus. Nearly all the formulas for the solemn blessing at Mass (Order of Mass, 142) rely on this passage for inspiration.

The second reading is the only passage in all of Paul's letters that refers to Mary, and she is simply called the woman of whom Jesus was born. The prayer after Communion gives her a similar title. When Eucharistic Prayer IV says that God sent the Son "in the fullness of time," it refers to Galatians 4:4.

Prayer over the Offerings

This prayer was also new to the post-Vatican II missal, but it started as a sixth-century oration for the consecration of a bishop. Revised for this day, the prayer eliminates the reference to that event and inserts the one for this solemnity. Coming at the start of the new year, the acknowledgment that God begins and brings all things to fulfillment is appropriate.

Preface

The preface can be found among the collection of prefaces later in the missal. To pray it, the priest chooses the option "on the Solemnity of the Motherhood." It was a new composition for the post-Vatican II missal, proclaiming that through a miraculous conception (Luke 1:26–35), she brought the light of Christ into the world (see John 1:9).

Communion Antiphon

Citing the Letter to the Hebrews, this antiphon has more to do with New Year's Day than anything else: Jesus Christ is the same yesterday, today, and forever. It was new to the post-Vatican II missal.

Prayer after Communion

This was a new composition for the post-Vatican II missal, and the construction is rather complex. The first line is an independent clause. The Sacramentary is translated in this style quite frequently, but it is rare in the revised missal. In this case, the independent clause appears in the Latin original of this prayer.

Blessing

The solemn blessing for Christmas is appropriate *(p. 11)*, but so is the one from the *Collection of Masses for the Blessed Virgin Mary* on pp. 201–202.

PRAYER OF THE FAITHFUL

Years A, B, C

God has promised to bless us when we invoke the name of the Lord. Let us make known our needs.

— *Intercessions* —

O God,
upon whose wonders Mary reflected
   in her heart,
show us your power and bring us
   into your presence.
Through Christ our Lord.

Second Sunday after the Nativity [Christmas]

Overview

This Mass is only used in countries where the Epiphany is a holy day of obligation and is thus celebrated on its traditional date, January 6, no matter what day of the week that is. In other countries, such as the United States, the Epiphany always moves to Sunday, and the celebration of the Second Sunday after Christmas is suppressed.

Entrance Antiphon

Back in the eighth century, this passage from the book of Wisdom used to start the Mass for the First Sunday after Christmas. Because it says that the Lord's all-powerful word bounded from heaven in the middle of the night, it seems to prophesy the time that Jesus was born. It also supports the long practice of celebrating a Christmas Mass at midnight.

Collect

This prayer was new to the post-Vatican II missal. It is based on one for the Epiphany from the Hadrian Sacramentary, retouched to avoid an explicit allusion to that feast. The resulting prayer anticipates the celebration of the Epiphany.

Prayer over the Offerings

A version of this prayer has existed since the Hadrian Sacramentary for various Masses for the Christmas season. For the post-Vatican II missal, one line was changed. It formerly said the fruit of the Nativity was a cleansing from the stain of sin. Now it says that the way of truth is shown, and the life of the heavenly kingdom is promised.

Preface

You may choose any of the three Christmas prefaces *(p. 11)*.

Communion Antiphon

Relying on a text from the Prologue to John's Gospel, this antiphon says that those who receive Jesus become children of God. It was new to the post-Vatican II missal.

Prayer after Communion

First found among the Hadrian Sacramentary's prayers for Lent and Palm Sunday, this one was adapted and adopted for use in the Christmas season. It still carries a penitential tone.

Blessing

You may use the solemn blessing for the Christmas season *(p. 11)*.

LECTIONARY

The refrain of the responsorial psalm may be replaced with the word "Alleluia," which appears in the body of Psalm 147. It is one of the biblical locations for the liturgical word used as the Gospel acclamation throughout most of the year (Order of Mass, 13).

The second Christmas preface shares some vocabulary with the end of the second reading.

All three preface options allude to today's Gospel. The Communion antiphon comes from here, too.

PRAYER OF THE FAITHFUL

Years A, B, C

The Word of God became flesh and dwelled
among us. Let us pray to see the glory of
Jesus Christ.

— *Intercessions* —

Enlighten the eyes of our hearts, O God,
and fill us with hope
by answering our prayers.
Through Christ our Lord.

The Epiphany of the Lord, at the Vigil Mass

Overview

The *Ceremonial of Bishops*, 240 says that the Epiphany "ranks among the principal festivals of the whole liturgical year." It is one of ten days from which conferences of bishops may select holy days of obligation. In countries where it is not a holy day, the Epiphany is celebrated on the Sunday that falls between January 2 and 8.

This Vigil Mass is new to the 2002 missal. It did not exist in the first editions after the Second Vatican Council, and hence did not appear in the 1985 Sacramentary. It should be celebrated for any evening Mass the night before the Epiphany.

If you are singing "We Three Kings," be sure to sing all the verses, so that the catechetical meaning of all three gifts is sung. The cathedral of Cologne, Germany, claims the relics of the magi.

The *Ceremonial of Bishops* suggests that there be a "suitable and increased display of lights" (240) today. It also suggests a "special presentation of the gifts." Perhaps this could include gifts for the poor, letters to legislators on behalf of the needy, and gifts for the homebound and the dying. Some groups in your parish could take responsibility for each of these categories, symbolically representing the gold, frankincense, and myrrh.

Entrance Antiphon

The text comes from the passage that served as the first reading for the Second Sunday of Advent in Year C. There it was prophecy; here it is fulfillment. All have come from east to west, as noted by the arrival of the magi. It is new to the 2002 missal.

Collect

The Gelasian Sacramentary offered this prayer as the collect for the Vigil of the Epiphany. Unused in *The Roman Missal* since the Middle Ages, it returned in 2002 and is being heard in English for the first time in history. Adopting the imagery of the star's light, it prays for light within our hearts.

Prayer over the Offerings

This prayer is new to the missal, though it bears some similarity to one from the *Rotulus of Ravenna*. It links our offerings with those of the magi, the first from the Gentile nations to recognize Christ.

Preface

Although this preface was new to the post-Vatican II missal, it drew on words and ideas from the Gelasian Sacramentary's preface for Epiphany. After Christ appeared in our mortal nature, he made us new by his immortal nature. The reference to Jesus as the light for the nations comes from Luke 2:29–32, and is prophesied in Isaiah 42:6–7. The appearance of Christ is noted in Colossians 3:4 and Titus 2:11–12.

LECTIONARY YEARS A, B, C

The Gospel inspired all the prayers of this Mass. They are filled with images of light, the nations, the star, and the treasure.

Communion Antiphon

This antiphon turns to the book of Revelation for a vision of all the nations walking in the light of God. The frequent reference to the "nations" in this liturgy alludes to the magi, who represent the coming of the Gentiles to honor Christ. This antiphon is new to the 2002 missal.

Prayer after Communion

A version of this prayer appeared in the Gelasian Sacramentary as a collect. It was simplified for the revised missal, but the imagery is still quite rich, drawing on the symbols of the star and the treasure.

Blessing

The solemn blessing for the Epiphany is not required, but the text is most appropriate. It draws on images from 1 Peter 2:9 and Matthew 2:1–12. It was new to the post-Vatican II missal.

PRAYER OF THE FAITHFUL

Years A, B, C

God will have pity on the lowly and the poor. Let us pray that every nation on earth will experience God's mercy.

— *Intercessions* —

O God,
who revealed your mystery
through holy apostles and prophets,
be faithful to your promise
and grant our prayers.
Through Christ our Lord.

The Epiphany of the Lord, at the Mass during the Day

Overview

See the comments at the Vigil Mass for when this feast is celebrated *(p. 26)*. This is still the Christmas season, so it is fitting to sing the Gloria.

After the Gospel, the deacon or a cantor may sing the table of moveable feasts for this year. The text and a musical tone are provided in the missal. This old custom announces to the community the upcoming dates for such moveable occasions as Ash Wednesday, Easter, and Pentecost. The proclamation is done on the first major gathering after the beginning of the new calendar year, and it includes the date for next Advent. If your parish handed out calendars last month, you probably don't need to do this, but it is a beautiful old custom that sanctifies the new year by letting people know the important forthcoming dates. The missal does not indicate what posture the people should take. Because the proclamation immediately follows the Gospel, they could remain standing, but if they sit out of habit, that would surely be acceptable.

If you are using Eucharistic Prayer I today, you insert the special *Communicantes* for this day. The key verb in this section is "appeared." Christmas celebrates the Incarnation, but "Epiphany" means "manifestation"—the revelation of Jesus' identity. He was brought forth, or "appeared," to the magi as God's only Son.

Entrance Antiphon

Inspired by prophecies from Malachi and First Chronicles, this text says that the Lord has come with power and dominion in hand. The magi are sometimes called kings, but the real king is the child they come to see. This antiphon has enjoyed continuous use since at least the eighth century.

Collect

The journey of the magi is compared with our journey of faith. They represent the Gentile nations, and they come to belief by the guidance of a star. We who have faith also hope to journey to sublime glory. This collect first appeared among the prayers for Epiphany in the Hadrian Sacramentary, and it has remained there ever since.

Prayer over the Offerings

On the day we remember the offering of gifts to the newborn Jesus, we compare ours to those of the magi. The prayer first appeared in the Hadrian Sacramentary.

Preface

See the comments for the Vigil Mass *(p. 26)*.

Communion Antiphon

Quoting the Gospel of the day, this antiphon puts the words of the magi on our lips: We have seen his star in the East and have come with gifts to adore the Lord. It has been used for this Mass since at least the eighth century.

LECTIONARY YEARS A, B, C

The collect borrows imagery from the second reading.

The Gospel for today influenced the collect, the prayer over the gifts, the preface, and the prayer after Communion.

Prayer after Communion

As the star's light led the magi, so this prayer asks that God's heavenly light will go before us always and everywhere. The prayer first appeared in the Gelasian Sacramentary for the Epiphany, but some traditions borrowed it as the text for blessing the fire at the Easter Vigil.

Blessing

A solemn blessing for the day is provided. It is optional, but recommended *(p. 27)*.

PRAYER OF THE FAITHFUL

Years A, B, C

The magi were overjoyed at seeing the star.
Let us pray for the light of God's glory,
that our hearts may be radiant with hope.

— *Intercessions* —

O God,
who showed the way to those
who sought your Son,
reveal your light to us
   who place our prayers before you.
Through Christ our Lord.

The Baptism of the Lord

Overview

Normally we celebrate the Baptism of the Lord on the Sunday after January 6. However, if Epiphany has been transferred to a Sunday, and if that Sunday falls on January 7 or 8, the Baptism of the Lord is observed on the following Monday. This gets Ordinary Time underway without unduly prolonging the season of Christmas.

The Lectionary expects you to change the Gospel each year of the cycle. However, you may always use the other readings and the psalm from Year A. The readings for Years B and C are optional. If you use those options, you give people the broadest hearing of the scriptures relating to this feast.

Entrance Antiphon

The four Gospels and the Acts of the Apostles all testify to the baptism of Jesus. The entrance antiphon chooses a passage from Matthew. It was new to the post-Vatican II missal.

Collect

You have a choice of two collects. The first asks that God may also be pleased with us who have been baptized. This is a new composition for a feast that was new to the first post-Vatican II missal. It is a little complex in the original Latin, as you can tell by the English translation. Some of the prayers that were composed after Vatican II were a bit wordy.

The second option originated in the Gelasian Sacramentary as a prayer for the Epiphany. It is also the collect you say on the Tuesday after Epiphany before the Baptism of the Lord. It

notes the outward appearance of Jesus' humanity, and it hopes that our inward appearance may be favorably transformed.

Prayer over the Offerings

We ask God to accept the offerings we have brought, and to transform our oblation into the sacrifice of Christ. The prayer was a new composition for the post-Vatican II missal. As is true of the collect, it is complex, as if the authors were trying to put a lot of ideas into a short prayer.

Preface

This preface was newly composed for the post-Vatican II missal because the previous one had nothing like it. There were some prefaces for this day in the Middle Ages, and this one was probably inspired by them, but the complete text was new in 1970. This preface retells the highlights of

---

LECTIONARY

The collect and the preface allude to the first reading of Year A, which tells of the pleasure God takes in his servant. The collect, preface, and prayer after Communion all refer to today's Gospel.

In Year B, the collect and the preface rely on the Gospel.

In Year C, the second reading is the passage that contributed a line to the embolism that follows the Lord's Prayer at every Mass: "we await the blessed hope" (Order of Mass, 125). The prayer after Communion reflects this Gospel.

this story from all its New Testament sources. The dwelling of God in Christ is in John 1:14, Ephesians 3:17, and Revelation 21:3. The "oil of gladness" appears in Psalm 45:7, and the anointing with the Spirit is in Isaiah 61:1, which Jesus reads in Luke 4:18, where he announces his mission to bring good news to the poor. The word "Servant" recalls the four servant oracles from Isaiah, the first of which begins in 42:1.

Communion Antiphon

The testimony of John the Baptist supplies the text for the Communion antiphon. It is one of several antiphons that indicate who says what. It was new to the post-Vatican II missal.

Prayer after Communion

In the Gospel, the voice of God asks the crowd to listen to Jesus. This prayer is offered by the people who have done just that. One phrase is echoed in the collect for Saint Jerome Emiliani on February 8, but otherwise this was a brand new prayer for the post-Vatican II missal.

Blessing

No solemn blessing is indicated, but you could make a case for reusing the one for the Epiphany (p. 27). Today marks another manifestation of Jesus Christ.

PRAYER OF THE FAITHFUL

Years A, B, C

Jesus went about doing good, healing all who were oppressed. We offer our prayers to God through him.

— Intercessions —

O God, who sent your Son
to open the eyes of the blind
and bring prisoners from confinement,
hear our prayers for those
who seek your aid.
Through Christ our Lord.

LENT

The season of Lent has two purposes. It is the time for those who are to be baptized at the Easter Vigil to make their final, spiritual preparations; and it is the time for those who are already baptized to exercise penance in preparation for the renewal of their baptismal promises at the same occasion. The whole season carries a penitent tone, and it still captures the goodwill of Christians all around the world.

The Gloria is omitted throughout the season of Lent, except when the community observes feasts and solemnities, such as Saint Joseph's Day (March 19) and the Annunciation (March 25). The Fridays of Lent are days of abstinence from meat for all Catholics over the age of fourteen. Exceptions are made whenever these same solemnities fall on a Friday (canon 1251). Catholics from their eighteenth to their fifty-ninth birthdays fast on Ash Wednesday and Good Friday. They eat only one full meal. The other meals should not equal a second meal. Snacking is not permitted on those two days. Many Catholics add to these rather minimal disciplines; it is their choice. The relaxation of the laws of abstinence on solemnities has made some Catholics decide to relax their other disciplines on the Sundays of this season. You may wish to include a brief announcement about the laws of fast and abstinence each week during Lent.

Appendix V includes two sample formularies for the Prayer of the Faithful in Lent. These may be used as they appear, or to inspire your composition of new prayers. The prayer that concludes the first refers to the first reading on Ash Wednesday, in which people are invited to turn to God with all their heart.

Special prefaces are designated for many of the Sunday Masses throughout Lent. There are four generic prefaces for this season; the first two of these are for Sundays when no other preface takes precedence. In practice, they are used for weeks three, four, and five in Years B and C when there is no scrutiny of the elect at that particular Mass. Both these prefaces were new to the post-Vatican II missal.

The first deals with the spiritual renewal that is ours during the season. It is more appropriate for a congregation of the Catholic faithful who are experiencing Lent for their own renewal, than for a Mass that features the elect preparing for their baptism. The "fullness of grace" recalls John 1:16, Galatians 4:4–5, and Ephesians 3:19. The word "reborn" appears in John 3:5. The idea of being God's own sons and daughters shows up in Romans 8:14–17 and 21–23. It is hard to see even in Latin, but the expression "more eagerly intent on prayer" may refer to the responsibilities of devout Christians outlined in 2 Peter 3:11, and the "works of charity" may allude to Ephesians 3:19 and 1 John 3:1–2. In the 1985 Sacramentary, this is the preface that called Lent "this joyful season." But the revised translation says more carefully that it is the season in which we "await the sacred paschal feasts with the joy of minds made pure."

Similarly the second general preface pertains to the renewed and purified heart that the faithful obtain through their participation in Lent. God's purification of the hearts of believers is found in Acts 15:9. The unacceptability of "disordered affections" appears in 2 Thessalonians 3:6, where the Lectionary for Mass 427 translates it as "a disorderly way." The passing nature of heaven and earth is mentioned in Matthew 23:35 and Hebrews 13:14.

The *Book of Blessings* includes an Order for the Blessing of Fields and Flocks (966–985) and an Order for the Blessing of Seeds at Planting Time (986–1006). These could be used at the appropriate local time.

You may use one of the two Eucharistic Prayers for Masses of Reconciliation on any day throughout the season of Lent. Whenever you do, you may use its own preface, or you may substitute it with a preface from Lent. Their prefaces are not as integral as the one for Eucharistic Prayer IV.

Violet vesture is worn by priests and deacons. If you have more than one set, you may wish to designate one for the entire season of Lent. Music and floral decorations should be restrained (*Ceremonial of Bishops*, 252 and *GIRM*, 313). The decorations in the church should look as though they are fasting, too. Instrumental music is to be avoided as well.

The back of the missal includes a selection of prayers of preparation for Mass. The last of them is about having the right intention. Those wanting to focus on their prayer during Lent might give it a look.

First Sunday of Lent

Overview

The forty-day fast of Jesus sets the penitential tone for this season. It invites the renewal of those who have already been baptized, even as it challenges those awaiting baptism to spend these days in spiritual preparation. They will be engaging their battle with the devil's trials during the scrutiny rites of this season.

The Rite of Election is celebrated on this day, but probably at the cathedral. If for some reason you are celebrating the Rite of Election in your parish church today, use the texts from the ritual Masses in the back of the missal. This is probably why the traditional papal Mass was celebrated at Saint John Lateran in Rome on this day. It is the cathedral church of that diocese.

For Ash Wednesday, the Hadrian Sacramentary implies that the pope walked from Saint Anastasia Church at the foot of Rome's Aventine hill to Saint Sabina Church at the top, where the Mass took place. To this day, the pope's Mass for Ash Wednesday takes place at Saint Sabina, but he usually starts the procession at Saint Anselm Church, just a few steps away—also on top of the hill. Perhaps in imitation of this custom, the *Ceremonial of Bishops*, 261 suggests a procession for all the Sundays of Lent wherever the bishop presides, and the *Circular Letter on Preparing and Celebrating the Paschal Feasts*, 23 says the Litany of the Saints might accompany the opening procession for the First Sunday of Lent. Even in a parish church, the litany may make an appropriate start to the season, while putting this important prayer in the repertoire of our people.

Entrance Antiphon

Unchanged since eighth-century sources, the antiphon that opens the first Sunday of the Lenten season prophesies where all this will end up: in deliverance, glory, and length of days.

Collect

We pray to grow in understanding this Lent, and to lead a worthy life. New to the post-Vatican II missal, this prayer recovered one from the Gelasian Sacramentary. Composed for the First Sunday of Lent, it had fallen into disuse until the late twentieth century.

LECTIONARY

The priest quotes verse four of Year A's responsorial psalm at every Mass during the washing of the hands (Order of Mass, 28). When Eucharistic Prayer IV says "when through disobedience he had lost your friendship" (Order of Mass, 117), it alludes to the conclusion of the second reading. Year A's Gospel inspired the preface and the prayer after Communion; it is quoted in the Communion antiphon.

When the Eucharistic Prayer refers to the "covenants" God made with humanity (Order of Mass, 117), it implies the inclusion of the one with Noah, found in the first reading of Year B. The Gospel inspired the preface.

The end of Year C's responsorial psalm is quoted in the entrance antiphon. This is a rare occasion when the psalm refers to the Gospel, not to the first reading. The devil quotes it in his final temptation. The Gospel inspired the preface. The second reading of Year C says that "Jesus is Lord." This is one reason he bears this title in the Kyrie (Order of Mass, 7).

Prayer over the Offerings

We ask God to make us ready to make these offerings at the beginning of this sacred time. This prayer first appeared in the Gelasian Sacramentary on the Wednesday before Ash Wednesday, but it was moved here for the post-Vatican II missal.

Preface

New to the post-Vatican II missal, this preface especially fits the celebration of the First Sunday of Lent. Citing the Gospel narrative of the abstinence of Jesus in the desert, it shows how this season will guide us to the eternal Passover. First Corinthians 5:8 tells about casting out the leaven of malice. In Luke 22:15–16, Jesus says he will eat the Passover with his disciples when it is fulfilled in the reign of God.

Communion Antiphon

Two antiphons are proposed. The second is the traditional one that can be traced to at least the eighth century. The first was added to the post-Vatican II missal because of an occasional custom that the Communion antiphon echoes the Gospel. Matthew's version is chosen.

Prayer after Communion

We pray that in this time of fasting we may hunger for him who is the true and living Bread. This prayer was newly composed for the post-Vatican II missal, and its dependence on the Gospel is clear.

Blessing

A prayer over the people is proposed for every day of Lent; only the ones on Sunday are assigned to those days. The ones for weekdays may be interchanged or even omitted. The Gelasian Sacramentary supplied a prayer over the people for every day of Lent. This custom had been abandoned, but it was revived in the 2002 edition of *The Roman Missal*. This particular prayer appeared in the Gelasian on the First Sunday of Lent, the same Mass where the collect for this day was first found. Both have been restored to this place after many centuries of disuse, and they appear together in English for the first time in history.

PRAYER OF THE FAITHFUL

Year A

Mindful of our sins, we pray for a clean heart.

— Intercessions —

O God,
whose Son resisted every temptation,
grant us the gifts that will please you.
Through Christ our Lord.

Year B

God placed a rainbow in the clouds as a sign of the covenant. In our desire to remain faithful, we seek the help that God alone can give.

— Intercessions —

Help us keep your covenant, O Lord.
Hear our prayers
and show us your ways of love and truth.
Through Christ our Lord.

Year C

God is our refuge and fortress. God rescues us in time of trouble. Trusting in the Lord, we cry out for mercy.

— Intercessions —

O God,
who promise salvation
to those who confess that Jesus is Lord,
hear our prayers, strengthen our belief,
and save your faithful people.
Through Christ our Lord.

There is a solemn blessing for Lent in the *Collection of Masses for the Blessed Virgin Mary*, p. 202. It might be appropriate if your community is under Mary's patronage, but otherwise the restored system of prayers over the people deserves attention.

Second Sunday of Lent

Overview

The Gospel each year recounts the story of the Transfiguration of Jesus in the presence of his closest followers. It still gives the community hope of the glory that awaits faithful disciples of Jesus.

In the United States, if you have baptized candidates preparing for reception into the full communion of the Catholic Church at the Easter Vigil, the *Rite of Christian Initiation of Adults* gives you a penitential rite you may celebrate with them today (459). It resembles a scrutiny. However, you may receive baptized Christians at any time of year, and this rite is optional. If you use it, it should look different from the scrutinies that will follow on the next three Sundays. Unbaptized catechumens, now called the "elect," celebrate the scrutinies in preparation for their baptism at the Easter Vigil.

In Rome, the stational Mass for this Sunday is celebrated at Santa Maria in Domnica. This is a place where Saint Lawrence is said to have distributed alms to the poor. As the Gospel for the First Sunday of Lent concerns fasting, so the traditional Roman location for the celebration of the Second Sunday of Lent suggests almsgiving.

Entrance Antiphon

Two options are given for the entrance antiphon. The second is the traditional one that dates before the Vatican II missal. The first expresses our longing to see the face of the Lord. On this day, the psalm suggests our desire to see the beauty of transfigured glory on the face of Jesus Christ.

LECTIONARY

Eucharistic Prayer IV says that Jesus "destroyed death and restored life" (Order of Mass, 117), referring to the ending of the second reading in Year A. The Gospel account of the Transfiguration inspired all the presidential prayers for this Mass.

Eucharistic Prayer I refers to "the sacrifice of Abraham" (Order of Mass, 93), which is described in the first reading of Year B, but see also the first reading of Year C. In the full text of this passage, Abraham tells Isaac that God will provide a lamb, and that lies behind the statement in Eucharistic Prayer IV: "Look, O Lord, upon the Sacrifice which you yourself have provided for your Church" (Order of Mass, 122). The conclusion of the second reading in Year B inspired the belief that Jesus sits at the right hand of the Father, as stated in both the Apostles' and the Nicene Creeds (Order of Mass, 18, 19); the third invocation in the third form of the penitential act makes a similar statement (Order of Mass, 6). The Gospel account of the Transfiguration inspired all the presidential prayers for this Mass.

In Year C's first reading, Abraham makes a sacrifice as part of the covenant with God, which is alluded to in the first Eucharistic Prayer (Order of Mass, 93), and in the fourth Eucharistic Prayer among the "covenants" God offered time and again (Order of Mass, 117). In Masses for the Dead, Eucharistic Prayer III includes an insert that says of Christ that he will "transform our lowly body after the pattern of his own glorious body" (Order of Mass, 115), referring to part of the second reading of Year C, Philippians 3:21. The Gospel account of the Transfiguration inspired all the presidential prayers for this Mass.

Collect

We pray for the spiritual vision that we need in order to see the glory of God. This prayer was newly composed for this Mass in the post-Vatican II missal. It draws on the accounts of the transfiguration of Jesus.

Prayer over the Offerings

We pray that the sacrifice will cleanse us and sanctify us to celebrate the paschal mystery. This prayer appeared in the Hadrian Sacramentary for the Third Sunday of Lent, among many other places, but the Vatican II missal moved it to the Second Sunday and replaced its other occurrences with different prayers from the broad library of possibilities in the history of the liturgy.

Preface

The promise of the Resurrection shone forth in the transfiguration of Jesus upon the holy mountain. This preface was new to the post-Vatican II missal. It was composed to echo the Gospels for each Sunday of the cycle. The "glory" of Christ appears in John 17:22, 2 Corinthians 4:6, Philippians 3:21, and Hebrews 2:9. The "holy mountain" is mentioned in 2 Peter 1:18.

Communion Antiphon

Citing Matthew's account of the Transfiguration, this antiphon was new to the post-Vatican II missal, and it supports the occasional tradition of linking this antiphon with the Gospel of the day.

Prayer after Communion

We thank God for letting us share now on earth the things of heaven. This prayer was assigned to Wednesday of the Third Week of Lent in the Gelasian Sacramentary. Unused for many centuries, it was restored to this Sunday in the post-Vatican II missal.

Blessing

We pray that we may desire and attain the glory that the apostles saw in the transfigured body of Jesus. The text originated in the Parisian Missal, published in the 1800s.

PRAYER OF THE FAITHFUL

Year A

Having listened to the word of the beloved Son of God, we bring our petitions.

— Intercessions —

Let your mercy be upon us, O Lord, as we place our trust in you, and grant these prayers. Through Christ our Lord.

Year B

God did not spare his own Son. God will give us everything else we ask.

— Intercessions —

O God, who revealed the glory of your only Son, hear our prayers as we await a share in the rising of the Son of Man. Through Christ our Lord.

Year C

Christ will change our lowly body to conform with his glorified body. With faith in the power of God, let us offer our prayers.

— Intercessions —

O God, whose voice announced that Jesus Christ is your chosen Son, look with mercy upon the prayers of your children, and grant them. Through Christ our Lord.

Third Sunday of Lent

Overview

If members of the elect will be baptized at the Easter Vigil, you celebrate the first scrutiny with them today. If this is Year A, this presents no problem. But if this is Year B or C, you use the Gospel from Year A at the Masses that include a scrutiny. The rubrics say nothing about the other readings and psalms, so presumably they remain those of Years B and C. For pastoral reasons, you may celebrate the scrutinies on a weekday, but Sundays are preferable.

At a scrutiny Mass, the presidential prayers are found in the back of the missal under Ritual Masses, Christian Initiation, Scrutinies. These replace the prayers for the Third Sunday of Lent only when scrutinies are celebrated at this Mass. If you use Eucharistic Prayer I, there is a special form of the commemoration of the living (85) that allows the priest to list the names of the godparents. There is also a special form of the section that begins "Therefore, Lord, we pray" (87). All these texts first appeared in the Gelasian Sacramentary for the scrutiny Masses, and they are still offered at these celebrations today. Eucharistic Prayers II and III also have special formulas that acknowledge the elect. Those familiar with these pages from the 1985 Sacramentary will notice that they are easier to follow in the revised missal, which splits them into independent Sundays and adds unique entrance antiphons. For the actual scrutiny ritual and texts, see the *Rite of Christian Initiation of Adults*, 150–156.

The traditional location for the stational Mass for this day is Saint Lawrence outside the Walls of Rome. It is regarded as the burial place of Saint Lawrence, deacon and martyr. The cemetery there was owned by the lady who lived in the house where Saint Lawrence distributed alms, and where the church associated with last Sunday's Mass now stands, Santa Maria in Domnica. Deacons still serve the church in the liturgy, preaching, and service. The ministry of almsgiving, so important to Lawrence, is a feature of Lenten renewal.

The elect should celebrate the presentation of the Creed this week. You may want to tie it in with some other parish event, making it the opening prayer service for any groups that are meeting. Whenever it will happen, be sure to announce it this weekend.

LECTIONARY

In Year A, the second reading's theme of charity recurs in the prayer over the people. The Gospel resonates with the entrance antiphon, the preface, and the Communion antiphon. The third memorial acclamation calls Jesus the Savior of the world (Order of Mass, 91), which is how the Samaritans acclaim Jesus at the end of the Gospel.

When Eucharistic Prayer IV says that God offered "covenants," it surely means to include the Sinai covenant with Moses, as told in the first reading of Year B.

Second reading: During the preparation of the gifts at every Mass, the priest says the wine "will become our spiritual drink" (Order of Mass, 25). The reference is inspired by the second reading in Year C. First Corinthians 10:4 calls water from the rock a spiritual drink.

Entrance Antiphon

Two options are given—or three, depending on how you count. The first is the traditional entrance antiphon for this celebration, existing already in the eighth century. You can imagine Jesus praying these verses for rescue from his pursuers. The second foreshadows the cleansing given to those who are to be baptized. In fact, the second option here is the first option for the entrance antiphon if you are celebrating a scrutiny at this Mass. See the ritual Masses in the back of the missal. The second option for a scrutiny Mass cites Isaiah, through whom the Lord invites those who thirst to come to the waters.

Collect

This highly penitential prayer asks God to lift up those who are "bowed down by our conscience," and who spend this season in fasting, prayer, and almsgiving. The Gelasian Sacramentary assigned this prayer to Saturday of the Fourth Week of Lent. It was restored to the missal after the Second Vatican Council and moved to this day.

The collect for the first scrutiny prays that the elect may worthily and wisely come to confess God's praise. This very prayer is found in the Gelasian Sacramentary for the first scrutiny on this same Sunday.

Prayer over the Offerings

To make our sacrifice pleasing, we ask that we may be pardoned as we forgive the sins of our neighbor. The Gelasian Sacramentary included this among the prayers of Masses for charity, but its message of forgiveness befits the season of Lent. The pre-Vatican II missal assigned it to the previous day—Saturday of the Second Week of Lent—but it is now prayed on the Third Sunday.

If you are celebrating a scrutiny at this Mass, see the special prayer over the offerings in the ritual Mass for scrutinies in the back of the missal. As the collect does, it comes from the Gelasian Sacramentary's prayers for the first scrutiny Mass on this Sunday. It uses a Latin adverb,

PRAYER OF THE FAITHFUL

Year A

God provided water in the desert at the request of Moses. Let us pray for sustenance on our journey this Lent.

— *Intercessions* —

Give us living water,
O God of all creation,
and send refreshment
to all who seek your aid.
Through Christ our Lord.

Year B

Christ is the power of God and the wisdom of God. We present our prayers through him.

— *Intercessions* —

God of power and might,
who raised up Jesus your Son from death,
lift us up to praise you for your goodness,
and mercifully grant our prayers.
Through Christ our Lord.

Year C

God witnessed the affliction of the chosen people, heard their complaint, and knew their suffering. God will welcome these prayers in our time of need.

— *Intercessions* —

Merciful and gracious God,
slow to anger and abounding in kindness,
secure the rights of all who are oppressed.
Through Christ our Lord.

competenter, related to the word *competentes*, which was one of the early words for catechumens: those making a petition (for baptism) together.

Preface

You have three choices for the preface. However, if the Gospel of the Samaritan woman is proclaimed, you use the one that recounts her story. That is the case in Year A and in all three years when a scrutiny is celebrated at this particular Mass. When the Gospels of Years B and C are proclaimed, you may choose from either of the first two prefaces for Lent *(pp. 32–33).*

The preface about the Samaritan woman was a new composition for the post-Vatican II missal, based on one from the Supplement to the Hadrian Sacramentary for Friday of the Second Week of Lent. The "gift of faith" is mentioned in Wisdom 3:14 and Ephesians 2:8. The image of fire in relationship to belief is in Luke 12:49, Luke 24:32, and Hebrews 12:29.

Communion Antiphon

Of the two options, the second is the one from eighth-century sources. Its mention of the Lord's altars probably made it suitable for Communion. The first option is to be used whenever the Gospel of the Samaritan woman is read. It is repeated in the ritual Mass for scrutinies in the back of the missal.

Prayer after Communion

We pray that the mystery at work within us will come to true completion. The earliest record of this prayer is in the Verona Sacramentary among texts for the month of April. The post-Vatican II missal assigned it to this day after centuries of neglect.

A different prayer is offered when you have celebrated a scrutiny at this Mass. See the back of the missal under ritual Masses. It too is taken from the Gelasian Sacramentary's Mass for the first scrutiny on the Third Sunday of Lent.

Blessing

We pray that God will direct the hearts of the faithful in the fulfillment of God's commands. The prayer refers to the two great commandments of Jesus. The text is a conflation of two prayers for vespers found in the Verona Sacramentary among those for the month of July. Originally prayers for the close of the day, they draw this Mass to its ending.

Fourth Sunday of Lent

Overview

Priest and deacon may wear rose vestments today, but it is not obligatory. Violet vesture is also appropriate. This day marks the midway point of Lent for those keeping the spirit of the fast, but for the elect, it is the day of the second scrutiny. This has more to do with their own spiritual preparation than with a mid-season respite.

The traditional location for the stational liturgy on this day is Rome's Church of the Holy Cross in Jerusalem, which houses relics of the passion of Christ. Helena, the mother of Constantine, is credited with discovering the true cross in Jerusalem. She brought the relics back and placed them in her palace chapel, which Pope Sylvester I named "Jerusalem." The traditional antiphons for entrance and Communion both mention the Holy City by name.

Omit the Gloria today and on all the Sundays of Lent. But you may use floral decorations today (*GIRM*, 305 and 313; *Ceremonial of Bishops*, 252).

If you have elect preparing for their baptism at the Easter Vigil, conduct the second scrutiny today. See the prayers under Ritual Masses, Christian Initiation, Scrutinies. Those replace the usual ones for the Fourth Sunday of Lent. The Gospel from Year A is used. During the Eucharistic Prayer, mention is made of the godparents and those to be baptized. See the Third Sunday of Lent for comments.

Entrance Antiphon

The first word of this antiphon has given this day its traditional title since the eighth century: *Laetare*. The liturgy cites Isaiah's summons to rejoice, be joyful and exult. For him the exile is approaching its end, as Lent is for us.

Even so, if you are celebrating a scrutiny at this Mass a different antiphon is proposed in the ritual Mass section of the missal. With the man born blind we direct our eyes ever toward the Lord, begging for mercy.

Collect

Midway through Lent, we pray to hasten toward the solemn celebrations to come. The first part of this prayer is inspired by one for Wednesday of the Second Week of Lent in the Gelasian Sacramentary, but the rest of it was a completely new composition for the post-Vatican II missal. It intends to mark the bridge from one part of Lent to the next.

An alternative prayer is supplied when the second scrutiny is celebrated. You find it in

---

LECTIONARY

Because of the Gospel, the theme of light from the second reading of Year A reappears in many of the prayers and antiphons for this Mass. The Gospel's themes appear in the collect, prayer over the gifts, preface, prayer after Communion, and first Communion antiphon.

Eucharistic Prayer IV says that the Father sent the Son because "you so loved the world" (Order of Mass, 117), quoting John 3:16. It can be found in the Gospel of Year B.

In Year C, a verse from the Gospel is quoted in the second Communion antiphon.

the ritual Masses. It prays for an increase in spiritual joy as new members are reborn. It first appeared in the Gelasian Sacramentary as the collect for the second scrutiny on this day. It was restored here for the post-Vatican II missal.

Prayer over the Offerings

The gifts we bring we will soon revere and present for the salvation of the world. This prayer also comes from the scrutiny Mass on this day in the Gelasian Sacramentary. It appears intact in the ritual Mass for the second scrutiny, but it was lightly edited to fit celebrations where there are no elect ("for the salvation of all the world"); that is the version that appears on the main page of the Fourth Sunday of Lent.

Preface

The preface concerning the man born blind is to be used in Year A or any year you are celebrating a scrutiny at this Mass. It was newly composed for the post-Vatican II missal, primarily based upon the account from John 9:1–41. Also in John 8:12 and 12:35, Jesus scorns those who walk in darkness. The comparison between baptism and adoption can be found in Romans 8:15–17 and Galatians 4:4–7. See also Ephesians 1:5.

If this is Year B or C, and if you are not celebrating a scrutiny at this Mass, you choose one of the first two Lenten prefaces. See above for comments *(pp. 32–33)*.

Communion Antiphon

Three options are given. The first is for Year A and during a scrutiny Mass in Years B and C. It is repeated in the texts for scrutinies in the back of the missal. The second option is for Year C when the Gospel of the prodigal son is read at a Mass where no scrutiny is taking place. The third option, which relates to none of the Gospels, is the antiphon that existed here since at least the eighth century. It directs our thoughts to Jerusalem, where Jesus heads toward his passion.

Prayer after Communion

We pray that this Communion will illuminate our hearts. The earliest version of this prayer, from the Gelasian Sacramentary, was offered on the Vigil of the Epiphany. The imagery of light made it a good candidate for this Mass, especially when hearing about the man born blind.

Predictably, the prayer after Communion for the second scrutiny Mass is taken from the Gelasian Mass of the same name, which supplied the other presidential prayers for this ritual celebration. The text prays for guidance; it is included here primarily because of its antiquity and for the integrity of the purpose of its composition.

Blessing

The prayer asks God to sustain the weak and help us all reach the highest good. It first appeared in the Verona Sacramentary among the prayers for the month of April, and was restored for this day in the post-Vatican II missal.

PRAYER OF THE FAITHFUL

Year A

Even though we walk in the dark valley, we
   fear no evil, for the Good Shepherd will
   hear our prayers.

— Intercessions —

O God,
who make your works visible
even through the infirmities of your people,
reveal your radiant kindness
upon the needs we lift to you.
Through Christ our Lord.

Year B

God did not send the Son to condemn
   the world, but that we might be saved
   through him. In confidence we present
   our needs.

— Intercessions —

O God,
who send your light into the world,
grant our prayers,
and help us to live in truth
that all may see the works you have done.
Through Christ our Lord.

Year C

We are a new creation in Christ. The old
   things have passed away; new things have
   come. In God's presence we present our
   prayers.

— Intercessions —

Boundless is your compassion, O God,
to those who repent and return to you.
Grant our needs and restore us to life.
Through Christ our Lord.

Fifth Sunday of Lent

Overview

The custom of covering crosses and images throughout the church may be retained from this day, but it is not obligatory. If crosses are covered, they remain so until after the celebration of the Passion on Good Friday. Other images are uncovered just before the Easter Vigil.

The third scrutiny is celebrated today for those to be baptized at Easter. The Gospel of the raising of Lazarus should be proclaimed at those Masses.

Saint Peter's is the traditional stational church in Rome for this day. This Sunday began Passiontide in the old calendar, so it was fitting to go to the place of Peter's crucifixion and burial in anticipation of participating in the paschal mystery of Christ.

The elect may celebrate the presentation of the Lord's Prayer this week, or you may transfer it to the preparation rites on Holy Saturday. You may want to connect it with some other parish event this week, making it the opening prayer service for any groups that are meeting. If so, announce it this weekend.

Before Mass begins this weekend, you might take a few minutes to rehearse any special music people will need to know for the Triduum. Some of the chants are used only once a year. Rehearsing will help prepare people to participate, and may even encourage them to attend these services.

Entrance Antiphon

The post-Vatican II missal kept the antiphon that used to introduce Passiontide since at least the eighth century. It offers a prayer that God will judge against a faithless nation, and grant rescue from the deceitful and cunning. However, if this is a scrutiny Mass, the antiphon comes from a different psalm and anticipates the account of the raising of Lazarus: "The waves of death rose about me."

Collect

The collect looks forward to the passion of Christ and begs for the same charity he showed

---

LECTIONARY

Year A's Gospel, the raising of Lazarus, inspired the antiphons and the preface.

The priest quotes verse 4 of Year B's responsorial psalm every time he washes his hands at Mass (Order of Mass, 28).

The third Communion antiphon comes from the Gospel of Year B. In Eucharistic Prayer IV, the priest says the sacrifice "brings salvation to the whole world," and that those who partake are "gathered into one body by the Holy Spirit" (Order of Mass, 117). These lines resonate with Jesus' statement at the end of this Gospel, "And when I am lifted up from the earth, I will draw everyone to myself."

In the first reading of Year C, the Lord speaks through Isaiah of "the people whom I formed for myself," and Eucharistic Prayer III refers to "the entire people you have gained for your own" (Order of Mass, 113). The Gospel provides the second Communion antiphon.

as he handed himself over to death. This prayer was new to the post-Vatican II missal, which reworked an older prayer from the Mozarabic tradition of the Catholic Church. It originated as part of the sign of peace, but it fittingly serves here as we fix our attention more closely on the cross of Christ.

If there is a scrutiny today, the collect comes from the ritual Masses in the back of the missal. It first appeared in its entirety for the same Mass in the Gelasian Sacramentary. Close to the day of their initiation, celebrating the final scrutiny, we pray that the elect will receive new life from their baptism.

Prayer over the Offerings

We pray that the faithful familiar with the teachings of the Christian faith may be purified by this sacrifice. The prayer is the same as the one from the Mass for the third scrutiny from the Gelasian Sacramentary—except for one word: "teachings." The original word was "first fruits," which can be found in the prayer from the ritual Mass used today if there is a scrutiny. The two versions of the prayer contrast those who have begun to learn the faith and those who have absorbed it—the elect and the faithful.

Preface

As a human, Jesus wept for Lazarus, but as God, he raised him from the tomb. Christ can bring us to new life. This preface was composed for the post-Vatican II missal, and it is used in Year A and whenever the scrutiny is celebrated in Years B and C. The preface relies on the Gospel account of Lazarus (John 11:1–46), but alludes to other passages. Jesus showed "pity" on the crowds in Matthew 14:14. The theme of new life appears in Romans 6:4.

If there is no scrutiny, and this is Year B or C, choose one of the first two Lenten prefaces. See comments on *pp. 32–33*.

Communion Antiphon

The three options were all new to the post-Vatican II missal, and they are drawn from the Gospels of Years A, B, and C. The first applies

---

PRAYER OF THE FAITHFUL

Year A

With the Lord there is mercy and fullness of redemption. Trusting in God's word, we present our prayers.

— *Intercessions* —

O God,
whose Son is the resurrection and the life,
restore our joy by granting these petitions.
Through Christ our Lord.

Year B

Christ Jesus offered prayers and supplications with loud cries and tears, and he was heard because of his reverence. Let us bring our prayers.

— *Intercessions* —

Glorify your name, O God;
in all our troubled hours,
hear our prayers and lift us from the earth.
Through Christ our Lord.

Year C

We are filled with joy when the Lord does great things for us. In hope of salvation we make known our needs.

— *Intercessions* —

Help us to sin no more,
O God of infinite mercy,
and turn not away from the needs
   of your people.
Through Christ our Lord.

---

to Year A and any year you have a scrutiny at this Mass. The second is for Year C, which has retained the pre-Vatican II Gospel for this day. The third, to be used when "another Gospel" is read (the same phrase appearing in last Sunday's Communion antiphon options), is logically reduced to non-scrutiny Year B usage. All the texts preserve the custom of linking the Communion antiphon to the Gospel of the day. They replace an antiphon that quoted Jesus' words over the bread and the wine at the Last Supper, which worked well when the Passion was read on this day, but now are premature in the slower evolution of this season.

Prayer after Communion

We pray to be counted among those sharing Communion in the Body and Blood of Christ. The original version of this prayer comes from the Verona Sacramentary, among the collection for prayers during drought in the month of October. By the next century it had moved to Monday of the Second Week of Lent, and the post-Vatican II missal assigned it here.

If you are celebrating a scrutiny, use the prayer from the ritual Masses. It is taken from the same Mass in the Gelasian Sacramentary, restored after centuries of disuse. We pray to live out the joy at being saved and to pray lovingly for those to be baptized.

Blessing

The prayer over the people asks God to grant what they are inspired to request. The original comes from the Gelasian Sacramentary, where it serves as a prayer over the people for the first scrutiny Mass.

Palm Sunday of the Passion of the Lord

Overview

Holy Week opens with the celebration of Palm Sunday. It is called "of the Passion of the Lord," as is Good Friday, because these are the days on which the community hears one Gospel account of the suffering and death of Jesus.

There are three options for the opening of this Mass. The first form—the procession—is meant to be done only at the principal Mass. Although Mass is "principal" for each person no matter when he or she comes, having one procession for the parish establishes one principal celebration, as there will be for the days of the Triduum. The priest and deacon wear red vesture.

In the first form, Mass begins in a chapel apart from the church. Prepare a lectern from which the Gospel may be read. Servers and ministers may hold the missal, the holy water, a decorated processional cross, candles, and incense. People hold branches. Traditionally, these are palms, but no kind of branch is specified. The priest may start the liturgy wearing a red cope.

After the entrance antiphon, the priest leads the sign of the cross and greets the people as usual. Then an introduction to the day is given. The rubrics do not specify who gives it; it could be spoken by the deacon, lector, or even a trained catechist. The priest says a prayer and then sprinkles the blessed branches. A deacon or priest proclaims the Gospel of Palm Sunday. Incense may be used. A brief homily may follow the Gospel. Almost no one exercises this option, but it is another way to preach on this day.

The invitation to join the procession may be given by the priest, deacon, or lay minister. All process to the church behind incense, if it is being used. The processional cross may be decorated with palm branches (here the type of branch is specified) and carried between two candle-bearers. The deacon carries the Book of the Gospels, the priest follows with ministers, and then the faithful. All sing during the procession. The priest venerates the altar. If he has been wearing a cope, he removes it and puts on the chasuble for Mass. The penitential rite and Gloria are omitted, but the Kyrie may still be sung before the opening prayer.

The second form is for places where the opening procession cannot take place. People gather outside the church if possible; if not, then inside, holding branches. The priest and ministers go someplace where at least some of the faithful can see them, and perform the rites outlined in the first form. This form may be repeated at any Mass this weekend.

The third form is for Masses with no blessing of branches or proclamation of the Palm Sunday Gospel. It moves from the introit to the opening prayer of the Mass. During the entrance antiphon, the priest processes to the sanctuary, venerates the altar, makes the sign of the cross, and greets the people from the chair. If there is no music, the priest reads the antiphon.

Regarding the proclamation of the Passion, no candles or incense are used, nor are the people greeted, nor is the book signed with the cross. A deacon or priest may read the entire Passion, or its parts may be distributed to other readers. The assembly may take part. If possible, the priest should read the part of Christ. Only a deacon asks the priest for a blessing. After the verse on the death of Jesus, all kneel and observe a brief silence; the book is not kissed after the Passion (*Ceremonial of Bishops*, 273). A brief homily may be given, or a brief silence may be kept. The rest of the Mass proceeds as usual.

The traditional stational church for this day is Saint John Lateran, the cathedral church of Rome, where the stational Mass for the First Sunday of Lent took place.

Appendix V offers a sample formulary for the Prayer of the Faithful during Holy Week. The introduction quotes the Letter to the Hebrews 5:7. The tabernacle needs to be empty on Holy Thursday. Refrain from consecrating unneeded Communion bread today. You may not celebrate marriage on Good Friday or Holy Saturday. If convalidations still need to be celebrated for catechumens or candidates in irregular marriages, make preparations to do so before the Triduum.

Entrance Antiphon

The antiphons at the beginning of this liturgy come from the pre-Vatican II missal and quote lines from the first Gospel of Palm Sunday. The hymn that follows them is also traditional; many parishes sing "All Glory, Laud and Honor" in its place, which is most appropriate, but other songs may be used. Some chants for the traditional texts appear in the missal; it would be good to work them into the repertoire of the congregation.

Collect

We pray for the same patient suffering that Jesus had, as well as a share in the Resurrection. This prayer has been in place for this day since at least the Gelasian Sacramentary.

Prayer over the Offerings

We pray for the mercy of God through this sacrifice. This prayer originated as one for the month of July in the Verona Sacramentary, and then was lost for many centuries. One theory is that it was composed for a Mass in Rome on February 7, 538, when Vigilius was pope, shortly before the Goths lifted their siege. The post-Vatican II missal placed this prayer here; its themes of reconciliation, mercy, and sacrifice make it a fitting choice for this day.

Preface

Innocent, Jesus suffered for sinners, and offered us forgiveness and a share in resurrection. Today's preface carries an allusion to Romans 4:23–25, where Paul says Christ rose for our justification. Several New Testament passages affirm that Christ was sinless and innocent:

LECTIONARY

The entrance antiphon comes from Year A's Gospel of Palm Sunday; the Communion antiphon comes from Year A's Passion. The introduction to the first sample Prayer of the Faithful for Lent in Appendix V refers to Matthew 26:40 when it invites people to watch more intently with Christ. The institution narrative of all the Eucharistic Prayers relies on Matthew 26:26–28.

In Year C's Passion, at the Last Supper, Jesus says he is one who serves, and he establishes a model that his followers are to imitate. This is one reason why a passage such as Order of Mass 85 in Eucharistic Prayer I prays for "servants"—the living whose faith and devotion are known to God.

2 Corinthians 5:21, 1 Peter 2:21–24, 1 Peter 3:18, and 1 John 3:5. This preface is based on one for Wednesday of Holy Week from the Supplement to the Hadrian Sacramentary.

Communion Antiphon

This antiphon is the traditional one from eighth-century sources. It quotes the Gospel that was proclaimed each year on Palm Sunday prior to Vatican II: The Passion according to Matthew.

Prayer after Communion

Looking beyond the Passion through this Communion, we pray for a share in the resurrection of Christ. This prayer was new to the post-Vatican II missal, but it combines elements of two prayers from the Palm Sunday Mass in the Gelasian Sacramentary. The second half comes from a prayer that survived for many centuries just before the procession with palms on this day. It was moved here together with a phrase from a Communion prayer so that it fit the purpose of this part of the Mass.

Blessing

As we recall that Jesus handed himself over for our sake, we ask God to look upon us. In the Hadrian Sacramentary this prayer concluded the Mass on Wednesday of Holy Week, when the Passion according to Luke was read. Now the Passions of Matthew, Mark, and Luke are proclaimed on Palm Sunday throughout the three-year Lectionary cycle. So the 2002 missal brought this traditional prayer back to the liturgy. It was not here in the 1985 Sacramentary.

There is a solemn blessing for Lent in the *Collection of Masses for the Blessed Virgin Mary*, p. 202. It has the Passion in mind, so this could be an appropriate occasion to consider it as an alternative.

PRAYER OF THE FAITHFUL

Year A

The Lord God is our help. We shall not be put to shame. Aware of God's love, we present our needs.

— *Intercessions* —

Open our ears, O God,
that we may hear
a word that rouses the weary.
Through Christ our Lord.

Year B

Christ Jesus became obedient to the point of death, even death on a cross. Through him, the Father's beloved Son, we lift our prayers.

— *Intercessions* —

O God,
who bestowed upon your Son
the name above every other name,
listen to the cries of those who hope
in your saving mercy.
Through Christ our Lord.

Year C

Jesus promised paradise to the repentant thief. God will not be deaf to our prayers.

— *Intercessions* —

O God,
remember us who long to enter
your kingdom,
and grant our prayers.
Through Christ our Lord.

Thursday of the Lord's Supper

Overview

In commemoration of the night that Jesus gathered with his disciples for the Last Supper before he died, we gather for the Eucharist he commanded us to keep in his memory.

The Mass takes place in the evening when the faithful, priests, and ministers can take part. Your bishop may permit a Mass earlier in the day for extreme cases when people cannot participate in the evening, but ordinarily that is not recommended. Communion may be brought to the sick at any time, but the ideal time is after this Mass, not before. No one else may receive Communion outside of Mass on this day. Flowers may adorn the altar in moderation. The tabernacle should be empty, its doors open wide. Extinguish or remove the sanctuary lamp. Prepare enough bread so that people can receive Communion today and tomorrow from what is consecrated at this Mass.

Sing the Gloria at this Mass, if at all possible. Ring bells, too—inside and outside the church. After this, the organ and other instruments should be used only to support singing, not to play solos.

The homily should treat the mysteries of this Mass: the institution of the Eucharist and the priesthood, as well as the command to love one another.

The washing of the feet may follow the homily; it is optional, but a powerful ceremony to include this evening. The rubrics call for the feet of designated men to be washed, probably in imitation of the Gospels' apostles. It never calls for "twelve" men, probably because this would be difficult to arrange in some small communities. In practice, the priest in some communities washes the feet of women and children, too. The priest may remove his chasuble, and then he approaches each of the seated participants, pours water on their feet, and dries them. Ministers may help, but it probably looks humbler if he does all this alone. In some communities, people who have their feet washed wash the feet of others. The rubrics do not invite this; Jesus probably did not expect the disciples literally to wash one another's feet, but to serve one another in a hundred other ways.

All the antiphons for this part of the ceremony are traditional ones from the pre-Vatican II missal, but they have been rearranged in chronological order of their appearance in the Gospel of John. The only exception is antiphons 5 and 6, which cite John 13:35 and 13:34 respectively, probably because this sequence leads more naturally into the surprisingly appropriate antiphon 7 from Paul's First Letter to the Corinthians, chapter 13. Most people expect to hear that passage at weddings: of faith, hope, and love, the greatest gift is love. After this ceremony, the priest washes and dries his hands, puts the chasuble back on, and goes to his chair for the Prayer of the Faithful. This washing of hands is new to the 2002 missal, though it was being practiced in other countries after the Council.

The procession of the gifts should include gifts for the poor, especially those collected as a fruit of Lenten penance (*Circular Letter Concerning the Preparation and Celebration of the Easter Feasts*, 52). Many parishes bring gifts for a local food pantry. The traditional hymn about charity is recommended for this part of the Mass. The Sacramentary Supplement of 2004 included here a presentation of the oils blessed at the Chrism Mass, but the missal is silent about this. You may still use it if you wish.

The missal reprints the entire text of Eucharistic Prayer I among the pages for Holy Thursday, showing its preference for this traditional text today. The special inserts, which have been in place for about fifteen hundred years with almost no variation, are worked right into the text. However, you may use Eucharistic Prayer II or III.

At Communion time, consecrated bread is entrusted to the ministers who will bring it to the sick and homebound. This requires some advance preparation—both to recruit the ministers and to set up times with those who wish to receive at what may be a late hour for them. But it extends the fruits of this special Mass to the entire parish community.

After Communion the consecrated breads are gathered into ciboria (not a monstrance) and placed on the altar. (This is about reservation of the Eucharist, not adoration of the Blessed Sacrament.) The priest says the prayer after Communion from the chair; normally he may choose to stand at the altar or the chair at this time, but not at this Mass.

There is no final blessing. After the prayer after Communion, all kneel. The priest incenses the Blessed Sacrament, puts on a humeral veil, approaches the altar, and picks up the ciboria with the veil. A procession forms, led by a cross-bearer and two candle-bearers. Other candles may be carried. The thurifer comes next, in front of the priest, who carries the Blessed Sacrament. All sing a Eucharistic hymn as the procession moves to a location preferably outside the nave to repose the Blessed Sacrament. The deacon may assist the priest in placing the ciboria in the tabernacle. The priest removes the humeral veil. Kneeling down, he incenses the Blessed Sacrament while another Eucharistic hymn is sung. Then the deacon or the priest closes the tabernacle door. All adore in silence. The priest and ministers genuflect and return to the sacristy.

Afterward the altar is stripped and crosses are carried away or veiled if possible. Candles—even those before images of the saints—are extinguished (*Circular Letter*, 57). The faithful should be invited to spend time in adoration. Perhaps the cantor could announce this before giving the page number for the processional hymn. The *Circular Letter* suggests that the Gospel of John, chapters 13–17, be read during the period of adoration (56); perhaps different groups from the parish could sign up for one hour of meditation on one of these chapters. Adoration concludes by midnight without any solemnity. But night prayer from *The Liturgy of the Hours* would be appropriate as the period of adoration come to an end.

If it is necessary to celebrate a funeral today, observe the form for a Funeral without Mass in the *Order of Christian Funerals*.

Entrance Antiphon

Although the focus will be on the Eucharist tonight, the entrance antiphon draws our attention immediately to the cross. These next three days depend on one another. This is the traditional antiphon for this Mass, in place since at least the eighth century.

Collect

We pray for the fullness of charity and life from the celebration of the Paschal Mystery.

This was a new composition for the post-Vatican II missal, and, as sometimes happened, the writers made it rather complex. It requires a purposeful delivery.

Prayer over the Offerings

We pray to participate worthily in these mysteries as we witness the work of our redemption. This began as a prayer for April in the Verona Sacramentary, presumably one for the Easter season.

Preface

Jesus instituted the Eucharist, offering himself as a sacrifice and commanding us to offer it as well. This preface was newly composed for the post-Vatican II missal. It is also the first of the two prefaces of the Most Holy Eucharist. Melchizedek is called an eternal priest in Psalm 110:4 and Hebrews 5:5–6 and 6:20. Ephesians 5:2 says Jesus offered himself as a victim; Hebrews 7:26 and 9:14–15 use similar language. Jesus commanded this memorial in Luke 22:19 and 1 Corinthians 11:24. The word "flesh" recalls John 6:54; the "sacrifice" of that flesh recalls 1 Corinthians 5:7. According to Matthew 26:28, Mark 14:24, and Luke 22:20, Jesus said he would pour out his blood. Revelation 1:5 says that Jesus Christ washed away our sins in his blood.

Communion Antiphon

This text comes from the second reading. If the Communion antiphon quotes one of the readings of the day, it usually cites the Gospel. But in this case, we hear Paul's account of the institution of the Eucharist, so the antiphon—which was new to the post-Vatican II missal—quotes him.

PRAYER OF THE FAITHFUL

Years A, B, C

Jesus loved his own in the world, and he loved them to the end. In service to his holy name we bring forth our prayers.

— Intercessions —

O God,
who give us a model in the service
 of your Son,
strengthen us to imitate his example
by answering our needs.
Through Christ our Lord.

Prayer after Communion

Renewed by sharing in this supper, we pray that we might feast at your Son's banquet in eternity. The text appeared in the Gothic Missal, a western, non-Roman prayer book, where it served as the prayer after Communion for the Mass of the Lord's Supper. The prayer went unused for many centuries, but was restored for the post-Vatican II missal to broaden the number of sources from which our prayers are drawn.

LECTIONARY YEARS A, B, C

Responsorial psalm: During Eucharistic Prayer I the priest offers "the Chalice of everlasting salvation" (Order of Mass, 92), and in Eucharistic Prayer II the "Chalice of salvation" (Order of Mass, 105). Both of these phrases refer to Psalm 116:13.

Second reading: The Communion antiphon comes from this text. The preface also alludes to it. The institution narrative in all the Eucharistic Prayers relies on the information in this passage. The second memorial acclamation (Order of Mass, 91) is a direct quote of 1 Corinthians 11:26.

Gospel: When Eucharistic Prayer IV says that Jesus loved his disciples to the end (Order of Mass, 119), it quotes John 13:1. Jesus takes on the role of a servant, and this is one reason why passages such as Order of Mass, 85 in Eucharistic Prayer I call the followers of Jesus "servants." Jesus tells Peter he will have no inheritance with him unless he submits to having his feet washed; Eucharistic Prayer IV hopes for the day when "we may enter into a heavenly inheritance" (Order of Mass, 122).

Friday of the Passion of the Lord

Overview

With a somber liturgy, the Church observes the day that Jesus died. Although the priest wears a chasuble, it is not a Mass. The ceremony is simply called "The Celebration of the Lord's Passion."

Today and tomorrow the sacraments are not administered, except for penance and the anointing of the sick. The convalidation of the marriages of anyone becoming a Catholic at the Easter Vigil this year should have been done already. The faithful may receive Communion only at this service, unless they are infirm. However, the liturgy does not promote bringing Communion to the sick as it does on Holy Thursday.

Today is a day of fast and abstinence. All Catholics over the age of fourteen abstain from meat all day. Those from their eighteenth through their fifty-ninth birthday limit themselves to one full meal and two smaller meals. Eating between meals is not permitted. You may wish to announce these regulations in the parish bulletin, at Mass on Palm Sunday, and even at the close of this celebration, if other announcements are made.

The preferred time for this celebration is 3:00 p.m., but it may be celebrated in the evening. The altar should be bare: no cross, no candles, and no cloths. You might remove from the sanctuary anything extraneous to this celebration. Priest and deacon wear red vesture and approach the altar in silence. There is no mention of any kind of procession with other ministers or candles; logically, though, servers would enter ahead of the clergy. The priest and deacon kneel or prostrate for silent prayer. Kneeling is listed first, suggesting it is preferable, but prostration is the more meaningful posture. All others in the church kneel. After a while the priest goes to his chair with the ministers; he extends his hands and offers an opening prayer. It is not called a collect.

During the Liturgy of the Word the proclamation of the Passion takes place as it is described on Palm Sunday; namely, without incense or candles, without a greeting of the people or the signing of the book. All kneel for a time of silent prayer at the announcement of the death of Christ. The book is not kissed. The options for the readers are the same as well. A brief homily or a short silence may follow the reading.

The Prayer of the Faithful takes on a more solemn form; in fact, it is thought that this was the common form for the weekly Sunday Prayer of the Faithful in the earliest stages of the Eucharist. A deacon or lay minister stands at the ambo and gives the intention. All pray silently. The priest at the chair or the altar says the prayer with arms extended. The faithful may remain kneeling or standing throughout, or they may kneel for the moments of silent prayer that follow the first half of each intention. In that case, the deacon or priest may invite people to kneel and stand. The conference of bishops may suggest other intentions; so may the local bishop. Music for these prayers appears in the missal; it would be good if ministers and faithful could all sing their parts.

The adoration of the cross may take place in one of two forms. In the first the deacon or another minister goes to the sacristy and processes out with the cross, veiled in violet. The procession moves through the church to the sanctuary, accompanied by two lighted candles. The priest stands in front of the altar, takes the cross, uncovers the top part, and sings, "Behold, the wood of the Cross." The deacon or a choir may sing instead. All respond, "Come, let us adore." Then all kneel for brief silence while the priest stands holding the cross aloft. Notes for the music are in the missal. The priest uncovers the right arm of the cross, while the dialogue is sung a second time; then the left arm. All kneel in silence each time.

In the second form, the priest or the deacon or another minister goes to the door of the church, takes up the unveiled cross, and processes with two candle-bearers through the church to the sanctuary. The sung dialogue takes place near the door, in the middle of the church, and before the entrance to the sanctuary. All kneel in silence each time.

For the adoration of the cross, the priest with two candle-bearers carries it to the front of the sanctuary or another appropriate place and sets it there, or he hands it to ministers who will hold it up. The candles are set on either side. The priest comes alone; his chasuble and shoes may be removed. The clergy, lay ministers, and faithful all process up and reverence the cross with a simple genuflection or another appropriate sign; for example, kissing the cross. Only one cross should be used.

If it is difficult for all to come forward, the priest and some ministers may adore it, and then he may invite everyone to adore together from their places, holding up the cross for silent adoration. Hymns should be sung. "We Adore Your Cross, O Lord" is recommended. Other texts may be used, including the traditional reproaches, but some people find these offensive to people of the Jewish faith. The traditional hymn "Faithful Cross" may also be used. New to the 2002 missal is the suggestion that *Stabat mater* may be sung, a hymn many parishes use at Stations of the Cross during Lent. Any song of the sorrowful Virgin is appropriate. After the adoration, the cross is carried by a deacon or another minister to its place at the altar, but not on it. Lighted candles are arranged around or on the altar, or near the cross.

For Communion, a cloth is placed on the altar, then a corporal and the missal. Meanwhile the deacon or priest puts on the humeral veil and carries the Blessed Sacrament from its place of reposition to the altar while all stand in silence. Two candle-bearers accompany this procession and place their candles around or on top of the altar. If a deacon has led this procession, he uncovers the ciborium, and the priest approaches the altar and genuflects. The priest conducts the Communion rite. No text is given for a Communion antiphon, though Psalm 21 is offered as a possibility. It is also entirely appropriate to have no singing at all during this particular Communion. The priest says the prayer after Communion and the prayer over the people. Then the ministers genuflect to the cross and leave.

After the service the altar is made bare again, but the cross may remain in place surrounded by two or four candles for the adoration of the faithful throughout the day.

If your parish needs to schedule a funeral today, use the Funeral without Mass from the *Order of Christian Funerals*. The *Circular Letter* says a Good Friday funeral should be celebrated without singing, music, or the tolling of bells (61). The absence of music is hard to explain; even morning prayer on Good Friday calls for music. But the tolling of bells might confuse the surrounding community to think you are observing a moment of silence at the death of Jesus Christ.

It is permissible to hear confessions today, but it would be more appropriate to keep these days clear for the observance of the Triduum liturgies.

Prayer

We ask the Lord to remember his mercies and sanctify his servants. This prayer is new to the post-Vatican II Good Friday service, but it started in the sixth century as a prayer for Friday of the Second Week of Lent, and was brought into place here. It serves as an alternative for the traditional pre-Vatican II prayer, which is still preserved in the missal. That prayer asks that we who bear the image of earthly humans may be conformed to Christ. This is a complex prayer that requires careful articulation. The appearance of the word "man" twice will not sound gender-inclusive to many, but the translators strove to preserve the poetic contrast in Latin between a man (or woman) of earth and the Man (Jesus) of heaven. This alternative prayer has been part of the Good Friday liturgy since at least the seventh-century Gelasian Sacramentary; even though it presents challenges, it was retained because of its antiquity and imagery.

Intercessions

I. For Holy Church

We pray that God will watch over the Church, that we may persevere in confessing the divine name. The text has been virtually unchanged since the Gelasian Sacramentary, which added the hope that principalities and powers would be subject to the Church.

II. For the Pope

We pray that God will protect the pope, so that, governed by God, we may grow under the pontiff. The original prayer from the Gelasian concerned all the bishops; now we concentrate on the pope.

III. For All Orders and Degrees of the Faithful

We pray that God will be faithfully served by the ministers of the Church. Originally a Gelasian prayer for those in major orders, minor orders, confessors, virgins, widows, and all the faithful, this was redrawn in the post-Vatican II missal to pray for the local bishop, all ordained ministers, and all the faithful.

IV. For Catechumens

We pray that catechumens will increase in faith and understanding and be added to the children of God through baptism. The word "our" is inserted if the parish has catechumens this year. The prayer for catechumens has remained unchanged since at least the seventh century.

V. For the Unity of Christians

We pray that all Christians may be joined by integrity of faith and united in the bond of charity. This prayer was a new composition in the post-Vatican II missal. It is the same as the first option for the collect of the Mass for the Unity of Christians.

LECTIONARY

During the institution narrative, the Eucharistic Prayers all quote Matthew and Mark that, at the Last Supper, Jesus said he poured out his blood "for many." This is an allusion to Isaiah 53:11–12, found at the end of today's first reading.

When Eucharistic Prayer IV says that Christ "shared our human nature in all things but sin" (Order of Mass, 117), it cites Hebrews 4:15 from today's second reading. The fifth appendix of the missal offers sample formularies for the Prayer of the Faithful. The one for Holy Week is not used today, but it cites Hebrews 5:7.

The Passion according to John sets the tone for this celebration. Jesus willingly accepts his cross, which becomes an image of the glory of God.

VI. For the Jewish People

We pray that the Jewish people may attain the fullness of redemption. This prayer was newly composed for the post-Vatican II missal. Its predecessor, which dates at least back to the Gelasian, contained offensive language. When Pope Benedict XVI expanded the usage of the pre-Vatican II missal, he drafted a new prayer to replace the offensive one, but it still presented challenges for interfaith dialogue. Because you are using the revised *Roman Missal*, you steer clear of the whole controversy because this post-Vatican II prayer has been much appreciated by our Jewish brothers and sisters.

VII. For Those Who Do Not Believe in Christ

We pray that those who do not know Christ but walk with a sincere heart may find the truth. This prayer was newly composed for the post-Vatican II missal.

VIII. For Those Who Do Not Believe in God

We pray that those who do not acknowledge God will be led to faith through natural desire and the witness of believers. This was another new composition for the post-Vatican II missal. This and the previous prayer replace one for those who worship false idols.

IX. For Those in Public Office

We pray that God will grant prosperity, peace, and freedom of religion through the good governance of those in public office. The Gelasian included a prayer for the emperor, which evolved into one for those in public office in the pre-Vatican II missal. That prayer was expanded for the revised rites after the Council.

X. For Those in Tribulation

We pray for people with various concerns: disease, hunger, imprisonment, travel, pilgrimage, and illness. This prayer has remained unchanged since it appeared in the Gelasian Sacramentary. However, it has been moved from the middle of the intentions to the end, where it serves as a final summary of various needs.

Prayer after Communion

We pray that this celebration may preserve within us the work of God's mercy. This prayer began in the Verona Sacramentary as a preface for days of fast in the month of September. Once a Communion rite was added to this liturgy, this text was recast as one of several prayers after Communion in the pre-Vatican II missal. After the Council, it became the only prayer after Communion for Good Friday.

Blessing

We pray for God's blessing, for pardon, comfort, an increase of faith, and everlasting redemption. The Verona Sacramentary preserved this prayer over the people as an option for fasting days in December. It appeared as a prayer after Communion in the pre-Vatican II missal for this day, when the phrases about the death and resurrection of Christ were added to the original prayer. The post-Vatican II missal restored it to its original purpose as a prayer over the people, but to conclude the Good Friday liturgy where it had found its home for the past many centuries.

The Easter Vigil in the Holy Night

Overview

On Holy Saturday the Church observes the day that Christ spent in the tomb, and the Easter Vigil celebrates his resurrection with a variety of symbols in the most complex, reflective, and joyous celebration of the year. If there is any Mass every Catholic should make a priority every single year, it is the Easter Vigil.

The Church recommends that we spend Holy Saturday in prayer and fasting. Most people know that Good Friday is a day of fast and abstinence, but not many realize that the same practice is advised for Holy Saturday. We keep vigil as we await the celebration of the resurrection of Jesus Christ. Holy Communion may be given today only to the dying.

The entire Vigil should take place at night, not beginning before dark, and finishing before dawn. Priest and deacon wear white vestments. Candles are prepared for all participants. Lights in the church should be out—including the votive candles.

A large fire is prepared outside the church in an appropriate place. People gather there; the priest approaches with ministers, one of whom carries the paschal candle, which must be made of wax (*Circular Letter*, 82). And it should be new; don't buy a new number to cover up the last digit on last year's candle. No other candles and no processional cross are used. If a fire cannot be lit outside, the priest stands at the door inside the church.

All make the sign of the cross and exchange the usual greeting. The priest introduces the Vigil; a suggested text is supplied, but he may use his own words. He blesses the fire, and then a minister brings him the paschal candle. The priest cuts a cross into it with a stylus, then cuts the Greek letters alpha and omega, and the numbers of the current year, proclaiming Christ yesterday, today, and forever. The priest may then insert five grains of incense into the candle while asking Christ to guard and protect us by his wounds. The priest lights the candle from the new fire, and incense is lit from charcoal taken from the fire.

The deacon or another minister takes the paschal candle. The thurifer goes in front of the paschal candle and the priest, the ministers, and the people follow. At the door of the church the person holding the candle sings, "The Light of Christ," and all respond, "Thanks be to God." Then the priest lights his own candle. The procession moves to the middle of the church, where the dialogue is repeated. All light their candles from the paschal candle. The procession goes to the front of the altar, and the dialogue happens a third time. Then the paschal candle is placed on a large candle stand near the ambo or in the middle of the sanctuary. The other candles in the church are lighted, except the altar candles.

The priest goes to his chair, hands his candle to a minister, puts incense in the thurible as at the Gospel at Mass, and blesses the deacon who will proclaim the Exsultet. If a lay person sings it, the priest does not give a blessing. The deacon incenses the book and the candle; all stand, holding lighted candles. If no deacon or priest can sing the Exsultet, a lay cantor may do so, omitting parts that belong to the clergy. A shorter version may be sung instead. This is a great piece of music in the repertoire of the Church, and it would be good to have someone sing it well.

After the Exsultet, all extinguish their candles and are seated. The priest gives an introduction to the next part of the service. The Liturgy of the Word has nine readings. If possible, they should all be used to establish the nature of this Vigil. For serious reasons the number of Old Testament readings may be reduced from seven to as few as three. Still, they have to represent texts from both the Law and the Prophets. Each Old Testament reading is followed by silence, a responsory, and a prayer. People are seated, but they stand for each of the prayers. Sacred silence may replace the psalms, and the words "Let us pray" may then be omitted. But the psalms add to the character of the Vigil.

Note that the proclamation of the Gospel is one of the key moments in the entire evening. After the New Testament reading, the *Ceremonial of Bishops*, 352 allows a deacon or reader to go to the bishop and say, "Most Reverend Father, I bring you a message of great joy, the message of Alleluia." Then all rise as the bishop intones the Alleluia three times, raising the pitch each time. It would not be inappropriate for something similar to happen in parishes to highlight the proclamation of the Gospel. In the Gospel procession, candles are not carried (*Ceremonial of Bishops*, 353).

The liturgy of baptism follows. For an extended commentary, see *Celebrating Initiation: A Guide for Priests* (WLP, 2008). Basically, though, if there are catechumens to be baptized, the Litany of the Saints accompanies a procession to the font, where water is blessed and baptism is celebrated. After the other rites, including confirmation, the entire assembly relights its candles, renews its baptismal promises, and is sprinkled with the water from the newly blessed font. You will need the *Rite of Christian Initiation of Adults* because the missal does not include the texts for administering the sacraments of baptism and confirmation.

Please note that the missal does not include the combined rite for baptism and the reception of baptized Christians into the full communion of the Catholic Church. For that, you still need to consult the appendix of the *Rite of Christian Initiation of Adults*. The sequence of events is different. After the baptisms, the assembly renews its baptismal promises with the candidates for reception, then all are sprinkled, and then the candidates make their statement of belief, and the priest receives them into the Catholic Church. Then the newly baptized are confirmed together with the newly received. Remember that baptized candidates may be received into the full communion of the Catholic Church at any time of year, but adult baptism ideally takes place at the Vigil.

If there is no one to be baptized, the parish still has the option of blessing the water in the font. If you do, go to the second half of #40 of the Easter Vigil and start there. You still sing the Litany of the Saints and then bless the water. If you do not bless the water in the font—for example, this liturgy takes place where baptisms never do—you may produce previously blessed water at this point, omit the prayer of blessing, and proceed to the renewal of baptismal promises and sprinkling. See #54 of this liturgy.

Appendix V of the missal offers sample formularies for the Prayer of the Faithful, including one for the Easter season that could be used at this Mass or at any time in the next fifty days.

If you are using Eucharistic Prayer I, II, or III, the presider should include the inserts concerning the newly baptized. The formulas are found in the third of the ritual Masses near the back of the missal. If Eucharistic Prayer I is used, there is a special formula for the section that begins "In communion with those" (81). This may be used every day for the Octave of Easter, including next Sunday. The formula for the section beginning "Therefore, Lord, we pray" (87) differs slightly from the one in the ritual Masses for baptism. It is designed to be used when no one has been baptized at this Vigil this year, but still prays for others who are newly baptized.

At the end of Mass, the two halves of the dismissal formula should conclude with a double Alleluia. If at all possible, sing the beautiful chant that appears on this page, and teach the response to the people—at least be sure the choir knows how it goes. Others will join in. The double Alleluia is added each day for the Octave of Easter, including next Sunday. Then it is retired until Pentecost, when it closes the Easter season.

The Easter candle remains in place until Pentecost, when it is moved to the baptistry. Of course, if your church is arranged in a way that the candle has been visible by the font throughout Easter, it stays put.

The *Book of Blessings* includes an Order for the Blessing of Food for the First Meal of Easter (1701–1723). This could be given at a reception following the Easter Vigil.

This is the first day on which people may complete their Easter duty. Catholics should receive Communion at least once a year during the fifty days of Easter.

If your parish needs to schedule a funeral today, use the Funeral without Mass from the *Order of Christian Funerals*. The celebration of marriage today is strictly forbidden by the *Circular Letter* (75). Convalidations for catechumens in irregular marriages should have been celebrated by now.

Blessing of the Fire

We pray that God will sanctify this new fire and inflame us with the desires that will bring us to the festivities of unending splendor. This prayer is the one from the pre-Vatican II missal, though it omits the previous designation of Christ as the "cornerstone," probably because that would mix metaphors.

LECTIONARY

Eucharistic Prayer IV says that God entrusted the whole world to the care of humans (Order of Mass, 117). It cites Genesis 1:26, which comes from the first reading.

The first Eucharistic Prayer refers to "the sacrifice of Abraham" (Order of Mass, 93), which is recounted in the second reading. In Eucharistic Prayer IV (Order of Mass, 122), we ask God to look upon "the Sacrifice which you yourself have provided for your Church," which alludes to Genesis 22:8, where Abraham tells Isaac that God himself will provide the sheep.

The responsorial psalm that follows the Epistle is 118, which has "Alleluia" as its refrain. It is one of the places in scripture that gives us the word we resume using as the Gospel acclamation tonight (Order of Mass, 13).

In Masses for the Dead, Eucharistic Prayers II and III pray "that he (she) who was united with your Son in a death like his, may also be one with him in his Resurrection" (Order of Mass, 105 and 115). The text refers to Romans 6:5, found in tonight's Epistle.

Prayer after the First Reading

We pray for the understanding that the sacrifice of Christ is even greater than the creation of the world. This prayer has remained virtually unchanged since it first appeared in the Gelasian Sacramentary, where it followed a reading about Noah. It seems to fit the reading of the creation of the world even better.

Alternatively, we may pray to turn away from sin and attain eternal joys. This prayer appeared after the first reading about the creation of the world in the texts for the Vigil in the Hadrian Sacramentary; it remained there in the pre-Vatican II missal. It is still kept, but as one of the options to follow the first reading.

Prayer after the Second Reading

We pray to enter worthily into the grace of God's calling, as members of a growing Church fulfilling the promise that Abraham would be the father of all nations. This prayer links the Old Testament promise to our current practice of baptism. The text has remained virtually unchanged since it first appeared in the Gelasian Sacramentary after the reading about Abraham.

Prayer after the Third Reading

There are two choices. In the first we pray that all the people of the world may become children of Abraham and inherit the dignity of Israel's birthright. This links the story of the Exodus to the experience of baptism. The prayer has remained virtually unchanged since it first appeared in the Gelasian Sacramentary after the reading about the the Exodus from Egypt.

In the second option, we pray that all nations may be reborn by partaking of God's Spirit. This prayer, too, links the Red Sea with the waters of baptism. The text appeared in almost exactly this form in the Gelasian Sacramentary, but as a prayer following the reading about the song of the Exodus at the Pentecost Vigil.

Prayer after the Fourth Reading

We pray that God will increase the children of the promise beyond what the Saints of old ever imagined. This prayer originated with very

---

PRAYER OF THE FAITHFUL

Years A, B, C

Through the wonders of the Red Sea, the chosen people feared the Lord and believed in him. Together with all those who rise from the waters of baptism tonight, let us present our prayers in faith and awe.

— *Intercessions* —

God of power and might,
hear our prayers.
Make us dead to sin
and alive for you in Christ Jesus our Lord.
Who lives and reigns for ever and ever.

---

minor variations in the Gelasian Sacramentary, where it followed a reading from Isaiah. It was not used anyplace in the pre-Vatican II missal.

Prayer after the Fifth Reading

Aware that God has fulfilled prophecies from of old, we pray that we might increase our longing and grow in virtue. This prayer has been unchanged since it appeared in the Gelasian Sacramentary, where it followed a reading from the prophet Daniel. The pre-Vatican II missal did not include this text at all.

Prayer after the Sixth Reading

God increases the Church by calling upon all the nations to respond. We pray that God will ever protect those who respond to this call in baptism. This prayer first appeared in the Hadrian Sacramentary, where it followed a reading from Isaiah. As with many previous prayers in this section, it had been lost for many centuries but was restored to the missal after the Second Vatican Council.

Prayer after the Seventh Reading

In a kind of summary prayer to all the readings, we address the God of unchanging power and eternal light, asking for the accomplishment of human salvation. The text has a more solemn tone and is a bit longer than the others, probably to set it apart as the conclusion of the series. It is taken from the Gelasian again, where it followed the first reading about the creation of the world, but the second half of this prayer began its life as part of a preface for the month of April in the Verona Sacramentary. This prayer was absent from the pre-Vatican II missal.

There is an alternative prayer. We ask to comprehend God's mercy, that receiving the gifts of this night may confirm our hope for the gifts to come. This prayer comes from the Gelasian Sacramentary, where it followed the reading from Ezekiel—as it does here. It was restored to the missal after the Second Vatican Council.

Collect

We ask God to stir up the spirit of adoption in the Church so that we may render undivided service. After hearing all these prayers that lay the foundation for our understanding of baptism, we are reminded that those of us adopted by the Spirit are also called to serve. The prayer has remained virtually the same since the Gelasian Sacramentary, and it was preserved in the pre-Vatican II missal for the collect of the Mass of the Easter Vigil. Only one verb has changed. We used to pray that God would keep the spirit of adoption—now we ask God to stir it up.

Litany Closing Prayer

As the Litany of the Saints draws to its close, we pray that God will send forth the spirit of adoption to create new peoples in the font of baptism. This is the prayer that preceded the blessing of the font in the Hadrian Sacramentary, and it was preserved in the pre-Vatican II missal. Surprisingly, it is missing from the *Rite of Christian Initiation of Adults*. So the priest should follow the missal for the Litany of the Saints and this prayer, and then turn to the *RCIA* for the texts pertaining to baptism.

Prayer over the Offerings

We pray that the events of this night will bring us eternal healing. This prayer appeared in the Gelasian Sacramentary exactly in this place, and it has served as the prayer over the offerings all through the life of *The Roman Missal*.

Preface

The first Easter preface is used for this Mass, and the word "night" replaces the word "day" for obvious reasons. The text has remained virtually unchanged since it appeared in the Gelasian Sacramentary. It praises Christ as the true Lamb who takes away the sins of the world, who destroyed death and restored life by his own death and rising. In John 1:29, John the Baptist calls Jesus the Lamb of God who takes away the sins of the world. The saving mission of Jesus' death and resurrection can be found in Romans 5:10–11, 1 Corinthians 15:3–4, and 2 Corinthians 5:14–15. This preface inspired the first English translation of one of the memorial acclamations. It is especially fitting throughout the Octave of Easter, but it may be used on any of the fifty days.

Communion Antiphon

The text comes from one of the passages that may be used as the second reading for tomorrow's Mass. It proclaims that Christ our paschal lamb has been sacrificed. You can hear the present tense, an invitation to participate in the saving mystery of Christ. It has been used for Communion on Easter Day since the eighth century.

Prayer after Communion

We pray for the Spirit of God's love, that we might be one in mind and heart. This is a true fruit of the paschal celebration, and a unity that the newly baptized will experience most profoundly through the Eucharist. The prayer originated in the Verona Sacramentary, where it refers to those who were satisfied by "the one bread." Its meaning was later amplified to include all the paschal sacraments. This prayer after Communion has been in continual use at the Easter Vigil for hundreds of years.

Blessing

Today's solemn blessing asks that we be preserved from sin, obtain the prize of immortality, and reach the eternal feasts. It was moved into place here for the 2002 missal. It used to be situated only in the collection of blessings; now it is easier to find. This blessing was newly composed for the post-Vatican II Church.

Alternatively, the solemn blessing may be taken from the *Rite of Baptism* for adults or for children. This instruction is new to the 2002 missal, and it is a lovely idea to have this option. However, there is no solemn blessing in the rite for adults, and the ones for children may not be appropriate if adults were baptized at this celebration.

EASTER TIME

The celebration of Easter extends for fifty days and culminates in Pentecost. The decorations, music, and vesture should exude a sense of joy throughout this season. You can add to the tone by starting Mass with the sprinkling rite and then singing the Gloria. There is a special version of the sprinkling for the Easter season, but it still presumes you are blessing the water, rather than using previously blessed water.

There are five choices for the preface throughout the Easter season. For commentary on the first, see *p. 62* above. It was the only Easter preface in the pre-Vatican II missal. Four additional prefaces have greatly enriched the texts available to the Roman Church throughout the Easter season.

The second preface is about new life in Christ. The children of light will rise to eternal life through him, and the halls of the kingdom are opened to the faithful. Our death was ransomed by his, and all life rises in his resurrection. The earliest version of this preface appeared in the Gelasian Sacramentary on Easter Day. Christians are called "children of light" in passages such as John 12:36, Ephesians 5:8–9, and 1 Thessalonians 5:5. Our participation in the death and resurrection of Christ is explained, among other places, in 2 Corinthians 5:14–15.

The third Easter preface concerns the living Christ who intercedes for us. He never ceases to offer himself for us and defends us with perpetual intercession. He no longer dies; the one who was slain lives forever. The earliest forms of this preface appeared in the Old Gallican and Gothic Missals. Jesus' role as intercessor appears in John 17:20, Hebrews 5:5–7 and 7:26–27, and 1 John 2:12. That Christ dies no more is stated in Romans 6:9; see also 1 Corinthians 5:7–8 and Revelation 5:12.

The fourth preface concerns the restoration of the universe through the paschal mystery. The old order has passed away and is renewed, and we are restored to life in Christ. This brief preface first appeared on Thursday of the Octave of Easter in the Gelasian Sacramentary. It has also been used in the Ambrosian Rite. Scripture background includes Romans 5:10 and 17, 2 Corinthians 4:9–11, 2 Corinthians 5:17, and Revelation 21:1 and 5.

The title of the fifth preface calls Christ priest and victim. But the text calls him priest, altar, and lamb. His offering fulfilled the sacrifices of old for the sake of our salvation. The Gelasian Sacramentary assigned this text to Tuesday of the Octave of Easter. It is based on a shorter Easter preface from the Verona Sacramentary. Christ's role as an offering priest is prophesied in Psalm 109:4. The nature of his sacrifice is found in 1 Corinthians 5:8; Ephesians 5:2; and Hebrews 7:26, 9:14, and 10:12. His identity as the Lamb of God is in John 1:29 and Revelation 5:6 and 12.

The solemn blessing for the season of Easter speaks of the promise of baptism. The earliest version comes from the Hadrian Sacramentary, where bishops used it during the season of Easter.

The *Book of Blessings* includes several blessings that may be appropriate on a Sunday during this season. Plan ahead if you wish to use the Order for the Blessing of Boats and Fishing Gear (880–898). The Blessing of Mothers on Mother's Day, Second Sunday of May (1724–1728) would fittingly close the Mass on that day. You may consider blessing motor vehicles (868C) before Memorial Day for the benefit of families planning a vacation by car this summer.

Easter Sunday of the Resurrection of the Lord

Overview

We celebrate the rising of Christ in a special Eucharist that announces the good news of resurrection. Although the Easter Vigil is a far richer liturgy, this one is preferred by many Catholics, and churches are usually full. A friendly welcome will mean more to people than a scolding.

The Easter Sequence should be sung at Mass today, though not at the Vigil the night before. It is very difficult to remember, because musicians are accustomed to moving from the second reading to the Gospel acclamation. But this Easter hymn should come between them. The Sequence is found in the Lectionary. It is best if everyone sings it. There are some settings of the text in the style of a hymn. Sometimes a search through hymn indexes under its Latin title, *Victimae Paschali Laudes*, will reveal several options. The rubrics are not clear whether people should sit or stand for the hymn. Standing is usually a good idea, especially if it will be sung. If no one can sing it, you can have a lector read it—but practice the music for next year! You may sing it again next Sunday if you wish.

If you are using Eucharistic Prayer I, there are special inserts at #81 and #87. The first emphasizes the significance of the day being celebrated. The second includes an intention for all the newly baptized.

Both parts of the dismissal formula close with a double Alleluia, as they will throughout this week and again on Pentecost. It is most effective when it is sung.

Entrance Antiphon

The antiphon quotes a particular Latin translation of Psalm 138 that uses the equivalent of the words "I have risen." Although recent scholarship translates these words in a different way, the antiphon has remained in place because it proclaims the mystery we celebrate this day. It is as if Christ himself, alive in the Church, sings this song: "I have risen,

---

LECTIONARY

The alternate antiphon for the responsorial psalm is "Alleluia," a word that opens the full text of this psalm in the Bible. Throughout most of the year it is the text for the Gospel acclamation (Order of Mass, 13).

The third form of the penitential act invokes the One who is "seated at the right hand of the Father" (Order of Mass, 6). This description comes from Colossians 3:1, which is part of the first option for today's second reading.

The Communion antiphon comes from the alternate second reading. The Communion rite at every Mass calls Christ the Lamb of God (Order of Mass, 130 and 132), and 1 Corinthians 5:7 is one of the reasons.

The entire Liturgy of the Word—and especially the homily—is similar to the conversation between Jesus and the disciples, found in the Gospel for afternoon and evening celebrations. In the Emmaus story, Jesus interprets all the scriptures that referred to him, and he was made known to them in the breaking of bread. The Lamb of God (Order of Mass, 130) is sung during the breaking of bread, a practice told in this Gospel.

---

and I am with you still." This is the traditional antiphon for this Mass, going back to at least the eighth century.

An alternative antiphon is offered, a composite from the Gospel of Saint Luke and the book of Revelation. This antiphon combines the first testimony of the apostles with a proclamation of John. It was new to the post-Vatican II missal.

Collect

The people celebrating the rising of Christ pray that they too may rise in the light of life. This is the first prayer for Easter Day from the Gelasian Sacramentary. It has remained in continual usage almost unchanged. After so many prayers at the Vigil that focus on baptism, this one turns the community's attention to eternal life.

Prayer over the Offerings

This prayer simply proclaims that we are offering the sacrifice by which we are reborn and nourished. It is an outburst of joy. The prayer is found in the Gelasian Sacramentary on Easter Monday, and it was moved up one day for the post-Vatican II missal. The reference to those who are reborn implies that those baptized at the Vigil have returned to celebrate the Eucharist and begin their mystagogy.

Preface

The first preface for the Easter season should be used for this Mass. See commentary above on *p. 62*. The words "day" and "night" are exchanged according to the time of day.

Communion Antiphon

This is the same text that appeared in the Vigil Mass. It is based on one of the options for the second reading at this Mass. The same text appeared in eighth-century sources for Mass on this day.

Prayer after Communion

Renewed through the paschal mysteries, the Church prays to reach the glory of the Resurrection. This simple, beautiful prayer is new to

---

PRAYER OF THE FAITHFUL

Years A, B, C

This is the day the Lord has made. Let us rejoice in the God who hears and answers our prayers.

— *Intercessions* —

O God,
who announced good news
through the mystery of the empty tomb,
fill the longing of our hearts
and grant these prayers.
Through Christ our Lord.

The Roman Missal, having been drawn from the Ambrosian Rite's Sacramentary of Bergamo. It is a sign of the Church's desire to reflect our many traditions on the most important day of the year.

Blessing

The solemn blessing created for the Vigil Mass may also be used for this one. *See p. 63.*

Second Sunday of Easter (or of Divine Mercy)

Overview

An earlier tradition called this Low Sunday because it seemed like a letdown after the brash celebration of Easter. It is still the Octave, and it still deserves festivity.

Although today is also known as Divine Mercy Sunday, the Votive Mass for Divine Mercy in the back of the missal may not be used. Those texts were created for other possibilities, such as a weekday in Ordinary Time. The liturgical texts for the Octave of Easter all take precedence over the ones for Divine Mercy.

The Easter Sequence is optional today. If your community is trying to learn a setting—or has already learned one—it may be a good idea to sing it again to be sure it is in the repertoire.

If you are using Eucharistic Prayer I, use the special inserts that refer to the season of the year and the newly baptized. Even if the ones from your community are not present, it is appropriate to pray for them and all the newly baptized at this Mass.

Both parts of the dismissal formula should conclude with a double Alleluia again today to close out the Octave of Easter. The Alleluias return only at the dismissal for Pentecost.

Entrance Antiphon

The first of the two options is the one in continuous use from eighth-century sources. As infants long for milk, so we are encouraged to long for pure spiritual milk. The Latin words for "Like" that open this antiphon gave this Sunday its popular name, Quasimodo Sunday. In Victor Hugo's novel *Notre Dame of Paris*, the hunchback is discovered on the steps of Notre Dame on the Sunday after Easter. He was named after the entrance antiphon: *Quasimodo*.

LECTIONARY

The Lamb of God (Order of Mass, 130) accompanies the breaking of bread. This action is mentioned in Acts 2:42, which appears in the first reading in Year A.

Eucharistic Prayer III prays for "an inheritance with your elect" (Order of Mass, 113), and Eucharistic Prayer IV asks for entry "into a heavenly inheritance" (122). Both refer to 1 Peter 1:3–4, which comes from the second reading in Year A.

In all three years, the alternative refrain for the responsorial psalm is the word "Alleluia," which appears at the beginning of the full text of this psalm in the Bible. The Gospel acclamation from the Order of Mass, 13 cites the word as it appears in the Bible here and in other passages.

Three times in the Gospel, Jesus greets his disciples with the words "Peace be with you." The Order of Mass, 2 assigns this greeting to the bishop, who represents the risen Christ as he greets the people. The Communion antiphon also quotes the Gospel text.

To this has been added an option from the apocryphal Fourth Book of Esdras, inviting the community to receive joy and give thanks. It was new to the post-Vatican II missal.

Collect

The community prays for an increase of grace so that all may rightly understand the One in whom they have been washed, reborn, and redeemed. This prayer originated in the Gothic Missal, and appeared in *The Roman Missal* for the first time after the Second Vatican Council. Its inclusion expands the sources from which we pray at Mass in the Roman Rite. It is also focused on the newly baptized, who should return to celebrate the Eucharist with the assembly of the faithful on this day. In the past, the neophytes wore their white garments again, giving this Sunday its former name, *Dominica in albis*.

Prayer over the Offerings

The people ask God to accept their oblations that they may be renewed and attain unending happiness. If the newly baptized are present for this Mass, the line in parentheses is added. It may be a good idea to add it at every Mass—it is possible that some visitor in the assembly has been recently baptized. This prayer first appeared in the Gelasian Sacramentary as an option for the Easter Vigil. It was restored to the Octave of Easter in the post-Vatican II missal.

Preface

The first Easter preface should be used because this is another Easter Day, the return of Sunday, especially in this case a renewed celebration of the Resurrection. See comments on *p. 62*. The words "night" and "day" are interchangeable depending on the time of day. Because this is still the octave, and hence still Easter Day in its broadest sense, it is not yet time to use the other option referring to Easter time. That one comes into use any time after today.

PRAYER OF THE FAITHFUL

Year A

The first disciples devoted themselves to teaching, community life, breaking bread, and prayers. Following their example, we make our petitions.

— *Intercessions* —

O God,
who each year increase the number
    of your faithful,
increase also your gifts to us
by granting these prayers.
Through Christ our Lord.

Year B

The first community of believers was of one heart and mind. Let us pray that there be no needy person among us.

— *Intercessions* —

O God,
who grant belief even to those
    who have not seen,
show your divine mercy
to all those we remember this day.
Through Christ our Lord.

Year C

God's love is everlasting. Let us give thanks as we present our prayers.

— *Intercessions* —

O God,
who cured the sick at the hand
    of your apostles,
work new signs and wonders for us.
Through Christ our Lord.

Communion Antiphon

In keeping with a tradition concerning Communion antiphons, this one quotes the Gospel of the day. That Gospel appears in the Lectionary every year on this day because it describes the miraculous event that took place on the octave day of the Resurrection. This particular antiphon encourages belief, an appropriate prayer in the presence of those who are newly baptized and all those who share faith in the Resurrection. It has been used on this day since at least the eighth century.

Prayer after Communion

We pray that our reception of Communion this Easter may have a continuing effect in our minds and hearts. This prayer originated in the Gelasian Sacramentary as one option for the prayer after Communion at the Easter Vigil. It appeared in the pre-Vatican II missal on a different day, but was restored to Easter.

Blessing

The solemn blessing from the Easter Vigil may be used again. *See p. 63.*

Third Sunday of Easter

Overview

We settle into the Easter season, putting the Octave behind us. Mass does not conclude with a double Alleluia in the dismissal. That will return at Pentecost.

The Blessing of Mothers on Mother's Day (*Book of Blessings*, 1724–1728) would be a fitting closing of the Mass on the second Sunday in May.

Entrance Antiphon

All the earth is called to cry out with joy to God. The post-Vatican II missal moved this antiphon from its traditional position at next week's Mass to this one. It is the first time it has moved since the eighth century.

Collect

We pray that we might exult forever in a youthful spirit, as we look forward to the day of resurrection. The prayer refers to the glory of adoption, a reference to the gift of baptism, which is still the focus of celebration these fifty days. It is a hybrid of an Easter prayer over the people from the Gelasian Sacramentary and a prayer for the dead in the Verona Sacramentary. It was created for the post-Vatican II missal. It will be offered again as one of the options for a prayer at the extended Pentecost Vigil. *See pp. 86–87.*

Prayer over the Offerings

As an exultant Church, we ask God to receive our offerings and bring us perpetual happiness. This prayer first appeared in the Gelasian Sacramentary for the Saturday following Easter. It was located here in the post-Vatican II missal.

Preface

Any of the five Easter prefaces may be used today. For commentary, *see p. 65.* The fifth one shares some vocabulary with the second reading each year.

LECTIONARY

In the second reading of Year A, Christ is called the Lamb, as he is in the fifth Easter preface, and in the Communion rite of the Order of Mass, 130 and 132. The third memorial acclamation says that Christ has "set us free" (Order of Mass, 91), which is affirmed in 1 Peter 1:18. The entire Liturgy of the Word—and especially the homily—is similar to the conversation between Jesus and the disciples in the Gospel of Year A, during which he interprets all the scriptures that referred to him, and after which he was made known to them in the breaking of bread. The Lamb of God (Order of Mass, 130) is sung during the breaking of bread, a practice told in this Gospel. The second Communion antiphon quotes this text.

In Year B the second reading notes Christ's role as the sacrificing priest. It is echoed in the fifth Easter preface. The first Communion antiphon quotes the Gospel.

In the first reading of Year C, Peter says God exalted Jesus "at his right hand," and this belief is repeated in the Creed each Sunday (Order of Mass, 18, 19). The second reading says Christ is the Lamb who was slain. This theme is taken up by the fifth Easter preface, in the Communion rite of the Order of Mass (130 and 132), during the Lamb of God, and in the invitation to Communion. The third Communion antiphon quotes the Gospel.

Communion Antiphon

Three options are given for the Communion antiphon, each of them citing the Gospel of that year's Lectionary cycle. The first option, though, may be used each year. These were new to the post-Vatican II missal.

Prayer after Communion

We pray that those who have been baptized may attain incorruptibility at the resurrection. This prayer was new to the post-Vatican II missal; it was composed of several ancient sources, including a sermon of Pope Leo the Great. The missal has already used this prayer on Saturday of the Octave of Easter and on Monday of the second week.

Blessing

The solemn blessing for the Easter season may be used. *See p. 65.*

PRAYER OF THE FAITHFUL

Year A

God worked mighty deeds, wonders, and
    signs through Jesus the Nazarene. In faith
    we speak our needs.

— Intercessions —

O God,
who granted faith to those
    who broke bread with your Son,
look kindly on the prayers we present
    at this Eucharist.
Through Christ our Lord.

Year B

Let us pray that the Lord will shine his face
    upon all those who look for mercy.

— Intercessions —

O God,
who sent forth witnesses
    to the resurrection of your Son,
make us witnesses of your mighty deeds
and grant these prayers.
Through Christ our Lord.

Year C

The Lord Jesus sent Peter to feed his lambs.
    Confident that Christ also cares for this
    faithful flock, we bring forth our prayers.

— Intercessions —

O God,
who gave us an example of love
in the suffering of your Son,
make us willing to love you
    above all things,
and receive these petitions with favor.
Through Christ our Lord.

Fourth Sunday of Easter

Overview

Traditionally this is called Good Shepherd Sunday because of the Gospel for the day, but it does not bear that title officially. This is also a traditional day to pray for religious vocations.

Entrance Antiphon

God's merciful love fills the earth; the word of the Lord made the heavens. Easter affects all creation—the world around us and the world above. This antiphon appeared on the previous Sunday in eighth-century sources, but the post-Vatican II missal switched it to this week for the first time in its history.

Collect

We pray for companionship in heaven, a humble flock led by a brave Shepherd. This prayer is based on one for an Easter evening from the Gelasian Sacramentary. It did not appear in the pre-Vatican II missal. The collect now unites with the theme of today's Gospel.

Prayer over the Offerings

We ask to delight in these paschal mysteries and obtain unending joy. The Gelasian Sacramentary presented this prayer over the offerings on Thursday of the Easter Octave.

Preface

Any of the five Easter prefaces may be used. *See p. 65* for comments. To avoid mixing metaphors, you may wish to choose an option other than the fifth one, which calls Christ the Lamb—not the Shepherd.

Communion Antiphon

With words not drawn from the scriptures, the antiphon proclaims that the Good Shepherd, who laid down his life for the sheep, has risen. The text was new to the post-Vatican II missal.

Prayer after Communion

The community asks the Good Shepherd for a place in eternal pastures. Normally we think of Christ as the Good Shepherd, but here the title is assigned to the Father. This prayer originated in the Verona Sacramentary as a prayer after Communion for a daily Mass in July. It did not appear in the pre-Vatican II missal.

Blessing

The solemn blessing for the Easter season may be used. *See p. 65.*

LECTIONARY

In Year B, the responsorial psalm's alternate antiphon is "Alleluia," which is found in Psalm 118 and is one of the sources for the Gospel acclamation (Order of Mass, 13). At Masses for the Dead, Eucharistic Prayer III says, "seeing you, our God, as you are, we shall be like you for all the ages" (Order of Mass, 115), which refers to the conclusion of today's second reading.

At Masses for the Dead, Eucharistic Prayer III says, "you will wipe away every tear from our eyes" (Order of Mass, 115), which refers to the conclusion of today's second reading in Year C. See also the Fifth Sunday of Easter, *p. 76.*

PRAYER OF THE FAITHFUL

Year A

The Good Shepherd spreads the table before
us in the sight of our foes. He longs to
hear our wants and needs.

— Intercessions —

O God,
whose Son is the gate of salvation,
grant these prayers and protect your flock.
Through Christ our Lord.

Year B

Christ the good shepherd has already laid
down his life for the sheep. He will not
refuse to answer our prayers.

— Intercessions —

O God,
who know us as your very own flock,
protect those for whom your Son died,
and grant the petitions we make.
Through Christ our Lord.

Year C

We are the sheep of God's flock. Let us turn
to our shepherd and present our petitions.

— Intercessions —

O God,
whose mighty hand holds the sheep
of your flock,
grant us your protection and grace.
Through Christ our Lord.

Fifth Sunday of Easter

Overview

The Gospels for the next few Sundays come from the farewell discourse Jesus gave at the Last Supper, according to the Gospel of John. Sequentially, the event took place before the Passion, but we meditate on these words in the light of the Easter mysteries.

Entrance Antiphon

The community is asked to sing a new song to the Lord who has worked wonders. This antiphon also appeared on this day in sources dating back at least to the eighth century. The liturgy sees in these verses a prophecy concerning the resurrection, open to all who put their faith in Christ.

Collect

We ask that our baptism may constantly accomplish the Paschal Mystery within us, bearing much fruit and coming to the joys of life eternal. This prayer is new to this day in the 2002 *Roman Missal*. Immediately after the Council, the prayer for the Fifth Sunday of Easter was repeated on the Twenty-third Sunday in Ordinary Time. The first English translation in the Sacramentary transposed one of the lines, adding very minimal variety to the two prayers. Now, the collect for this day has been replaced, and the one for the Twenty-third Sunday in Ordinary Time remains. This collect first appeared in the post-Vatican II missal on Saturday of the Fourth Week of Easter. It has now been moved to the next day. That missal turned to the Ambrosian Rite for this prayer, creating a new one from two different prayers for Tuesday of Holy Week in the Sacramentary of Bergamo.

Prayer over the Offerings

As we share this sacrifice we pray to come to know God's truth by a worthy way of life. This prayer, which is also offered on some weekdays of Easter, is found first in the Gelasian Sacramentary, where it is proposed as the prayer over the gifts for the third Sunday after the close of Easter. Assuming that that refers to the close of the Easter Octave, this is that same Sunday.

LECTIONARY

Year A's first reading describes the origins of deacons, who have an important liturgical role throughout the Order of Mass. The second reading inspired the whole theology of full, conscious, and active participation. For example, during the preparation of the gifts, when the priest invites the people to pray "that my sacrifice and yours may be acceptable" (Order of Mass, 29), he implies their role as members of the royal priesthood in 1 Peter 2:9. Eucharistic Prayer III prays for an inheritance "with your elect" (Order of Mass, 113), and the same passage at the end of this reading calls the readers "a chosen race."

Eucharistic Prayer I refers to the people "fulfilling their vows to you" (Order of Mass, 85), a phrase inspired by the first line of today's responsorial psalm in Year B. The Communion antiphon quotes the Gospel of Year B.

The vision from the book of Revelation in Year C's second reading shares a theme with the fourth preface of Easter. In Masses for the Dead, Eucharistic Prayer III looks for the day when God "will wipe away every tear from our eyes," a reference to Revelation 21:4. See also the Fourth Sunday of Easter, *p. 74.*

Preface

You may choose any of the five Easter prefaces. *See p. 65* for comments on them.

Communion Antiphon

The antiphon is inspired by a passage from the Gospel of Year B for this day. As comforting as it is to think of being branches on the vine, it is disquieting to think just how we might be expected to bear fruit and what that will cost us. The antiphon was new to the post-Vatican II missal.

Prayer after Communion

Having participated in the heavenly mysteries, the people pray to pass from the old to a new way of life. As with the prayer over the offerings, this one is also used on other occasions of Easter. This prayer began in the Verona Sacramentary as a pre-Pentecost prayer for safety from enemies, but it evolved into an appeal for spiritual growth.

Blessing

The Easter solemn blessing may be used. *See p. 65.*

PRAYER OF THE FAITHFUL

Year A

We are a holy priesthood offering spiritual sacrifices. Let all the faithful exercise their baptismal ministry by praying for the needs of the world.

— *Intercessions* —

O God,
who show us the way in your Son,
    Jesus Christ,
help us to grasp the truth,
and grant us eternal life.
Through Christ our Lord.

Year B

Jesus says, "If you remain in me, ask what you want, and it will be done for you."

— *Intercessions* —

O God,
who gave us Christ the true vine,
hear our prayers
and let us bear fruit.
Through Christ our Lord.

Year C

With love for one another, we pray for the needs of the Church and all the world.

— *Intercessions* —

O God,
source of love and glory,
hear these petitions that all may know
the love you hold for the world.
Through Christ our Lord.

Sixth Sunday of Easter

Overview

If your community celebrates the Ascension on Sunday, rather than on Thursday this week, you may use the second reading and the Gospel from the Seventh Sunday of Easter at this Mass. They continue the sequence of readings that have been proclaimed the last few weeks, so the choice is yours. The first reading of the Seventh Sunday of Easter, however, is taken from the first chapter of Acts of the Apostles each year, and the events reported there presume that the Ascension has taken place. Hence, it should not be proclaimed before your community celebrates that feast.

Entrance Antiphon

People are asked to proclaim a joyful message that the Lord has freed his people. As with almost all the other entrance antiphons of the Easter season, this one is addressed to the community in the plural, exhorting its members to some action in the light of Easter Day. This is the same antiphon that appeared on this day in sources dating to the eighth century.

Collect

We ask God to help us celebrate these Easter days of joy. One of the fruits of this season is its joy. The prayer combines texts that originally appeared in the Verona Sacramentary. Some lines were originally composed for the period of fast following the celebration of Easter, others for the feast of Saint John the Evangelist. The Gelasian Sacramentary moved some of these words into its prayers for Easter. The form that appears in the missal today was a creation of the post-Vatican II missal, and was probably inspired by the joyful spirit of the Council.

Prayer over the Offerings

The community prays that God will accept its prayers and offerings and make its members conformed to the mysteries of God's love. This prayer is repeated on some weekdays of the Easter season. Like the collect, this prayer was created for the post-Vatican II Church out of two texts from the Verona Sacramentary, one for the Ascension and the other for the feast of Saints Clement and Felicity in November. The first word in Latin is *Ascendant*—rendered in English as "May [our prayers] rise up." But the word is probably there to lead us into the mystery soon to be celebrated, the Ascension of the Lord.

Preface

Any of the five Easter prefaces may be used for this day. *See p. 65.*

Communion Antiphon

Quoting the promise of Jesus to send another Paraclete, this antiphon anticipates the

---

LECTIONARY

The second reading of Year A shares some themes with the second Easter preface. The mission of the Spirit is told in today's Gospel. Eucharistic Prayer IV says Christ sent the Holy Spirit (Order of Mass, 117) and that this Spirit gathers us into one body (Order of Mass, 122). The Communion antiphon quotes this text.

The vision from the book of Revelation in the second reading of Year C shares themes with the fourth Easter preface. The Communion rite of every Mass quotes today's Gospel in Year C when the priest prays, "Lord Jesus Christ, who said to your Apostles, Peace I leave you, my peace I give you" (Order of Mass, 126).

coming of the Holy Spirit at Pentecost. The complete text is in the Gospel of this day in Year A. The antiphon was new to the post-Vatican II missal.

Prayer after Communion

The community prays for an increase in the fruits of this Communion, here called the "paschal Sacrament." Ready to serve God, the people pray for the strength that this saving food brings. This same prayer is used on several other days of the Easter season. It is based on an Easter prayer after Communion from the Gelasian Sacramentary. It was lightly edited and presented in *The Roman Missal* for the first time after the Second Vatican Council.

Blessing

The solemn blessing of the Easter season may be used again at Mass this day. *See p. 65.* The *Collection of Masses for the Blessed Virgin Mary* includes a solemn blessing for the Easter season as well. Because it mentions how Mary and the apostles awaited the coming of the Holy Spirit, it may be more appropriate near the end of the Easter season.

PRAYER OF THE FAITHFUL

Year A

The Father will reveal himself to those who love him. Let us express our care for all the needy of the world.

— *Intercessions* —

O God,
who gave us the Advocate
    at the request of your only Son,
grant also these prayers
    from those who trust in him.
Who lives and reigns for ever and ever.

Year B

Jesus commanded us to love one another. In a spirit of true concern, let us make known the needs of all our brothers and sisters.

— *Intercessions* —

O God,
who revealed your saving power
    to the nations,
show us your might and grant our prayers.
Through Christ our Lord.

Year C

Jesus promised that the Holy Spirit would teach us everything. Fully aware of the needs of the world, let us give voice to our prayers.

— *Intercessions* —

O God,
who give peace to those
    whose hearts are troubled,
comfort all those we remember this day.
Through Christ our Lord.

The Ascension of the Lord, at the Vigil Mass

Overview

Depending on where you live, this Mass takes place on Wednesday night of the Sixth Week of Easter, or on Saturday night of Ascension weekend. If the Ascension is not among your holy days of obligation, it moves from Thursday to Sunday.

This entire Mass is new to the 2002 *Roman Missal*. This is the first English translation of these texts.

If your community is to hear Eucharistic Prayer I, the priest should use the special insert at paragraph 86, starting with "Celebrating the most sacred day."

Entrance Antiphon

The kingdoms of the earth are asked to sing to God who ascends. This verse from Psalm 67 is a prophecy of the ascension of Jesus, to whom all are called to give praise. As with other antiphons of the season, this one shouts a command to the community. It is new to the 2002 *Roman Missal*.

Collect

We pray that Christ, who ascended on this day, will live with us on earth, and we with him in heaven. The prayer is lightly adapted from one in the Gelasian Sacramentary for the Ascension.

Prayer over the Offerings

Christ the High Priest is seated at the right hand of God. We ask to approach the throne of grace and obtain mercy. The prayer is a new composition for the 2002 missal, drawing from the Letter to the Hebrews 4:14–16, 7:25, and 8:1.

Preface

There are two choices for the preface today. The first proclaims Jesus Lord, King of glory, conqueror of sin and death, mediator, judge, Lord of hosts, Head and Founder. He has ascended not to distance himself from us, but that we might hope to follow. The text is inspired by an Ascension preface in the Verona Sacramentary, but is largely a new composition for the post-Vatican II Church. When proclaiming the preface on this day, the word "today" should be inserted.

The second option is the preface from the pre-Vatican II missal. It is also based on one from the Verona Sacramentary, and it was rewritten after the Council of Trent. The only change in the post-Vatican II missal was in the lines about paschal joy just before the *Sanctus*. The text acknowledges Christ, who was taken up to heaven in the sight of the disciples to make us sharers in his divinity.

LECTIONARY

The first reading inspired all the texts of this day. The forty-day interval between the Resurrection and the Ascension of the Lord is recorded in Acts of the Apostles.

Communion Antiphon

Christ offers one sacrifice for sins and sits forever at the right hand of God. The text quotes the Letter to the Hebrews, explaining the role Christ assumes at his ascension. It was new to the 2002 *Roman Missal*.

Prayer after Communion

We pray for a longing for heaven, driving us to follow Christ where he has gone first. This prayer was newly composed and added to the missal in 2002. This is its first appearance in English.

Blessing

The solemn blessing for the Ascension may be used today. It sounds again the theme of Christ ascending to heaven so that we might follow. It comes from the Hadrian Sacramentary and was restored to usage after the Second Vatican Council.

PRAYER OF THE FAITHFUL

Year A

The Holy Spirit makes us witnesses to the ends of the earth. We pray that we may hear and see again the wonders of God's love.

— Intercessions —

O God,
who fulfilled your promise in the mission
   of your Son,
be faithful to us as we await the coming
   of your Spirit.
Through Christ our Lord.

Year B

When the disciples went into the world after the Ascension, great signs accompanied them. Let us ask God to work such wonders for us.

— Intercessions —

O God,
whose Son has taken his seat
   at your right hand,
confirm his word by signs of your mercy.
Through Christ our Lord.

Year C

The promise of God is trustworthy. Let us pray, holding unwaveringly to hope.

— Intercessions —

O God,
whose Son entered heaven
to appear before you on our behalf,
hear the prayers we offer.
Through Christ our Lord.

The Ascension of the Lord, at the Mass during the Day

Overview

After the Resurrection, Jesus appeared to his disciples to confirm their faith. Then he ascended into heaven. If your community celebrates the Ascension on Sunday, it replaces the texts for the Seventh Sunday of Easter. If you are using Eucharistic Prayer I today, use the special insert at paragraph 86, starting with "Celebrating the most sacred day."

Entrance Antiphon

People are staring into heaven, and they have to be told—not what has happened, but what to expect: Christ will come again. The verse is taken from the first reading from Acts of the Apostles. This is the same antiphon that was in use since at least the eighth century.

Collect

There are two options for the collect. The first was added to the missal after the Second Vatican Council. It was created for the contemporary Church out of a sermon that Leo the Great preached on this feast in the year 444. The community asks God for the gift of joy because the Body of Christ is called to follow where its Head has gone.

The second option is the one from the pre-Vatican II missal that the first one replaced. It has now been restored in the 2002 missal. Its intention is similar. We believe that Christ has ascended, so we pray that we may dwell with him in heaven. The earliest version of this prayer comes from the Gellone Sacramentary, a later edition of the Gelasian, dating to the eighth century.

Prayer over the Offerings

We pray that our offering may help us rise to heavenly realms. The petition is similar to the one in the collects of this day. The Gelasian Sacramentary records this prayer among those for the Ascension. It did not appear in *The Roman Missal* until after the Second Vatican Council.

LECTIONARY

The entrance antiphon comes from the first reading. In fact, that reading inspired all the texts of this day.

The third form of the penitential act invokes Jesus "seated at the right hand of the Father" (Order of Mass, 6). The second reading says this in Ephesians 1:20. The same passage inspired statements in the Creeds (Order of Mass, 18 and 19). In Year B, the longer form of the alternate second reading says Jesus "descended into the lower regions of the earth," and this inspired the words of the Apostles' Creed that Jesus "descended into hell" (Order of Mass, 19). When Eucharistic Prayer III prays that we "may become one body, one spirit in Christ" (Order of Mass, 113), it cites Ephesians 4:4.

The Gospel gave us the words to the sign of the cross (Order of Mass, 1). It also provides today's Communion antiphon. One of the reasons the priest and deacon greet the community with the phrase "The Lord be with you" (Order of Mass, 2, 15, 31, and 143) is because of the promise Jesus made in Matthew's account of his ascension: "I am with you always."

Preface

Either preface for the Ascension may be used, but the Latin edition of the missal seems to prefer the first one by printing it on the page with the other presidential prayers. For comments *see p. 80.*

Communion Antiphon

Jesus promises to remain with his followers until the end of the age. The text comes from the Gospel of Year A. It was new to the post-Vatican II missal.

Prayer after Communion

The community prays that its Christian hope may lead them to the place where they are united with God. In the Incarnation, Jesus took on our human nature; in the Ascension, he brings our human nature to a new level. We pray that our humanity may be united with God in that place where our nature is redeemed. One reason this prayer seems so dense is that it combines two different prayers from the Verona Sacramentary, one for the martyrdom of Saint Stephen and the other for the day before Pentecost. This new prayer was composed for the post-Vatican II missal.

Blessing

The solemn blessing for the Ascension may be used. *See p. 81.*

PRAYER OF THE FAITHFUL

Year A

The Holy Spirit makes us witnesses to the ends of the earth. We pray that we may hear and see again the wonders of God's love.

— Intercessions —

O God,
who fulfilled your promise in the mission of your Son,
be faithful to us as we await the coming of your Spirit.
Through Christ our Lord.

Year B

When the disciples went into the world after the Ascension, great signs accompanied them. Let us ask God to work such wonders for us.

— Intercessions —

O God,
whose Son has taken his seat at your right hand,
confirm his word by signs of your mercy.
Through Christ our Lord.

Year C

The promise of God is trustworthy. Let us pray, holding unwaveringly to hope.

— Intercessions —

O God,
whose Son entered heaven
to appear before you on our behalf,
hear the prayers we offer.
Through Christ our Lord.

Seventh Sunday of Easter

Overview

This day falls within the original novena of the Church—the nine days of prayer stretching from Ascension to Pentecost. In those parts of the world where the Ascension is celebrated on Sunday, this devotional nuance is lost—as is this Mass.

Entrance Antiphon

An intense prayer, this antiphon asks God to listen to the one who is seeking the divine face. One can imagine the disciples offering this prayer in the days between the Ascension and Pentecost. Taken from Psalm 26, this verse has supplied this antiphon from at least the eighth century.

Collect

Acknowledging that Jesus is ascended into heaven, we pray to experience his abiding presence. The earliest version of this prayer comes from the Verona Sacramentary as a collect for the Ascension. Unused for many centuries, it was restored to the *Roman Missal* after the Second Vatican Council.

Prayer over the Offerings

The faithful ask God to receive their prayers and offerings in order to pass over to the glory of heaven. The theme of the Ascension is repeated. The text first appeared in the Hadrian Sacramentary for Tuesday in the Octave of Easter.

Preface

Any preface from the Easter or Ascension collection may be used. You have seven options. In the spirit of the season, one from the Ascension is more appropriate, but any of them may be used. *See p. 65 and p. 80.*

Communion Antiphon

Jesus prays that the disciples may be one as he and the Father are. This is excerpted from the Gospel in Year C. It was new to the post-Vatican II missal.

Prayer after Communion

The community prays that through this Communion the Body of Christ may accomplish what its Head has already achieved. The original version of this comes from the prayers for the Ascension in the Verona Sacramentary.

LECTIONARY

Year A's first reading is one of the passages where the names of the apostles are given. If you use Eucharistic Prayer I today, you may wish to read the entire bracketed list in Order of Mass, 86.

Eucharistic Prayer I says that Jesus prayed "with eyes raised to heaven" (Order of Mass, 89). The four institution narratives in the New Testament do not indicate this. However, in Years A, B, and C, in today's Gospel John says Jesus raised his eyes at the Last Supper as he prayed on behalf of his followers. The opening words of that prayer are echoed in Eucharistic Prayer IV (Order of Mass, 119), "For when the hour had come for him to be glorified by you, Father most holy." Earlier in Eucharistic Prayer IV, the priest addresses "the one God living and true" (Order of Mass, 116), and Jesus calls the Father "the only true God" in John 17:3.

The Communion antiphon quotes the Gospel of Year C. Jesus' prayer "that they may all be one" is echoed in Eucharistic Prayer IV, "gathered into one body by the Holy Spirit" (Order of Mass, 122).

Blessing

The solemn blessing from the Ascension may be used again today. *See p. 81.*

PRAYER OF THE FAITHFUL

Year A

Jesus prayed for us while he was in the world. As his followers, let us pray for all who need God's aid.

— Intercessions —

O God,
who grant eternal life to those
    who know Jesus Christ,
grant also these prayers
    for those who long for him.
Through Christ our Lord.

Year B

Before choosing a new companion in apostolic ministry, the disciples prayed. Let us pray that God will guide the actions of all the world.

— Intercessions —

O God,
who remain in those who love one another,
dwell with us, grant our prayers,
and keep us one with you.
Through Christ our Lord.

Year C

We thirst for the gift of life-giving water. Let us pray that Jesus will come soon.

— Intercessions —

O God,
who desired that all would believe
that you sent us your only Son,
show your wonders
    and grant these petitions.
Through Christ our Lord.

Pentecost Sunday, at the Vigil Mass

Overview

Fifty days after the Resurrection, the promised Holy Spirit descended upon the disciples, and they zealously began their mission to proclaim the Gospel to the world. The Church has been in prayer for the last nine days, asking for a new outpouring of the Holy Spirit to enlighten our hearts this Pentecost Day.

The Vigil Mass may be celebrated either before or after vespers. It is not meant to be a Saturday morning Mass. There are other texts for that celebration.

The 2002 missal now offers an extended Pentecost Vigil for those who wish to experience more intently this hunger for the Spirit. It includes extra readings, psalms, and prayers, imitating the Liturgy of the Word during the Easter Vigil. This Mass may be incorporated into First Vespers. The hymn for vespers or one of the entrance antiphons of the solemnity may start the service to accompany the procession. The psalms from evening prayer take place, and the penitential act is omitted, but the Kyrie may be either sung or omitted. The traditional opening prayer for the Vigil is then offered ("Grant, we pray, almighty God, that the splendor"). It is the second option for the collect of the Vigil Mass.

If vespers is not included, then Mass begins in the usual way through the same collect. Then the priest introduces the celebration using words like those found in the missal. The Old Testament readings from the Lectionary follow, together with the responsorial psalms. (These may be replaced by a period of silence.) All stand after each psalm for the oration. After the four readings, the Gloria is sung. Then the priest says the first option for the collect of the Vigil Mass. The lector reads from Romans, and Mass continues as usual. If this Mass includes vespers, the Magnificat is sung after the Communion hymn. Both parts of the dismissal formula conclude with a double Alleluia.

Even if you do not celebrate the extended Vigil, the missal's presidential prayers for this Mass should be used. The Sequence, which is obligatory for Pentecost, is not obligatory for its Vigil. If you are using Eucharistic Prayer I today, use the special form of paragraph 86, starting with "Celebrating the most sacred day."

Entrance Antiphon

The Spirit dwells within us, and God's love is poured out into our hearts. The text alludes to the optional second reading for tomorrow's Mass in Year C. It was new to the post-Vatican II missal.

Collect

Two options are given. In the first, the community prays that the Holy Spirit will gather into one the different tongues of the nations, in order to confess God's name. The prayer mentions the fifty days that give us the word "Pentecost." The prayer first appeared in the Verona Sacramentary, and it was restored for use in *The Roman Missal* for the first time after the Second Vatican Council.

The second option prays that the Holy Spirit's light will confirm the hearts of those born again in baptism. It is more fitting if those baptized at Easter are present again for this Mass, or if baptisms are taking place. (In the early centuries of Christianity, baptisms were recommended on both Easter and Pentecost.) This day used to be called Whitsunday because the newly baptized wore their white robes again to the Eucharist and then turned them in after the service. This prayer first appeared in the Hadrian Sacramentary as the collect for Mass "after rising from the font" on this day. It was in use at the Pentecost Vigil prior to the Second Vatican Council, but was removed from the first post-Vatican II missal.

The extended vigil of Pentecost requires two collects. This may explain why the one that had been removed from the missal has been restored as an option.

Prayer after the First Reading

The community prays that the Church may remain a holy people and show God's holiness to the world. The prayer was new to the post-Vatican II missal, where it appeared as one of the options under Masses for Various Needs and Occasions as a collect offered for the sake of the Church. It was placed here for the first time in the 2008 reprint of the 2002 missal. Its theme has more to do with the Church than with this particular reading; however, it makes a good pair with the psalm.

Prayer after the Second Reading

Because God appeared in fire both on Mount Sinai and in the gift of the Spirit at Pentecost, the faithful pray that they may be aflame with that same Spirit. This prayer was newly composed for the 2008 reprint of the

PRAYER OF THE FAITHFUL

Years A, B, C

The Spirit comes to the aid of our weakness, for we do not know how to pray as we ought.

— *Intercessions* —

Let your Spirit intercede for us, O God. Search our hearts, and find the intentions that agree with your will. Through Christ our Lord.

missal. Its length and complexity suggest the haste with which it may have been prepared. Its theme is directly related to the reading it follows and the occasion of its proclamation.

Prayer after the Third Reading

There are three options. In the first, the community prays for an increase of the people to be renewed by God's name. The prayer is especially appropriate when the recently baptized or those to be baptized are present. It echoes the theme of the reading of the dry

LECTIONARY

Among the options for the first reading, the second tells of the Sinai covenant. It is one of those alluded to in Eucharistic Prayer IV in the phrase, "Time and again you offered them covenants" (Order of Mass, 117). This passage also calls the people God's "special possession," as Eucharistic Prayer III refers to the "elect" (Order of Mass, 113). Calling the people "a kingdom of priests" inspires the priestly role of the people in passages such as Order of Mass 29, where the priest calls for "my sacrifice and yours" to be acceptable, inviting the priestly people to exercise their function. They also do this in the Prayer of the Faithful (Order of Mass, 20).

Eucharistic Prayer IV calls the Holy Spirit "the firstfruits for those who believe" (Order of Mass, 117). It cites Romans 8:23, found in today's second reading. In Eucharistic Prayer I, the phrase "in hope of health and well-being" (Order of Mass, 85) is probably an allusion to Romans 8:24, "in hope we were saved." So is the phrase "through the prophets [you] taught them to look forward to salvation" (Order of Mass, 117) in Eucharistic Prayer IV.

The Communion antiphon cites the Gospel.

bones from Ezekiel. It was newly composed for the 2008 reprint of the missal.

In the second option the community prays for the Holy Spirit, in order to attain the incorruptible resurrection of the flesh. Again, the prayer echoes the passage from Ezekiel. It is new to the 2008 missal.

The third option repeats the collect from the Third Sunday of Easter. A prayer for the newly baptized, it works well with the reading from Ezekiel. *See p. 72.*

Prayer after the Fourth Reading

The faithful pray for a fulfillment of God's promise that the Holy Spirit will make them witnesses to the gospel. This is one of the alternative collects when administering the sacrament of confirmation. The 2008 reprint adopted it in this place to follow the reading from Joel, who prophesied the pouring out of the Spirit. The prayer was newly composed after the Second Vatican Council.

Prayer over the Offerings

We pray that the blessing of the Spirit will be poured out upon these gifts so that the truth of God's saving mystery may shine forth. This prayer, new to the 2008 reprint, was inspired by lines from a Christmas preface found in the Verona Sacramentary. Advent parallels the week before Pentecost. During Advent we pray for the coming of our Savior, and before Pentecost we pray for the coming of the Spirit. Those familiar with the chant settings of the O Antiphons from the last week of Advent know that the antiphon for the Magnificat at Second Vespers for Pentecost imitates the same structure and content.

Preface

On the first Pentecost the Father bestowed the Holy Spirit and united his adopted children to his Son. The Spirit imparted the knowledge of God to all people, united languages, and brought the Church to birth. Today's celebration is more than a historical event; these gifts are still happening today. For many centuries the Roman Rite had no special preface for Pentecost. This one was added to the missal right after the Second Vatican Council. It was inspired by a preface for the Vigil of Pentecost in the Gelasian Sacramentary. Scriptural allusions include Acts of the Apostles 2:1–4, Romans 8:15–16 and 23 and 9:4, 2 Corinthians 4:5–6, Galatians 4:4–5, and Ephesians 1:3, 5–6.

Communion Antiphon

Jesus invites the thirsty to come to him and drink. The antiphon is an abbreviated version of the one that appeared in sources since the eighth century. It quotes the Gospel used at the Vigil Mass.

Prayer after Communion

The community prays that the gifts received in this Communion will help its members be aflame with the Spirit. The text is inspired by the Ambrosian Rite's Sacramentary of Bergamo.

Blessing

The solemn blessing for Pentecost may be used. We pray that God will bestow on the community the gifts of faith received on the first Pentecost, purify the hearts of believers, and grant them perseverance. This threefold blessing is based on one from the Supplement to the Hadrian Sacramentary.

Pentecost Sunday, at the Mass during the Day

Overview

The Church gathers on this day to celebrate the outpouring of the Holy Spirit. Remembering the first Pentecost Sunday, we pray that the Spirit may come renew our hearts today.

The Sequence is obligatory after the second reading. The words are found in the *Lectionary for Mass*. There are various settings for it. Look in the indexes of hymnals under the title *Veni, Sancte Spiritus*.

If you are using Eucharistic Prayer I today, use the special form of paragraph 86, starting with "Celebrating the most sacred day." The dismissal formulas conclude with the double Alleluia today to close the Easter season.

This is the last day on which people may complete their Easter duty. Catholics should receive Communion at least once a year during the fifty days of Easter.

Entrance Antiphon

There are two options. The first announces that the Spirit of the Lord has filled the whole world. This is the same antiphon that has been in use continuously since the eighth century.

The second option was added to the missal after the Council. One fruit of the Spirit is the love of God poured out into our hearts. The same antiphon is used for the Pentecost Vigil, and it alludes to several verses of Paul's Letter to the Romans, the second reading for the Vigil Mass.

Collect

The community asks God to pour out the gifts of the Spirit across the face of the earth to fill once again the hearts of believers. The text is based on a prayer for Pentecost from the Gelasian Sacramentary. It was brought into *The Roman Missal* for the first time after the Second Vatican Council. The prayer is lengthy and its meaning dense.

LECTIONARY

The first reading inspired all the main prayers of the day.

The Kyrie (Order of Mass, 7) developed from the belief that Jesus is Lord, a declaration that opens the second reading. The alternative second reading for Year C inspired the entrance antiphon for the Vigil Mass. Near the end of Eucharistic Prayer IV (Order of Mass, 122) we express our hope to enter "a heavenly inheritance," and the conclusion of this passage from Romans says that we are heirs of God and joint heirs with Christ.

Year A's Gospel gives the origin of the greeting given by a bishop at the beginning of Mass (Order of Mass, 2). He quotes the greeting Jesus makes after the Resurrection.

The optional Gospel for Year B contributed to the words of the prayer over the offerings. The opening verse of this passage inspires the belief that the Spirit proceeds from the Father (Order of Mass, 18).

The optional Gospel for Year C contributed to the words of the prayer over the offerings. It also records the promise that the Father will send the Spirit, which is implied in the secondary epiclesis such as the one in Eucharistic Prayer IV (Order of Mass, 122).

Prayer over the Offerings

We pray that the Holy Spirit will reveal the mystery of this sacrifice and lead us into all truth. The prayer relies on two passages from Jesus' farewell discourse in John's Gospel, both of which appear as optional Gospels for Years B and C. It comes from the Ambrosian Rite's Bergamo Sacramentary, which has supplied several prayers for the modern Roman Church.

Preface

The preface of Pentecost should be used. See comments on *p. 88*.

Communion Antiphon

On the first Pentecost, all were filled with the Holy Spirit, speaking the marvels of God. Communities today do the same. This is a shortened version of the Communion antiphon from eighth-century sources, still quoting the first reading for this feast, which tells the story we need to hear on this day.

Prayer after Communion

We pray that the gift of the Holy Spirit may retain all its force, and that our Communion will gain us eternal redemption. The prayer is based on one from the month of July in the Verona Sacramentary. It was amplified after the Second Vatican Council to include a reference to the Holy Spirit.

Blessing

The solemn blessing for Pentecost may be used. See comments on *p. 88*.

PRAYER OF THE FAITHFUL

Year A

To the disciples who prayed in the upper room, God sent the Holy Spirit. Let us pray for all that the world needs to experience the power of God.

— *Intercessions* —

O God,
who enabled all the world
    to hear the Gospel,
grant our prayers
and open more ears to hear your word.
Through Christ our Lord.

Year B

Jesus fulfilled his promise to send the Advocate. Let us ask him in the Holy Spirit to grant our prayers.

— *Intercessions* —

O God,
whose Spirit testifies to Jesus,
grant these prayers
that we too may testify in your name.
Through Christ our Lord.

Year C

Jesus asked the Father for another Advocate, and we received the Holy Spirit. Let us petition the Father through Christ.

— *Intercessions* —

O God,
whose Spirit reminds us what Jesus taught,
mercifully grant the petitions we offer.
Through Christ our Lord.

Ordinary Time

Overview

When we are not celebrating the seasons of the year, our calendar rests in Ordinary Time. It is the quiet period that offers a breather between the intense celebrations of the mysteries of the birth, death, and rising of Jesus Christ.

According to the *General Norms for the Liturgical Year and Calendar*, 58 and the *Ceremonial of Bishops*, 380, celebrations that fall on weekdays of Ordinary Time may be transferred to Sunday if they have special appeal to the devotion of the faithful, and if they take precedence over Ordinary Time Sundays in the general calendar. For example, if your parish feast day or anniversary of church dedication occurs on a Wednesday in the Seventeenth Week of Ordinary Time, you may transfer it to a nearby Sunday, complete with the readings and prayers.

Sample formularies for the Prayer of the Faithful are given in the fifth appendix of the missal. The ninth and tenth are recommended for Ordinary Time. The first two, called "general," seem to be permissible at any time of year, but the rubric after sets nine and ten implies that they are intended for Ordinary Time also.

The Prefaces

There are eight optional prefaces for the Sundays of Ordinary Time. The first is called "The Paschal Mystery and the People of God." God has freed us from sin and death by the death and resurrection of Christ, calling us a chosen race, a royal priesthood, a holy nation, a people of God's own possession. As a result we proclaim God's mighty works. The earliest version of this preface comes from the Verona Sacramentary, where it is listed in the month of October for periods of drought—perhaps due to the baptismal imagery of this text. The revised preface was added to the post-Vatican II missal. This preface relies on many scriptural passages, including Exodus 19:5–6 and Isaiah 43:20 (a royal priesthood, a holy nation, chosen by God). These themes reappear in a Christian context in 1 Peter 2:9 and Revelation 1:5–6 and 9–10. The call of God is mentioned in 1 Peter 5:10 and 2 Peter 1:3–4.

The second preface is "The mystery of Salvation." Christ had compassion for our sins, humbled himself to a human birth, suffered death, and rose to give us eternal life. The entire Paschal Mystery is summarized here, along with its motivation: divine compassion. The earliest version of this preface comes from the Gelasian Sacramentary, where it was used on the Sunday after the Easter Octave. Perhaps because it includes a reference to the Incarnation, it was assigned to Ordinary Time in the post-Vatican II missal. The compassion of Jesus is noted in Matthew 14:13. His virginal conception is in Luke 1. The gift of eternal life is noted in John 10:28. The call to freedom is in Galatians 5:13. The hymn in Philippians 2:6–8 carries a theme similar to this preface.

The third preface concerns "The salvation of man by a man." God's divinity provided a healing remedy for mortality out of mortality itself. Through Christ, God turned the nature that led to our downfall into the means of our salvation. The earliest version of this preface comes from the Verona Sacramentary. Like the first option, this one is found among the prayers in October for periods of drought—in this case, perhaps because of its reassurance that God comes to our aid. It was added to *The Roman Missal* after the Second Vatican Council. God's search for the lost is a theme in Luke 19:10. The contrast between Jesus and Adam is found in Romans 5:12–17 and in 1 Corinthians 15:20–26.

"The history of salvation" is the title of the fourth preface; however, it deals mostly with the birth of Christ and the Paschal Mystery. By his birth Jesus brought renewal to our fallen state, by suffering he canceled out our sins, by rising he opened the way to eternal life, and by ascending he unlocked the gates of heaven. The earliest version of this preface is in the Gelasian Sacramentary, where it appears among the prayers for the Ascension. However, its inclusion of the mystery of the Incarnation may have influenced the decision to list it among the prefaces for Ordinary Time in the post-Vatican II missal. The birth of Jesus is announced in Luke 2:10. The change from the old way of life to new is told in Romans 6:6, 2 Corinthians 5:17, and Colossians 3:9–10. The remission of sins is noted in Ephesians 2:5, 1 Peter 2:24–25, and 1 John 4:10.

The fifth preface is called "Creation." God laid the foundations of the world and arranged the changing of times and seasons. God formed humanity in the divine image to rule over the world and to praise God's mighty works. This preface was newly composed for the post-Vatican II missal, though it bears some resemblance to one in the Ambrosian tradition. God's creation is told in Genesis 1–2 and Psalm 8. The praise of God's works is noted in Psalm 104:31, 111:2, and 145:17.

The sixth preface is "The pledge of the eternal Passover." We live and move and have our being in God. We experience daily care and the pledge of eternal life. Sharing the firstfruits of the Spirit, we hope to share in the Paschal Mystery for ever. The opening line comes from a collect in the Verona Sacramentary, once again from the collection of prayers in October during a time of drought. The original, however, included a specific petition for rain. The opening was adopted and turned into a preface for Ordinary Time Sundays in the Prague Sacramentary, and from there was brought into *The Roman Missal* after the Second Vatican Council with a new conclusion. Paul argued with the Athenians that we live, move, and have our being in God (Acts 17:28). The work of the Holy Spirit is noted in Romans 8:11 and 23 (where the firstfruits is mentioned). The pledge of the Spirit comes from 2 Corinthians 1:21–22 and 5:1–7, as well as Ephesians 1:14.

The seventh preface is "Salvation through the obedience of Christ." God so loved the world that he sent us the Redeemer to live like us in all things but sin, so that God might love in us what he loves in Christ. The obedience of Christ restored what we lost through disobedience. The line "that you might love in us what you loved in your Son" comes from a prayer in the Mozarabic Rite, but the rest of this preface was newly composed after the Second Vatican Council. It opens with a direct reference to John 3:16. The obedience of Christ is noted in Romans 5:15–19 and Philippians 2:7–9. Hebrews 4:15 says Jesus was like us in all things but sin, a theme repeated in 1 Peter 2:21–22.

The eighth and final option of prefaces for Ordinary Time is called "The Church united by the unity of the Trinity." God gathered the children scattered by sin through the Son and the Spirit, so that the unified Church could be visible through the unity of the Trinity. As the Body of Christ and the temple of the Spirit, the Church praises God's wisdom. This preface was newly composed after the Council. It relies on a passage from Cyprian's *Treatise on the Lord's Prayer*. Commenting on the line "forgive us our sins as we forgive those who sin against us," Cyprian says the resultant peace in the Church shows the unity of the Trinity. This same passage is cited by Vatican II's *Dogmatic Constitution on the Church* (4) to sum up the opening section, which shows how the Church is the fruit of the Trinity. The theme of gathering into one can be seen in John 11:51–52 and 17:20–21, and also in Luke 13:34. The Church as temple of the Spirit is found in 1 Corinthians 6:19. The effects of the blood of Christ are told in Ephesians 2:13–18 and Colossians 1:19–20. God's manifold wisdom is noted in Ephesians 3:9–10. The image of the Church as the Body of Christ is in 1 Corinthians 12:12–30, Romans 12:4–7, and Ephesians 4:15–16 and 5:29–30.

The Communion Antiphons

Throughout Ordinary Time, two alternative Communion antiphons are given, one from the psalms and the other from one of the Gospels for the day. The "I AM" statements of Jesus in John's Gospel appear as Communion antiphons on various Sundays of Ordinary Time; so do the Beatitudes.

The Blessings

The blessing that concludes Mass may be expanded into a threefold solemn blessing or a prayer over the people. In a solemn blessing, the priest addresses the people, and they answer "Amen" to each of the three sections. The prayer over the people is addressed to God, and everyone answers "Amen" as they do to the other prayers of the Mass. In both forms, the deacon or priest commands the people to bow their heads, and after the prayer the priest gives the blessing with the sign of the cross.

There are six choices for solemn blessings during Ordinary Time. The first is the most foundational to them all. It prays that God will keep the people from harm, show mercy to them, and give them peace. In Numbers 6:22–27, this is how God wants the Old Testament priests to bless the people. Most of the other solemn blessings follow a similar three-part structure. Among Christian liturgical books, this blessing first appears in the Hadrian Supplement in a collection for ordinary days. There it has obtained its responsive nature: each part of the blessing concludes with an Amen.

The second option is inspired by Philippians 4:7. "May the peace of God . . . keep your hearts and minds in the knowledge and love of God." This one solemn blessing abandons the three-part structure in order to retain Paul's original format. It was perhaps added here as a New Testament blessing to parallel the one from Numbers.

The third option asks for an outpouring of God's saving wisdom, nourishment with the teachings of the faith, perseverance in holy deeds, and the discovery of the path of peace and charity. The text is taken almost word for word from the Hadrian Supplement, where it appears as the first option after the blessing from Numbers.

The fourth blessing prays for peace; good works; the gifts of hope, faith and charity; and eternal life. It is inspired by another of the many solemn blessings from the Hadrian Supplement.

The fifth option asks for protection from adversity, gifts of blessing, attention to God's words, everlasting gladness, following God's commands, and an understanding of what is good and right in order to be coheirs with the citizens of heaven. It is also inspired by one of the blessings from the Hadrian Supplement. The final petition alludes to Ephesians 2:19 and perhaps to Hebrews 12:23.

The sixth and final option prays that the community may be holy and pure, receive the riches of God's glory, learn God's words of truth and the gospel of salvation, and become rich in charity. It was newly composed for the post-Vatican II missal from Ephesians 1:3–14. As with the second option, it abandons the three-part structure of a solemn blessing in order to present a text more in keeping with its biblical source.

The prayers over the people are found in two places in the missal: near the end of the Order of Mass, and throughout the season of Lent. The Gelasian Sacramentary includes one of these for each day of Lent. That tradition, abandoned for centuries, was restored to the Roman Rite with the 2002 missal.

The 2002 missal made a few changes to these prayers. A number of the ones you may know from the 1985 Sacramentary were moved to a new location during the season of Lent: the second one to Wednesday of the Second Week; the fifth to Saturday of the First Week; the ninth to Friday of the Third Week; the tenth to the Fifth Sunday; the thirteenth to Saturday of the Third Week; the fifteenth was lightly edited and moved to Thursday of the Fifth Week; the sixteenth became the prayer on Monday of the Third Week; the seventeenth moved to Palm Sunday; the eighteenth to Wednesday of Holy Week; the twenty-third to Monday of the Second Week; and the twenty-fourth to Thursday of the Fourth Week of Lent.

Two prayers from the 1985 Sacramentary were removed, the eighth and the twentieth. The eighth was a version of the collect for the

Eighteenth Sunday in Ordinary Time (see *p. 130*), which remains in place there. Several are new to the 2002 missal: the sixth, and all those from the seventeenth to the twenty-sixth. The two prayers for feasts of the saints remain unchanged.

The first prayer over the people asks for consolation in this life. It comes from the Verona Sacramentary's prayers for fasting in December. This is a revised translation of the first prayer in the 1985 Sacramentary.

The second asks that Christians understand what they profess and love: the heavenly liturgy. It comes from the Gelasian Sacramentary's prayers at the ordination of a priest or deacon. This is a revised translation of the third prayer in the 1985 Sacramentary.

The third asks that people may spurn what would harm them and obtain what they desire. It comes from the daily prayers for July in the Verona Sacramentary. It retranslates the fourth prayer in the 1985 Sacramentary.

The fourth prays for the people to turn back wholeheartedly to God, who sustains those who serve with undivided heart. It first appeared on Monday of the Second Week of Lent in the Gelasian Sacramentary. This is a new translation of the sixth prayer in the 1985 Sacramentary.

The fifth asks the Lord to enlighten his family, that they may accomplish all that is good. It comes from the Gelasian Sacramentary, where it served the Second Sunday of Lent. This is a new translation of the seventh prayer in the 1985 Sacramentary.

The sixth prays for pardon and peace, and for cleansing from every offense in order to serve God with untroubled hearts. It was used at vespers on the Sunday after Easter in the Hadrian Sacramentary. It was newly added to the 2002 missal.

The seventh prays for an increase in the numbers and obedience of those who subject themselves to God. It was used on Thursday of the Third Week of Lent in the Hadrian Sacramentary. It is a new translation of the eleventh prayer in the 1985 Sacramentary.

The eighth prays that the people may serve God with all their heart. It comes from a collection of Sunday prayers over the people in the Gelasian Sacramentary. This retranslates the twelfth prayer in the 1985 Sacramentary.

The ninth asks that God's family may rejoice and persevere to attain the effects of redemption. It comes from the collection of Sunday prayers over the people in the Gelasian Sacramentary. This is a new translation of the fourteenth prayer in the 1985 Sacramentary.

The tenth asks the Lord God to provide mercy for his servants that they may abound in thanksgiving and exultation. This also comes from the Sunday prayers over the people in the Gelasian. It retranslates the nineteenth prayer in the 1985 Sacramentary.

The eleventh prays for God's constant care, that people may be free from all troubles. This originated in the Gellone Sacramentary, and was newly added to the 2002 missal.

The twelfth prays for purity in body and mind, a feeling of compunction, the avoidance of what is harmful, and a feast of God's delights. This comes from the Gelasian's collection of Sunday prayers over the people. This is a new translation of the twenty-first prayer in the 1985 Sacramentary.

The thirteenth asks that the minds of all be prepared with spiritual sustenance for the strength to do charity. The prayer is based on one from an ordinary Mass in the Gelasian Sacramentary. This is a new translation of the twenty-second prayer in the 1985 Sacramentary.

In the fourteenth prayer, the faithful ask to know what is right and to receive all they need for their good. The Verona Sacramentary listed this among the prayers for Saint Cecilia's Day in November. It is newly added to the 2002 missal.

The fifteenth prays for strength in human weakness, as well as healing in this life and the life to come. The prayer originated as one for fasting in the Verona Sacramentary. It was newly added to the 2002 missal.

The sixteenth prays for mercy, that the Lord's family may obey his saving commands. It originated among prayers for a bishop's ordination in the Verona Sacramentary. It was newly added to the 2002 missal.

The seventeenth prays for grace to praise God with our lips, souls, and lives. It is based on a fasting prayer for December in the Verona Sacramentary and was newly added to the 2002 missal.

The eighteenth asks for heavenly instruction, to avoid evil, pursue good, and obtain God's mercy. It comes from the blessing at the consecration of a bishop in the Verona Sacramentary. It is new to the 2002 missal.

The nineteenth prays for protection, that God's people may remain faithful in holiness of life and be heirs of the promise for eternity. It originated among the prayers for fasting in September. It is new to the 2002 missal.

In the twentieth, the people pray for grace, that God who formed them and restored them may also save them. It is based on a Christmas blessing from the Verona Sacramentary. It is new to the 2002 missal.

The twenty-first asks the Lord that the people may respond to his love, gladly do his command, and receive what he promises. The original comes from the Verona's prayers in times of drought. It is new to the 2002 missal.

The twenty-second asks for God's generous pardon to people who are weak but faithfully pleading. It comes from the Verona's prayers for the consecration of a bishop. It is new to the 2002 missal.

The twenty-third prayer asks the Lord to defend his children, that they may be protected by his care. It is based on the Verona Sacramentary's blessing for the feast of Saints Cornelius and Cyprian in September. It is new to the 2002 missal.

The twenty-fourth prayer asks that those strengthened by divine help may persevere in confessing God's name. It comes from the Verona's fasting prayers in September. It is new to the 2002 missal.

The twenty-fifth prays that God's family will be kept safe and may find growth through the teachings and gifts of heaven. It is based on an October prayer in times of drought from the Verona Sacramentary. It is new to the 2002 missal.

The twenty-sixth asks that the people progressing in the Christian life may delight in good things now and in the time to come. It is one of the Verona Sacramentary's last prayers in September on the occasion of the consecration of a bishop. It is new to the 2002 missal.

Second Sunday in Ordinary Time

Overview

Green vestments return today. They have been worn on weekdays last week, but this is their first appearance on Sunday. Keep the liturgy simple.

The second reading today begins a series of passages from Paul's First Letter to the Corinthians in all three years of the cycle. The Gospel is always taken from John.

Consider using Eucharistic Prayer IV today because it has not been used on Sunday since at least November.

Entrance Antiphon

Let all the earth bow down and sing to God the most high. This verse from Psalm 65 served as the entrance antiphon for the Second Sunday after Epiphany since at least the eighth century. Although this Sunday has a new title, the antiphon appears in the same place in the liturgical year.

Collect

We ask God who governs all things to bestow peace on our times. As with the entrance antiphon, this prayer appeared in the pre-Vatican II missal on the Second Sunday after Epiphany. It has remained unchanged since it first appeared in the Hadrian Sacramentary as a non-seasonal daily prayer. The words "heaven and on earth" appear in Genesis 1:1 and in Colossians 1:16.

Prayer over the Offerings

We ask to participate in these mysteries worthily, as the work of our redemption is being accomplished. This is the same prayer over the offerings offered on Holy Thursday (*see p. 51*). It comes from the Verona Sacramentary.

Preface

Any preface from Ordinary Time may be used. *See pp. 92–93.* The eighth option calls the Church "the temple of the Holy Spirit," a phrase that occurs near the end of the second reading in Year B.

Communion Antiphon

The first choice comes from the most popular psalm, "The Lord is my shepherd." This verse recalls the table and cup that God prepared. Eucharistic Prayer I refers to this line

---

LECTIONARY

Verses 6–8 of Year A's responsorial psalm foreshadow the self-offering of Jesus Christ, according to the Letter to the Hebrews 10:8–9. This lies in the background of the phrase in Eucharistic Prayer IV, "the sacrifice acceptable to you" (Order of Mass, 122). One of the options for the greeting at the beginning of Mass appears numerous times in the writings of Saint Paul. One example is the close of today's second reading. During the breaking of the bread we address Jesus as the Lamb of God (Order of Mass, 130), a title he receives in this Gospel, and the invitation to Communion (Order of Mass, 132) quotes John the Baptist directly.

Verses 6–8 of the responsorial psalm in Year B foreshadow the self-offering of Jesus Christ, according to the Letter to the Hebrews 10:8–9. This lies in the background of the phrase in Eucharistic Prayer IV, "the sacrifice acceptable to you" (Order of Mass, 122).

when it says Jesus took the "precious chalice" (Order of Mass, 90). The second choice, surprisingly, comes from First John, not from one of the Gospels. We recognize the love that God has for us. The first antiphon stresses the symbols of Communion, the second its fruit of charity. Both antiphons were new to the post-Vatican II missal.

Prayer after Communion

We pray that God will pour the Spirit of love into us, making us one in mind and heart. The prayer echoes the second option for the Communion antiphon as well as Romans 5:5. It originates in the Verona Sacramentary as a prayer after Communion for the ordination of a bishop in September.

Blessing

Any of the solemn blessings or prayers over the people may be used. *See pp. 94–96.*

PRAYER OF THE FAITHFUL

Year A

Jesus Christ is the Lamb of God who takes away the sin of the world. Through him we ask forgiveness and an answer to our prayers.

— *Intercessions* —

O God,
whose servant John baptized
in order to make Christ known to Israel,
hear the prayers of your servants
and make him known to all the world.
Through Christ our Lord.

Year B

As Samuel grew up, the Lord did not permit any word of his to be without effect. May the Spirit make effective the prayers we bring to God.

— *Intercessions* —

O God,
whose Son invited disciples to follow him,
be faithful to the prayers
of those who find in him
the Lamb of God they seek.
Through Christ our Lord.

Year C

The Spirit is given to each individual for some benefit. Let us pray that the gifts of the Spirit may flourish in our midst.

— *Intercessions* —

O God,
whose Son worked his first miracle
at the wedding feast in Cana,
be present at this banquet
and work new wonders for us.
Through Christ our Lord.

Third Sunday in Ordinary Time

Overview

Today's Gospel comes from the evangelist from whom you will hear the most this year. You may want to call attention to his appearance.

A few weeks before Lent begins, you may wish to invite people to return their old palm branches to church. You can burn these to make the ashes for Ash Wednesday.

Invite people to bring candles to your celebration of the Presentation of the Lord (February 2). These can be included in the blessing of candles at church, and brought home to be lighted at prayer time. If February 2 falls on a Sunday next week, cantors may want to rehearse the congregation on any special music they will be asked to sing. You may also alert churchgoers that next week's Mass may take a little more time than usual, in order to celebrate the crowning event in the infancy of Jesus Christ.

Entrance Antiphon

All the earth is summoned to sing a new song to the Lord. This text from Psalm 95 follows a pattern, in which the opening words of the Mass often issue a command to the community. This antiphon was new to the post-Vatican II missal.

Collect

We ask God to direct our actions and make us abound in good works. The prayer is lifted directly from the Hadrian Sacramentary, where it was offered on a Sunday in January. The recently celebrated events of the Christmas season are a sign of God's good pleasure (Ephesians 1:9). The reference to the "beloved Son" links this prayer to the same passage (Ephesians 1:6), as well as to the recent celebration of the Baptism of the Lord, where the voice from heaven gives this title to Jesus. The request to abound in good works relates to Ephesians 1:8 and 2:10.

Prayer over the Offerings

We ask God to accept our gifts and to sanctify them for our salvation. This prayer first appeared in the Verona Sacramentary among the daily prayers for the month of July.

Preface

Any of the prefaces from Ordinary Time may be used. *See pp. 92–93.* The eighth option calls the Church the Body of Christ, which is affirmed in the second reading in Year C.

Communion Antiphon

From the psalms, the community is invited to be made radiant by God. From the Gospel we hear Jesus say he is the light of the world. This is one of a series of Communion antiphons that cite the "I AM" statements of Jesus. Both use the recent Epiphany theme of light. Both were new to the post-Vatican II missal.

LECTIONARY

Second reading: One reason we hear "The Body of Christ" when receiving Communion (Order of Mass, 134) is Paul's statement in Year C's second reading: "You are Christ's body" (1 Corinthians 12:27). The Gospel of Year C is cited in Eucharistic Prayer IV (Order of Mass, 117) as it describes the mission of Jesus to the poor, the prisoners, and the sorrowful. It also inspired the introduction to the sample Prayer of the Faithful for Advent, found in the fifth appendix of the missal.

Prayer after Communion

We pray that we who have received new life may glory in God's gift. This prayer comes from the Gelasian Sacramentary, where it appears during both Lent and Easter. Its meaning is generic enough to serve in Ordinary Time.

Blessing

Any of the solemn blessings or prayers over the people may be used. *See pp. 94–96.*

PRAYER OF THE FAITHFUL

Year A

The people who sit in darkness have seen a great light. Let us pray for all who stand in need of the radiant love of God.

— *Intercessions* —

O God,
whose Son preached the nearness
    of your kingdom,
be close to your people in every necessity.
Through Christ our Lord.

Year B

This is the time of fulfillment. The kingdom of God is at hand. Let us fervently pray for the needs of the world.

— *Intercessions* —

O God,
whose Son called followers
    to fish for people,
let our hearts be filled with praise
for the answers you give our prayers.
Through Christ our Lord.

Year C

Jesus proclaimed liberty to captives, sight to the blind, and freedom for the oppressed. Let us bring our prayers to God through him.

— *Intercessions* —

O God,
whose Son fulfilled the hopes of ages past,
restore our hope and grant these prayers.
Through Christ our Lord.

Fourth Sunday in Ordinary Time

Overview

If February 2 falls this week, see the note about candles above *(p. 100)*.

The *Book of Blessings* includes the Order for the Blessing of Throats on the Feast of Saint Blaise, February 3 (1630–1635). When the feast falls on a Sunday, the Ordinary Time Sunday is observed, but it would be appropriate to include the blessing of throats.

Entrance Antiphon

From the psalms, we ask God to save us and gather us together that we might give thanks to his holy name. The verse works as a generic song of praise. It was new to the post-Vatican II missal.

Collect

We ask that we might honor God and love others. This prayer originated in the Verona Sacramentary among daily prayers for July, but scholars believe this particular prayer was written by Pope Gelasius specifically for the Sunday liturgy of January 29, 495. If so, it was intended to help Christians counter the upcoming pagan Roman Lupercalia celebrations. Although the threat of these particular pagan celebrations has passed, the prayer is still being used on a Sunday close to the same date each year. The prayer is probably based on the two great commandments from Mark 12:30, Matthew 22:37, and Luke 10:27, encouraging Christians to love the one true God.

Prayer over the Offerings

We ask God to transform these offerings into the Sacrament of our redemption. The complexity of this brief prayer forced the translators to break it into two independent clauses. This prayer first appeared in the Verona Sacramentary as a prayer for July.

Preface

Any preface for Ordinary Time may be used. *See pp. 92–93.*

Communion Antiphon

With the psalmist, we ask God to shine his face upon his servant. This antiphon appeared in eighth-century sources for Septuagesima Sunday (the third Sunday before Ash Wednesday). The date fluctuated with the Easter cycle. The custom of observing three Sundays before Lent was discontinued after the Second Vatican Council. However, many of the antiphons were retained for the Sundays that occur around the same time of year.

From the Gospel we hear Jesus proclaim that those who are poor in spirit are blessed. That antiphon is favored in Year A when the Gospel of the Beatitudes is proclaimed on this day. It is the first of several Communion antiphons in Ordinary Time that cite the Beatitudes.

LECTIONARY

The full text of Psalm 146, the responsorial psalm in Year A, includes the word "Alleluia." It serves as an alternative antiphon this weekend. This is one of the biblical sources for the word we use as the Gospel acclamation on most days (Order of Mass, 13).

Prayer after Communion

Nourished by this Communion, we pray that true faith may ever increase. The prayer comes from the Verona Sacramentary's collection of orations for daily use in the month of July.

Blessing

Any solemn blessing from Ordinary Time may be used, or even a prayer over the people. *See pp. 94–96.* The fourth solemn blessing specifically asks for the gifts of hope, faith, and charity, which appear at the end of the second reading in Year C.

PRAYER OF THE FAITHFUL

Year A

The Lord gives sight to the blind. The Lord raises up those who are bowed down. In confidence we present our petitions.

— Intercessions —

O God,
who promised great reward in heaven
for those who are blessed on earth,
receive these prayers
    from your faithful people.
Through Christ our Lord.

Year B

Throughout his life, Jesus demonstrated power over all the forces of nature. We bring our prayers to God through him.

— Intercessions —

O God,
whose Son taught with authority
and controlled the forces of evil,
send goodness into the world
and kindly answer our prayers.
Through Christ our Lord.

Year C

God's love is patient and kind. To the One who loves us more than we can love another, we present our needs.

— Intercessions —

O God,
who revealed your plan of love
in the coming of your only Son,
show us your care
    and grant these petitions.
Through Christ our Lord.

Fifth Sunday in Ordinary Time

Overview

Keep an eye out for the last Sunday in Ordinary Time before Lent begins. It may be a good occasion to use Eucharistic Prayer IV, which should not be used again until Ordinary Time returns after the Solemnity of the Most Holy Body and Blood of Christ. Similarly, you may want to sing hymns that include Alleluias in the text. It should be the last occasion to sing those until Easter.

Entrance Antiphon

The community is invited to come worship God. This psalm serves as an invitatory to start the Liturgy of the Hours. It was also the entrance antiphon for the observance of the Saturday ember day in Lent in eighth-century sources.

Collect

We ask the Lord to watch over his family and defend them with protecion. The text comes from the Hadrian Sacramentary, where it is a prayer over the people to conclude a Mass. In some early sacramentaries, it was used to open the Mass on the Fifth Sunday after the Epiphany, which usually calculates to this day.

Prayer over the Offerings

God created bread and wine to sustain us in our frailty; we pray that they may become the sacrament of eternal life. The text comes from the Verona Sacramentary, where it is a prayer from a time of fasting in the month of September.

Preface

Any of the prefaces of Ordinary Time may be used. *See pp. 92–93.*

Communion Antiphon

From one of the historical psalms, people thank the Lord for his mercy and for the wonders he has done, satisfying the hungers and thirst of the people. From the Gospel, Jesus blesses those who hunger and thirst for justice. The text is drawn from the previous Sunday's Gospel in Year A. It is part of the series of Communion antiphons in Ordinary Time that cite the Beatitudes. Both antiphons were new to the post-Vatican II missal.

Prayer after Communion

Sharing one bread and one cup, being made one in Christ, the community asks that it may bear fruit for the world's salvation. The prayer is inspired by 1 Corinthians 10:17 and has a parallel in paragraph 122 of Eucharistic Prayer IV. It is a new composition, based on the first

LECTIONARY

Verse 5 of Year B's responsorial psalm and the refrain exclaim that the Lord heals the brokenhearted. This line influenced the first invocation in the third form of the penitential act: "You were sent to heal the contrite of heart" (Order of Mass, 6). The same phrase appears in the introduction of the sample Prayer of the Faithful for Advent in the fifth appendix of the missal.

When the priest prepares himself to proclaim the Gospel (Order of Mass, 14), he says a prayer inspired by the first reading in Year C, Isaiah 6:5–7 ("Cleanse my heart and my lips"). The *Sanctus* quotes the angels whom Isaiah hears singing in his vision (Order of Mass, 31). The angels sing to one another about God, not directly to God. The punctuation of the *Sanctus* leaves the first line ambiguous. It could be either a statement about God or one addressed to God.

part of a prayer from the Dominican Missal of 1933 for the feast of Blessed Hosanna of Kotor. It also relies on scriptural passages such as Romans 12:5, John 15:16, and John 17:11 and 21. This little prayer shows the variety of sources from which the post-Vatican II missal was devised.

Blessing

Any of the solemn blessings or prayers over the people for Ordinary Time may be used. *See pp. 94–96.*

PRAYER OF THE FAITHFUL

Year A

If we remove oppression, lies, and malice, if we feed the hungry, light shall rise in the darkness. As God's own people, we lift our prayers.

— Intercessions —

O God,
whose Son commanded us to be light
    for the world,
hear our prayers
and let our hearts radiate the joy
    of your love.
Through Christ our Lord.

Year B

Jesus cured many who were sick and drove out many demons. Believing in his power, we pray to God through him.

— Intercessions —

O God,
who revealed your compassion
in the ministry of your Son,
show us your love
by granting these prayers.
Through Christ our Lord.

Year C

Jesus provided a miraculous catch of faith to stir up belief in his followers. Filled with faith we present our prayers.

— Intercessions —

O God,
whose Son worked wonders
to stir up faith and to send forth believers,
send us forth,
strengthenèd by a faith made firm
through an answer to our prayers.
Through Christ our Lord.

Sixth Sunday in Ordinary Time

Entrance Antiphon

The psalm verse asks God for protection, leadership, and guidance. Unlike many other entrance antiphons, this one is in the first person singular. Between the eighth century and the Second Vatican Council, this antiphon began the liturgy of Quinquagesima Sunday, the Sunday before Ash Wednesday.

Collect

God abides in hearts that are just and true. We ask that we might be the kind of people in whom God is pleased to dwell. The prayer originated in the Gelasian Sacramentary for the Sunday after the Ascension of the Lord; hence the concern about God's abiding presence, after the ascension of Christ. There is perhaps a resonance with the image of the vine and branches in John 15:10. A version of this prayer also appears in the missal's collects for the Common of Virgins, focusing on the virtue of purity of heart.

Prayer over the Offerings

We pray that the oblation will cleanse and renew us, giving us a source of eternal reward. The prayer is based on a preface from the Verona Sacramentary, used at the consecration of a bishop in September.

Preface

Any preface from Ordinary Time may be used. *See pp. 92–93.* There is a slight connection between the third option and the close of the second reading in Year C.

Communion Antiphon

From the historical Psalm 77, we hear of the Israelites in the desert who ate and had their fill of manna. This was the Communion antiphon for Quinquagesima Sunday between the eighth century and the Second Vatican Council. The alternative antiphon quotes Jesus saying God so loved the world that he gave his only-begotten Son.

Prayer after Communion

Having fed on this Communion, we ask to long always for the food by which we truly live. This prayer comes directly from the Gelasian Sacramentary, where it is a generic prayer after Communion for Mass.

Blessing

Any solemn blessing from Ordinary Time may be used, or even a prayer over the people. *See pp. 94–96.*

LECTIONARY

The long version of year A's Gospel includes Jesus' admonition to make peace before coming to offer a gift. This passage lies behind the practice of offering a sign of peace at the liturgy (Order of Mass, 128).

In Year B, the second reading is the last in the series of readings from Paul's First Letter to the Corinthians.

PRAYER OF THE FAITHFUL

Year A

Before we bring our gifts to the altar, let us seek peace with those we have offended. Let us pray for the needs of the Church and the world.

— Intercessions —

O God,
the source of all righteousness,
make us worthy
to receive a favorable answer
    to our prayers.
Through Christ our Lord.

Year B

The faith of a leper brought him healing. As we present our needs to God, let us be filled with a confident faith.

— Intercessions —

O God,
to whom we turn in times of trouble,
hear our prayers
and fill us with the joy of salvation.
Through Christ our Lord.

Year C

Jesus proclaimed blessings for the poor, the hungry, and the sorrowful. We anticipate a favorable response as we present our needs.

— Intercessions —

O God,
who blessed those who hope in you,
plant us beside the running waters
    of your word
and fill our hearts with the joy
    of your unending care.
Through Christ our Lord.

Seventh Sunday in Ordinary Time

Entrance Antiphon

The psalmist trusts in God's mercy, rejoices in salvation, and sings to the Lord who has been bountiful. As with last Sunday's, this antiphon is in the first person singular. Up to this point, many of the entrance antiphons came from traditional sources for the Sundays after Epiphany and the Sundays before Lent. This one was used for the first Sunday after Pentecost from at least the eighth century. It responds to the remote possibility that today's observance will follow the Lent and Easter seasons.

Collect

We ask to carry out what is pleasing to God in word and deed. This prayer comes from the Gelasian Sacramentary, where it was offered at special Masses in times of strife. In some early sacramentaries it was used for the Fifth or Sixth Sunday after Epiphany. It may contain an allusion to Jesus' criticism that the Pharisees do not practice what they preach (Matthew 23:3).

Prayer over the Offerings

We ask that what we offer may profit us for salvation. The prayer comes directly from the Verona Sacramentary's collection of orations for ordinary usage in the month of July. It was new to the post–Vatican II missal.

Preface

Any preface from Ordinary Time may be used. *See pp. 92–93.* The sixth option says we receive pledges of eternal life. The end of the second reading in Year B says that God's seal is upon us who receive the Spirit.

Communion Antiphon

The psalmist sings and rejoices in God's wonderful deeds. This is the traditional antiphon for the First Sunday after Pentecost, linking it with the entrance antiphon. From the Gospel of John, we hear Martha, who has lost her brother Lazarus, profess her faith that Jesus is the Christ, the Son of the living God.

Prayer after Communion

In Communion we receive a pledge of salvation. We ask to experience its effects. This very dense prayer comes from the Hadrian Sacramentary, where it was offered during Lent.

Blessing

Any solemn blessing from Ordinary Time may be used, or even a prayer over the people. *See pp. 94–96.*

LECTIONARY

In Year B's first reading from Isaiah, God speaks about "the people I formed for myself," which is related to the phrase in Eucharistic Prayer III, "the entire people you have gained for your own" (Order of Mass, 113). The second reading is the first in the series from Paul's Second Letter to the Corinthians. Although all three years of the cycle start Ordinary Time with passages from Paul's First Letter to the Corinthians, this is the only year that offers the Second. The theme of this passage resonates with that of the prayer after Communion.

PRAYER OF THE FAITHFUL

Year A

The sun rises on the bad and the good; rain
  falls on the just and the unjust. Seeking
  perfection, we reveal the needs we hold
  within.

— Intercessions —

O God,
whose Son loved his enemies,
hear our prayers even for those
  who persecute us,
and make us your children.
Through Christ our Lord.

Year B

Jesus cured the paralytic and forgave his sins.
  We pray for the grace of a clean heart that
  our petitions may find favor with God.

— Intercessions —

O God,
whose Son helped the sick
  and removed ailments,
have pity on us, heal us,
and grant our prayers.
Through Christ our Lord.

Year C

Jesus asked his followers to pray for those
  who mistreat them. Let us seek to possess
  the compassion of God as we make known
  our needs.

— Intercessions —

O God,
merciful and gracious,
slow to anger and abounding
  in compassion,
show us your love
and grant our prayers.
Through Christ our Lord.

Eighth Sunday in Ordinary Time

Entrance Antiphon

The psalmist says the Lord has brought protection and freedom. The antiphon sets a note of reassurance at the start of this Eucharist. From the eighth century, this was the antiphon for the Second Sunday after Pentecost on the pre-Vatican II calendar.

Collect

We pray that God will direct the world in peace, and that the Church may rejoice in untroubled devotion. The original text was recommended for morning or evening prayer in the Verona Sacramentary. It is thought to have been composed for Quinquagesima Sunday (the Sunday before Ash Wednesday), February 14 of the year 538, during a truce under a siege of Rome. The vocabulary may be related to 1 Timothy 2:1–2. When there is an Eighth Sunday in Ordinary Time before Lent, this prayer is offered at the time of year when it was possibly first used.

Prayer over the Offerings

Our oblations are a sign of our devoted service. We pray for an eternal reward. The prayer uses the word "merit," which is easy to misunderstand. In liturgical language it refers to some benefit that comes to us undeserved, not earned. This prayer assumes that God has given us gifts that make us appealing to him. We ask that these same gifts will guide us toward heaven. This first appeared among the daily prayers for July in the Verona Sacramentary.

Preface

Any preface from Ordinary Time may be used. *See pp. 92–93.*

Communion Antiphon

The psalmist sings to the Lord who has been bountiful—including the giving of this Eucharist. This antiphon comes from the Second Sunday after Pentecost in the pre-Vatican II tradition, beginning in the eighth century. From the end of Matthew's Gospel, we hear Jesus promise to remain with his disciples to the end of the age. He does this sacramentally in our Communion. This is one of the antiphons in which we hear Jesus speak in the first person.

Prayer after Communion

We pray that God will make us partakers of life eternal through the sacrament that feeds us in this life. This comes from the daily prayers for July in the Verona Sacramentary. The same prayer is also now used on two weekdays near the end of Lent.

Blessing

Any solemn blessing from Ordinary Time may be used or even a prayer over the people. *See pp. 94–96.*

LECTIONARY

Year A's second reading is the last in this year's series from Paul's First Letter to the Corinthians.

In the Nicene Creed we express our belief in the Holy Spirit, "the giver of life" (Order of Mass, 18). The attribute is acknowledged in the close of Year B's second reading.

Year C's second reading is the last in this year's series from Paul's First Letter to the Corinthians.

PRAYER OF THE FAITHFUL

Year A

Jesus commands us not to worry about our life. Let us place our trust in the One who can answer our needs.

— Intercessions —

O God,
whose kingdom and righteousness
we seek above all other things,
help us on our way
by granting these prayers.
Through Christ our Lord.

Year B

God has already espoused us in love and mercy. We present our petitions to the One who already looks after our needs.

— Intercessions —

O God,
whose love for us provides the model
    for married couples,
hear these prayers
    and show us your love anew.
Through Christ our Lord.

Year C

Saint Paul asks us to be firm, steadfast, and devoted to the Lord. Because of God, our labor is never in vain, and our prayers rise up in hope.

— Intercessions —

O God,
our guide and teacher,
remove the blindness from our eyes
and make our prayers more favorable
    in your sight.
Through Christ our Lord.

Ninth Sunday in Ordinary Time

Entrance Antiphon

The psalmist asks God for mercy, being poor and alone. The theme is very close to that of the season of Lent. The antiphon comes from eighth-century sources and was always used on the Third Sunday after Pentecost.

Collect

We ask our provident God to keep away what would harm us and to grant what works for our good. The prayer comes from the Gelasian Sacramentary, among those composed for Sundays outside the main seasons of the year. It was reassigned to that position after the Second Vatican Council.

Prayer over the Offerings

Trusting in God's compassion, we ask for cleansing through God's grace in these mysteries. This prayer was composed out of ideas from three different sources in the Verona Sacramentary. The same prayer is now used on December 22 each year.

Preface

Any preface from Ordinary Time may be used. *See pp. 92–93.*

Communion Antiphon

The psalmist asks God to turn an ear and listen. As with the entrance antiphon, this one implies our need for God's assistance. It comes from eighth-century sources for the Third Sunday after Pentecost, though it was not carried over into *The Roman Missal* tradition until after the Second Vatican Council. Almost in response, the alternative antiphon from the Gospel offers Jesus' comforting words about prayer—believe that you will receive and it will be yours.

Prayer after Communion

We ask God to govern us by the Spirit, and to make us fit for heaven. This prayer was added to the post-Vatican II missal from the late medieval Paris Missal.

Blessing

Any solemn blessing from Ordinary Time may be used, or even a prayer over the people. *See pp. 94–96.*

LECTIONARY

Year A's second reading is the first in the long series from Paul's Letter to the Romans.

Year C's second reading is the first in the series from Paul's Letter to the Galatians. Before receiving Communion, everyone says a line inspired by Year C's Gospel, "only say the word and my soul shall be healed" (Order of Mass, 132).

PRAYER OF THE FAITHFUL

Year A

Those who do the will of God will find an answer to their prayers. As faithful followers of Christ, let us present our petitions.

— *Intercessions* —

O God,
the rock of our faith,
hear our prayers
and be the foundation on which we stand.
Through Christ our Lord.

Year B

Jesus demonstrated his lordship over illness and cares, times and seasons. We lift our needs through him to God.

— *Intercessions* —

O God,
who care for us with a strong hand
  and outstretched arm,
work new wonders for your people
and graciously grant these prayers.
Through Christ our Lord.

Year C

Jesus cured the centurion's servant because of the master's faith. Let us renew our faith in God's power as we present our needs.

— *Intercessions* —

O God,
whose Son was pleased
with the centurion's faith and service,
look kindly upon our worship at your altar,
and grant the requests we make this day.
Through Christ our Lord.

Tenth Sunday in Ordinary Time

Entrance Antiphon

The psalmist has no fear, for God is light, salvation, and stronghold. A confident verse initiates the texts for this Mass. This was the antiphon for the Fourth Sunday after Pentecost from the eighth century to the pre-Vatican II missal.

Collect

All good things come from God. We pray to discern what is right and to do it. The earliest version of this prayer comes from the Gelasian Sacramentary on a Sunday of the Easter season. The text may be inspired by a saying of Jesus, that God gives good things to the faithful (Matthew 7:11), and a passage from James, that God is the source of every perfect gift (James 1:17), which in turn inspired a popular hymn text, "All Good Gifts."

Prayer over the Offerings

We ask that our oblation may be acceptable and lead to our growth in charity. This prayer originated in the Verona Sacramentary among those for times of drought in October, but the final line was changed from "help our weakness" to "lead us to grow in charity."

Preface

Any preface from Ordinary Time may be used. *See pp. 92–93.*

Communion Antiphon

The Lord is the rock, fortress, deliverer, and strength of the psalmist. The confidence of the entrance antiphon reappears here. This was the antiphon for the Fourth Sunday after Pentecost from the eighth century to the pre-Vatican II missal. From the First Letter of John—not from the Gospel—the alternative antiphon proclaims that God is love. We experience that love profoundly in Communion.

Prayer after Communion

We ask for God's healing work to turn us from evil to what is right. The Gelasian Sacramentary included this one among prayers for any day. It fits Ordinary Time.

Blessing

Any solemn blessing from Ordinary Time may be used, or even a prayer over the people. *See pp. 94–96.*

LECTIONARY

In the first Eucharistic Prayer, the priest says, "We offer you this sacrifice of praise," and "fulfilling their vows to you" (Order of Mass, 85). Both phrases come from Year A's responsorial psalm, verse 14. The second invocation of the third form of the penitential act (Order of Mass, 6) refers to the close of Year A's Gospel: "You came to call sinners."

PRAYER OF THE FAITHFUL

Year A

Jesus came to call not the righteous, but sinners. Though we are bowed down by our faults, we remain confident in God's goodness as we present our prayers.

— *Intercessions* —

O God,
who still show mercy
on those unworthy of your call,
let us praise the goodness you show
by answering these petitions.
Through Christ our Lord.

Year B

With the Lord there is mercy and fullness of redemption. We present our prayers in confidence.

— *Intercessions* —

O God,
who triumph over evil
and welcome all who do your will,
drive away whatever would harm us
and show mercy to your family.
Through Christ our Lord.

Year C

The Lord is our helper. Let us ask God to hear us, have pity on us, and change our mourning into dancing.

— *Intercessions* —

O God,
who create life and raise the dead,
sustain us in our times of need.
Through Christ our Lord.

Eleventh Sunday in Ordinary Time

Overview

The *Book of Blessings* includes an Order for the Blessing of Fathers on Father's Day (1729–1733). The prayer over the people may conclude the Mass on the third Sunday of June.

Entrance Antiphon

The psalmist asks God to listen, to be a helper, and not to forsake the one crying out. In contrast to last week's confidence, the psalmist of this antiphon needs assistance. This was the antiphon for the Fifth Sunday after Pentecost from the eighth century to the pre-Vatican II missal.

Collect

We ask help to please God in resolve and deeds. The prayer comes from the same collection of Easter season prayers in the Gelasian Sacramentary that gave us last week's collect. It was offered on Sundays after Pentecost in various medieval sacramentaries. The phrase "without you [we] can do nothing" recalls John 15:5, where Jesus says the branches can do nothing apart from the vine. Our "mortal frailty" recalls Romans 8:26, where Paul says the Spirit helps us in our weakness.

Prayer over the Offerings

The gifts nourish and renew us. We pray that this sustenance not fail us in body and spirit. The prayer comes from the Verona Sacramentary, among those that invite people to fast in the month of December.

Preface

Any preface from Ordinary Time may be used. *See pp. 92–93.* Note that the first option cites the last line of the first reading in Year A. The sixth option speaks about the present time "while in this body," an allusion to the beginning of the second reading in Year B.

Communion Antiphon

The psalmist asks one thing: to live in the house of the Lord forever. As we enjoy our Communion in the house of God, we long for this moment to last. This was the antiphon for the Fifth Sunday after Pentecost from the eighth century to the pre-Vatican II missal. In the alternative antiphon, Jesus prays to his Father that his disciples may be one as he and the Father are one. This unity is sublimely achieved in Communion.

Prayer after Communion

This Communion foreshadows our complete union with God; we pray it will unify the Church. This prayer has long been part of the tradition in the Roman Rite.

Blessing

Any solemn blessing from Ordinary Time may be used, or even a prayer over the people. *See pp. 94–96.*

LECTIONARY

Eucharistic Prayer IV says that God offered "covenants" to the people, and Year A's first reading tells about one of them.

PRAYER OF THE FAITHFUL

Year A

Jesus empowered his disciples to cure the
sick, raise the dead, and drive out demons.
Enlivened by the Spirit of Christ, we bring
our prayers.

— *Intercessions* —

O God, master of the harvest,
hear the prayers of those you have called
to be disciples of your Son,
and enrich the world
with your unfailing word.
Through Christ our Lord.

Year B

The kingdom of God spreads of its own ac-
cord. As disciples of Jesus Christ, called
into service, we pray for the needs of the
world.

— *Intercessions* —

O God,
whose trees bear fruit by your providence,
hear our prayers
and let your kingdom spread to the ends
of the earth.
Through Christ our Lord.

Year C

God knows our sins and forgives those who
show love. In imitation of the love of Jesus,
we pray for the needs of the world.

— *Intercessions* —

O God,
who forgive the sins of those who love you,
look kindly upon the prayers
of those who believe in you.
Through Christ our Lord.

Twelfth Sunday in Ordinary Time

Entrance Antiphon

The Lord is the strength of his people, a saving refuge for his anointed one. We pray for salvation and blessing under the governance of God. This was the antiphon for the Sixth Sunday after Pentecost from the eighth century to the pre-Vatican II missal.

Collect

We ask to revere and love God's holy name, for we know it will bring God's guidance. The text appeared in the Gelasian Sacramentary for the Sunday after the Ascension. In some medieval sacramentaries it appeared on the Second Sunday after Pentecost, within the octave of the celebration of the Most Holy Body and Blood of Christ. In Latin the prayer joins fear and love, though 1 John 4:18 says love casts out fear. After all, Psalm 110:10 says the fear of the Lord is the beginning of wisdom, and Deuteronomy 10:12 summons Israel to fear and love the Lord. The mention of fear in this post-Ascension prayer may relate to the apostles' reaction to the absence of the risen Jesus as noted in John 20:19.

Prayer over the Offerings

As God receives this sacrifice, we pray that he will cleanse the desires of our hearts, making us acceptable, too. The prayer comes from those in the Verona Sacramentary for fasting in December. It is related to another prayer in April.

Preface

Any preface from Ordinary Time may be used. See pp. 92–93. The third option says the nature that led to our downfall became the means of salvation, and the second reading of Year A also makes that contrast between Adam and Christ. The seventh option contrasts the sin of disobedience with the obedience of Christ, a theme that also appears in the second reading of Year A. The fourth option says that the death of Jesus opened the way to eternal life, and this is proclaimed in the second reading of Year B.

Communion Antiphon

The eyes of all look to the Lord, who gives food—this line from the psalms is sometimes used as a meal prayer. This antiphon was new to the post-Vatican II missal. From the Gospels, Jesus says he is the good shepherd, laying down his life for the sheep. His sacrifice is recalled in this Communion. This is one of the series of Communion antiphons citing the "I AM" statements of Jesus. This was the antiphon for the Third Sunday after Easter from the eighth century to the pre-Vatican II missal.

Prayer after Communion

Renewed by this Communion, we ask to attain the pledge of redemption. The prayer is listed among those for April in the Verona Sacramentary.

Blessing

Any solemn blessing from Ordinary Time may be used, or even a prayer over the people. See pp. 94–96.

LECTIONARY

Eucharistic Prayer IV says, "that we might live no longer for ourselves but for him who died and rose again for us," which refers to 2 Corinthians 5:15 from Year B's second reading.

PRAYER OF THE FAITHFUL

Year A

No sparrow falls to the ground without God's
   knowledge. We present our prayers to the
   One who cares for every creature above,
   below, and upon the earth.

— Intercessions —

O God,
present to us in darkness
that we may speak in the light,
grant these prayers
that we may tell your mighty deeds.
Through Christ our Lord.

Year B

Those who are terrified show little faith. Let
   us be confident as we present our needs.

— Intercessions —

O God,
Lord of wind and waves,
still the troubles of our hearts
and restore calm to those
   who make these prayers.
Through Christ our Lord.

Year C

With Saint Peter, we believe that Jesus is the
   Christ of God. We take up our cross and
   present our prayers.

— Intercessions —

O God,
whose Son suffered, died, and was raised,
look mercifully upon the prayers
of those who place their faith in him.
Who lives and reigns for ever and ever.

Thirteenth Sunday in Ordinary Time

Entrance Antiphon

The psalmist invites all peoples to clap their hands and cry out to the Lord in shouts of joy. The entire assembly joins in song to send out the message. This was the antiphon for the Seventh Sunday after Pentecost from the eighth century to the pre-Vatican II missal.

Collect

Children of the light, we pray to stand in the bright light of truth, freed from the darkness of error. This prayer comes from the Bergamo Sacramentary, the Ambrosian tradition, where it was used on rogation days. In the Roman Rite, rogation days preceded the celebration of the Ascension, but in the early Ambrosian Rite they preceded Pentecost. The Easter imagery of light is plain. One of the scripture passages that may have inspired this is 1 John 1:5–7, which mentions light, darkness, and the moral life. First John 2:10 stresses love of neighbor with the same images. This prayer was newly added to the Roman Rite after the Council.

Prayer over the Offerings

We pray that our service may be worthy of these gifts. The prayers of the Mass frequently draw a parallel between the ones making the offering and the gifts being offered. We ask God to be pleased with the gifts, but we also mean we hope God will be pleased with us. The text is lifted directly from the Verona Sacramentary, where it appears in July among the prayers for felt needs.

Preface

Any preface from Ordinary Time may be used. *See pp. 92–93.* The fourth option has a thematic connection with the second reading in Year B. The second option says Christ freed us from death, a theme that appears at the start of the second reading in Year C.

Communion Antiphon

With all that is within, the psalmist blesses God and the divine name. These generic words of praise spring to the lips of communicants in their moment of gladness. From the Gospels, Jesus prays for the unity of his followers, so that the world may have faith. Our Communion is an expression of the unity Jesus desired; through it, our mission is to help others believe. Both antiphons were new to the post-Vatican II missal.

Prayer after Communion

We pray that this Communion will bring us life so that we may ever bear fruit in charity. This prayer comes down through the tradition of the Roman Rite, and it seems to be inspired by Jesus' saying of the vine and the branches in John 15:16.

Blessing

Any solemn blessing from Ordinary Time may be used, or even a prayer over the people. *See pp. 94–96.*

LECTIONARY

Eucharistic Prayer I asks God to welcome the dead "into the light of your face" (Order of Mass, 105), which refers to Year A's responsorial psalm (89:16). Verses 2–3 speak of the covenant God established with David, which is included in the "covenants" mentioned in Eucharistic Prayer IV (Order of Mass, 117).

PRAYER OF THE FAITHFUL

Year A

Whoever gives a cup of cold water to God's little ones will not lose a reward. Mindful of the needs of the world, we present our prayers.

— Intercessions —

O God,
whose faithfulness reaches
   through all generations,
look upon us kindly in our times of distress.
Through Christ our Lord.

Year B

"Do not be afraid," Jesus said to the synagogue official. "Just have faith." In confidence we turn to the One who answers all our needs.

— Intercessions —

O God,
who bring us up from the netherworld
and preserve us from those going down
   into the pit,
rescue us in our times of distress
and let us sing your praise.
Through Christ our Lord.

Year C

No one who looks back is fit for the kingdom of God. With Jesus, let us turn our face resolutely toward our future, relying on God for support in times of stress.

— Intercessions —

O God,
who summon us to follow your Son,
supply us with all that we need
to walk each day with him.
Who lives and reigns for ever and ever.

Fourteenth Sunday in Ordinary Time

Overview

On Independence Day weekend, you may include appropriate music for the celebration. Include petitions for our nation in the Prayer of the Faithful. The Mass texts, though, should be those of the Sunday in Ordinary Time.

Entrance Antiphon

From the psalms we proclaim that we have received mercy in God's temple. As God's name and praise reach to the ends of the earth, so may the justice of God's right hand. The verse lifts the minds of the faithful beyond personal cares to God's will. This was the antiphon for the Eighth Sunday after Pentecost from the eighth century to the pre-Vatican II missal.

Collect

God's Son humbled himself to raise a fallen world. We ask God to rescue us from sin to eternal gladness. The text is based on a prayer for Sunday after the Octave of Easter in the Gelasian Sacramentary. The rescue of a fallen world recalls the story of Adam and Eve and Paul's commentary on it (Genesis 3, Romans 5:12–17, and 1 Corinthians 15:21–22). The "abasement" of the Son is the subject of the hymn in Philippians 2:7–9.

Prayer over the Offerings

We ask that this oblation will purify us and draw us daily closer to the life of heaven. The original version appears three times in the Gelasian Sacramentary, twice in the Easter season and once among the prayers for Ordinary Time Sundays.

Preface

Any preface from Ordinary Time may be used. *See pp. 92–93.* The sixth option says that we possess the firstfruits of the Spirit, and this is affirmed in the second reading in Year A.

Communion Antiphon

The psalmist invites us to taste and see the goodness of the Lord. Those who seek refuge in God are blessed. This is one of the most famous antiphons for the Communion rite. In fact, the earliest record of singing at Communion mentions exactly this verse. It comes from the description of the Eucharist in the third- to fourth-century *Apostolic Constitutions* (8:13, 16). This was the antiphon for the eighth Sunday after Pentecost from the eighth century to the pre-Vatican II missal. From the Gospels, Jesus promises refreshment to those who come to him when they are labored and burdened. The promise of refreshment is realized in this Communion. This verse quotes the Gospel of the day in Year A.

LECTIONARY

The second Communion antiphon comes from the Gospel of Year A.

Year B's second reading is the last in the series from Paul's Second Letter to the Corinthians.

Year C's second reading is the last in the series from Paul's Letter to the Galatians. It is one of four of Paul's epistles that conclude with a sentence that third-century Christians reworked into the liturgical dialogue, "The Lord be with you," "And with your spirit" (Order of Mass, 2, 15, 31, 143).

Prayer after Communion

Replenished by this Communion, we pray to attain salvation and never cease to praise God. The text is lifted from the Gelasian Sacramentary, where it is listed among those for the Sixth Sunday after Easter, just before the Ascension.

Blessing

Any solemn blessing from Ordinary Time may be used, or even a prayer over the people. *See pp. 94–96.*

PRAYER OF THE FAITHFUL

Year A

Because the Son has revealed the Father to us, we have come to know the Father. To the One who alone provides true rest for the weary, we present our needs.

— *Intercessions* —

O God,
whose Son gives us a yoke that is easy,
a burden that is light,
lift our spirits by granting these prayers.
Through Christ our Lord.

Year B

Our eyes are fixed on God, pleading for mercy. In faith we present our needs.

— *Intercessions* —

O God,
whose Son performed no mighty deed
for those who lacked faith,
see the faith of those
    who make these prayers,
and work wonders for us.
Through Christ our Lord.

Year C

Jesus commanded his disciples to eat what was set before them, to cure the sick, and to proclaim the kingdom of God. Let us ask for strength to do God's will.

— *Intercessions* —

O God,
who bid us bring peace
    to every household,
set your love in our hearts
    by granting these prayers.
Through Christ our Lord.

Fifteenth Sunday in Ordinary Time

Entrance Antiphon

In justice, the psalmist shall behold God's face and be filled with the vision of glory. The community aims to enter this celebration in the proper frame of mind. This was the antiphon for Friday of the Second Week of Lent from the eighth century to the pre-Vatican II missal.

Collect

God shows the light of truth to those who go astray. We pray that all Christians may reject what opposes the name of Christ and follow what does it honor. In the Gelasian Sacramentary this prayer appears among those in the Octave of Easter; hence, the image of light and faith. It could be related to scripture passages about the good shepherd and straying sheep (Isaiah 53:6, John 10:11–16, 1 Peter 2:21–25). Christ the light appears in John 1:4 and 9, 1 John 2:9, and Ephesians 5:8–9. Jesus says he is the way in John 14:6.

Prayer over the Offerings

We ask God to look upon these offerings for the greater holiness of believers. The prayer is based on one for the fourth Sunday after Pentecost in the Hadrian Supplement.

Preface

Any preface from Ordinary Time may be used. *See pp. 92–93.* The sixth option says that we possess the firstfruits of the Spirit, and this is affirmed at the end of the second reading in Year A. The same preface links to the conclusion of the longer form of the second reading in Year B, which says we were sealed with the promised Holy Spirit, the first installment of our inheritance. The eighth option says God's scattered children were gathered by the blood of Christ, and the conclusion of the second reading in Year C shares this theme.

Communion Antiphon

As a sparrow finds a home, so believers find the altars of the Lord. The house of God is our true home. This verse from the psalm tells the affection we feel for today's altars, from which we share Communion. It was the antiphon for the Third Sunday of Lent from the eighth century to the pre-Vatican II missal. *See p. 40.*

LECTIONARY

Eucharistic Prayer IV concludes with a prayer that we may be "freed from the corruption of sin and death," which relies on a verse from Year A's second reading, Romans 8:21. It expresses the hope that creation will be set free from slavery to corruption (Order of Mass, 122). Earlier, the same Eucharistic Prayer speaks of the Holy Spirit as "the firstfruits," the one who will "sanctify creation to the full" (Order of Mass, 117). These lines rely on Romans 8:22–23.

Year B's second reading is the first in a series from Paul's Letter to the Ephesians. Eucharistic Prayer IV says that Jesus came "to accomplish your plan" (Order of Mass, 117), a reference to Ephesians 1:10. The longer form of this reading includes verse 12, which inspired a phrase from the same Eucharistic Prayer, that the community "may become a living sacrifice in Christ to the praise of your glory" (Order of Mass, 122).

Year A's second reading is the first in the series from Paul's Letter to the Colossians. In the Nicene Creed (Order of Mass, 18), we express our belief in the God who made things visible and invisible, citing Colossians 1:16.

From the Gospels, Jesus says that those who eat his flesh and drink his blood remain in him, and he in them. He reminds us of the true meaning behind this Communion. This was the antiphon for Thursday of the Second Week of Lent and the Fifteenth Sunday after Pentecost from the eighth century to the pre-Vatican II missal.

Prayer after Communion

We pray that the saving effects of this mystery may grow. This prayer comes from the Gelasian Sacramentary on the Sunday after the Ascension.

Blessing

Any solemn blessing from Ordinary Time may be used, or even a prayer over the people. *See pp. 94–96.* The sixth solemn blessing is based on the second reading in Year B.

PRAYER OF THE FAITHFUL

Year A

The seed that fell on good soil produced fruit. We have opened our ears to hear God's word. In confidence we present our needs.

— *Intercessions* —

O God,
who speak your word
    as a sower scatters seed,
mercifully grant our prayers,
and help us spread your word
wherever ears are open to do your will.
Through Christ our Lord.

Year B

The Twelve drove out demons and anointed the sick and cured them. Let us ask God to work such wonders in our day.

— *Intercessions* —

O God,
who bestow authority over unclean spirits,
drive from us whatever keeps us from you,
and work wonders through the hands
    of all who believe.
Through Christ our Lord.

Year C

If we turn to the Lord in our need, we shall live. Let us seek the constant help of God.

— *Intercessions* —

O God,
who make us neighbor to all
    who are in need,
make us respond to those who suffer
by granting us your unfailing help.
Through Christ our Lord.

Sixteenth Sunday in Ordinary Time

Entrance Antiphon

The psalmist offers sacrifice to God, who is a helper in times of need. The verse explains one of the reasons we gather for prayer and sacrifice. This was the antiphon for the Ninth Sunday after Pentecost from the eighth century to the pre-Vatican II missal.

Collect

We ask for gifts of grace that we may keep God's commands in hope, faith, and charity. This prayer was brought into the Roman Rite after the Second Vatican Council from the Ambrosian tradition's Bergamo Sacramentary. Only three Ordinary Time collects come from that source. It was one of the prayers on the Ambrosian rogation days that precede Pentecost. The three theological virtues are mentioned in 1 Corinthians 13:13 and 1 Thessalonians 1:3 and 5:8, but hope is mentioned first in this prayer. The keeping of God's commands is mentioned in 1 John 5:3. The "vigilance" of the first Christians is noted in Acts 1:14 and 2:42, as well as in Hebrews 12:7.

Prayer over the Offerings

We ask God to make this sacrifice holy as he blessed the gifts of Abel, so that each one's offering may benefit the salvation of all. The Gelasian Sacramentary included it among the prayers for Ordinary Time Sundays. It refers to the pleasure God took in Abel and his offering in Genesis 4:4.

Preface

Any preface from Ordinary Time may be used. *See pp. 92–93.* The eighth option says that God's scattered children were gathered through the blood of Christ, an image that comes from the opening of the second reading in Year B.

Communion Antiphon

From the psalms we acknowledge that God showed mercy by giving food to those who feared him. This Communion is a sign of God's care for believers. The alternative antiphon comes from Revelation instead of the Gospels this week. We still hear the voice of Jesus, standing at the door and knocking because he wishes to dine with us. Our Communion is a sharing at table with the Lord. Both antiphons were new to the post-Vatican II missal.

Prayer after Communion

We pray to pass from former ways to newness of life . The prayer was new to the post-Vatican II missal. It was inspired by one from the Verona Sacramentary for the Pentecost Vigil, and also from a preface in the same source for fasting in December. The same prayer is used on the Fifth Sunday of Easter and on many weekdays of the Easter season. *See p. 77.*

Blessing

Any solemn blessing from Ordinary Time may be used, or even a prayer over the people. *See pp. 94–96.*

LECTIONARY

The theme of the blood of Christ appears in Year B's second reading and in the eighth option of the preface for Ordinary Time Sundays.

PRAYER OF THE FAITHFUL

Year A

We do not know how to pray as we ought,
but the Spirit comes to aid our weakness.

— Intercessions —

O God, Lord of the harvest,
look favorably upon your Church
and upon the prayers we offer you.
Through Christ our Lord.

Year B

We have come away by ourselves to rest
awhile with Christ. Through him we lift up
our petitions.

— Intercessions —

O God,
whose Son was moved with pity
at the sight of the crowds,
show us your kindness
and grant our prayers.
Through Christ our Lord.

Year C

Like Mary, we have been seated before the
Lord and listened to him speak his word.
Let us bring forth our prayers.

— Intercessions —

O God,
who reveal the mystery hidden
from ages past
in the coming of your Son,
listen to the prayers of those
who put their hope in him.
Who lives and reigns for ever and ever.

Seventeenth Sunday in Ordinary Time

Overview

The prayers of thanksgiving after Mass in the back of the missal include one attributed to Ignatius of Loyola, whose feast falls this week.

Entrance Antiphon

The psalmist proclaims that God is in his holy place. He unites those who dwell in his house, giving people might and strength. At the start of this Eucharist we gather as one in God's house. This antiphon opened the Mass for the Eleventh Sunday after Pentecost from the eighth century to the pre-Vatican II missal.

Collect

We ask for God's mercy that we who use temporal things may hold fast to the things that endure. This prayer was newly composed for the post-Vatican II missal. The first part comes from the Hadrian Supplement, where it appears on the fourth Sunday after Pentecost. But the ending is borrowed from ideas in a preface for daily use in the Verona Sacramentary. Psalm 17:31 calls God the protector of those hoping in him. First Corinthians 7:31 says this world is passing away.

Prayer over the Offerings

We ask God to accept the offerings, so that these mysteries may sanctify us now and lead us to eternal gladness. The Gelasian Sacramentary includes it among its prayers for Ordinary Time Sundays. The vocabulary shares words with the blessing prayers during the preparation of the gifts at every Mass.

Preface

Any preface from Ordinary Time may be used. *See pp. 92–93.*

Communion Antiphon

The psalmist blesses the Lord, and does not forget the Lord's benefits. In the midst of this Communion, we are very aware of God's love for us. From the Gospels, Jesus blesses the merciful and the clean of heart. As we share the Body and Blood of Christ, we experience God's mercy and behold him among us. This is one from the series of Communion antiphons citing the Beatitudes. Both antiphons were new to the post-Vatican II missal.

Prayer after Communion

Having consumed this Communion, we pray that this gift of God's love may profit us for salvation. This prayer was newly added to the post-Vatican II missal. It comes from the Dominican propers for the feast of Saint Louis de Montfort, who wrote about these themes of the passion of Christ and the Blessed Sacrament. His optional memorial, now observed on

---

LECTIONARY

In Year A's second reading, Paul says God glorified those he justified, and Eucharistic Prayer IV concludes with a prayer that we may "glorify you through Christ our Lord" (Order of Mass, 122).

Eucharistic Prayer III prays that we "may become one body, one spirit in Christ" (Order of Mass, 113), citing a verse from Year B's second reading, Ephesians 4:4.

We recite the Lord's Prayer at each Eucharist (Order of Mass, 124). We use Matthew's version in the daily liturgy; today's Gospel in Year C offers Luke's.

April 28, was added to the universal calendar in 2002 missal. Pope John Paul II's motto, *Totus tuus*, came from the writings of Louis.

Blessing

Any solemn blessing from Ordinary Time may be used, or even a prayer over the people. *See pp. 94–96.*

PRAYER OF THE FAITHFUL

Year A

The head of the household brings from the storeroom both the new and the old. In the tradition of our faith we present the needs we have today.

— Intercessions —

O God,
whose kingdom gathers believers
   of every kind,
be pleased to grant the prayers we offer
   in faith.
Through Christ our Lord.

Year B

Jesus fed the crowds of people who were hungry for food and for wisdom. We present our needs to God through him.

— Intercessions —

O God,
who wondrously satisfy the hungers
   of your people,
fill us with your wisdom
   and grant these prayers.
Through Christ our Lord.

Year C

Jesus says that those who ask will receive, those who seek will find. Let us knock upon the door of heaven, and ask God to open its treasures for us.

— Intercessions —

O God,
who give the Holy Spirit to those who ask,
enliven us with your Spirit
as you give ear to these prayers.
Through Christ our Lord.

Eighteenth Sunday in Ordinary Time

Entrance Antiphon

The psalmist prays for God's fast assistance. This is the versicle that opens each session of the Liturgy of the Hours. From at least the eighth century until the pre–Vatican II missal, this antiphon started the Mass for the Twelfth Sunday after Pentecost.

Collect

We ask God to draw near and to answer our prayers, so that all creation may be restored and kept safe. The earliest version comes from the Verona Sacramentary prayers announcing a fast in September, perhaps during a sixth-century siege of Rome. The 2002 Latin edition of the missal corrected a small error in the spelling of one word in the previous editions. The prayer shows similarities to Psalm 104:30, which says God sends forth the spirit to renew the face of the earth, and to Romans 8:17, which says God frees creation from its slavery to corruption. A version of this prayer appeared in the 1985 Sacramentary among the prayers over the people, #8. The 2002 edition removed it.

Prayer over the Offerings

We ask God to sanctify the gifts, accept the oblation, and make us an eternal offering. This same prayer appears several times on weekdays in the Easter season, and a variation of it appears in the Mass for charity, located in the back of the missal. It originated as a baptismal prayer on Pentecost in the Verona Sacramentary.

Preface

Any preface from Ordinary Time may be used. *See pp. 92–93.* The second option notes the compassion of Jesus, a theme found in the Gospel for Year A. The fourth option says that the birth of Jesus renewed humanity's old nature, and this theme is applied to the Christian life near the end of the second reading in Year C.

Communion Antiphon

The first option comes not from the book of Psalms, but from the book of Wisdom. It proclaims that God has given us bread from heaven. This versicle used to be part of Benediction of the Blessed Sacrament. From the eighth century until prior to the Council, this was the antiphon for the Thirteenth Sunday after Pentecost. From John's Gospel, Jesus says he is the bread of life, and all who come to him will not hunger. We are refreshed as we share this spiritual food. The line quotes the Gospel in Year B, and it is part of a series of Communion antiphons citing the "I AM" statements of Jesus. It was new to the post–Vatican II missal.

Prayer after Communion

Through this Communion we ask God's constant protection, that we may be worthy of eternal redemption. It comes from a Mass in a monastery in the Gelasian Sacramentary.

LECTIONARY

Referring to the last line of Year B's Gospel, Eucharistic Prayer I calls Christ "the holy Bread of eternal life" (Order of Mass, 92), and Eucharistic Prayer II says we offer "the Bread of life" (Order of Mass, 105). The priest's prayer at the start of the preparation of the gifts says, "it will become for us the bread of life" (Order of Mass, 23). The alternative Communion antiphon for today comes from this passage.

Year C's second reading is the last in the series from Paul's Letter to the Colossians. The third invocation of the third form of the penitential act addresses the Lord who is "seated at the right hand of the Father" (Order of Mass, 6). This reading opens with that image.

Blessing

Any solemn blessing from Ordinary Time may be used, or even a prayer over the people. *See pp. 94–96.*

PRAYER OF THE FAITHFUL

Year A

Jesus satisfied the hungers of those who came to hear him speak. Having listened to his Gospel, we present our needs.

— Intercessions —

O God,
from whose love nothing can separate us,
help us conquer all things
through the love you show us in your Son.
Who lives and reigns for ever and ever.

Year B

God provided bread from heaven to those who wandered in the desert. In our times of anxiety, we turn to God for help.

— Intercessions —

O God,
who commanded that we believe
in the One you have sent,
look upon the prayers
    of your faithful people,
and grant them.
Through Christ our Lord.

Year C

God has raised us up in Christ. We think of what is above, not of what is on earth, as we present our prayers.

— Intercessions —

O God,
for whom a thousand years
    are as yesterday,
prosper the work of our hands
and graciously supply our needs.
Through Christ our Lord.

Nineteenth Sunday in Ordinary Time

Overview

If the holy day of the Assumption of the Blessed Virgin Mary falls this week, be sure to announce Mass times.

Entrance Antiphon

The psalmist asks God to look to the covenant and care for the poor. Mass opens with a request for God's aid. From at least the eighth century until the pre-Vatican II missal, this antiphon opened the Mass for the Thirteenth Sunday after Pentecost.

Collect

We dare to call God Father at the teaching of the Holy Spirit. We ask for the perfect spirit of adoption and our promised inheritance. This prayer comes from the Bergamo Sacramentary. The post-Vatican II missal brought it from the Ambrosian Rite into the Roman Rite for the first time. It was also assigned to Monday of the Second Week of Easter, but the 2002 missal replaced it there with another prayer, so this is now its only occurrence in the missal. In the Ambrosian Rite it was offered on Saturday of Easter Week. It appeared in the seventh century in the Padua Sacramentary for the Seventh Sunday after the feast of Saint Michael, which justifies its use in Ordinary Time. The main inspiration comes from Romans 8:14–17. In

Matthew 6:9 and Luke 11:1–2, Jesus teaches the disciples to pray by calling God "Father." Jesus promises the Spirit who will teach the disciples in John 14:26. Another comparison between baptism and adoption is in Galatians 4:4–7 and Ephesians 1:5.

Prayer over the Offerings

We ask God to accept the gifts he provided and transorm them into the mystery of our salvation. The Gelasian Sacramentary assigned this prayer to Wednesdays in December and the Second Sunday of Lent.

Preface

Any preface from Ordinary Time may be used. *See pp. 92–93.*

Communion Antiphon

The psalmist calls upon Jerusalem to glorify the Lord who gives the finest wheat. Feasting on this Eucharistic food, we join in praise. This antiphon was new to the post-Vatican II missal.

From John's Gospel, Jesus says the bread he gives is his flesh for the life of the world. The

---

LECTIONARY

The preparation of the gifts uses a blessing formula that stems from Jewish roots, "Blessed be God for ever" (Order of Mass, 23 and 25). Year A's second reading ends with the same formula.

In Year B's Gospel, Jesus calls himself the bread of life in verse 48. The priest's prayer at the start of the preparation of the gifts says, "it will become for us the bread of life" (Order of Mass, 23). Eucharistic Prayer I calls Christ "the holy Bread of eternal life" (Order of Mass, 92), and Eucharistic Prayer II says we offer "the Bread of life" (Order of Mass, 105). The alternative Communion antiphon comes from this passage.

Year C's second reading is the first in this year's series from the Letter to the Hebrews. It picks up where last year's series ended on the Thirty-third Sunday of Ordinary Time.

text comes from today's Gospel in Year B. From at least the eighth century until the pre-Vatican II missal, this antiphon was used for the Fourteenth Sunday after Pentecost and Thursday of the First Week of Lent.

Prayer after Communion

We pray for this Communion to save us and confirm us in the light of God's truth. The prayer is first found in the Hadrian Sacramentary for the feast of Saint Hippolytus on August 13.

Blessing

Any solemn blessing from Ordinary Time may be used, or even a prayer over the people. *See pp. 94–96.*

PRAYER OF THE FAITHFUL

Year A

We believe with Peter that Jesus is the Son of God. Let us ask him to save us from all that could bring us harm.

— *Intercessions* —

O God,
Lord of earth, sea, and sky,
command the forces of nature
   to do your will,
and let our prayers be pleasing to you.
Through Christ our Lord.

Year B

We gather here to taste and see the goodness of the Lord. In confident expectation, we present our prayers.

— *Intercessions* —

O God,
who provide food and drink
   for the journeys of our life,
make our hearts rejoice in an answer
   to these prayers.
Through Christ our Lord.

Year C

The Son of Man will come at an hour we do not expect. Let us keep a prayerful heart as we await the fulfillment of God's promise.

— *Intercessions* —

O God,
whose Son will return to us
as from a wedding banquet,
grant what we truly need
and make us ready to welcome him.
Through Christ our Lord.

Twentieth Sunday in Ordinary Time

Overview

If the holy day of the Assumption of the Blessed Virgin Mary falls this week, be sure to announce Mass times.

Entrance Antiphon

The psalmist asks God to look upon the face of his anointed, for one day in God's courts is better than a thousand elsewhere. We gather within the courts of God's house to sing this psalm of praise. From at least the eighth century until the pre-Vatican II missal, this antiphon opened the Mass for the Fourteenth Sunday after Pentecost.

Collect

We ask our provident God to fill our hearts with love that we may attain his promises. This prayer comes from the Gelasian Sacramentary's collection of texts for Sundays. It was used in many other sources on the fifth Sunday after Pentecost. It recalls the great commandment to love God above all else (Exodus 20:3, Deuteronomy 6:5, Matthew 22:37, Mark 12:30, Luke 10:27). Human desires are mentioned in Philippians 4:19. God's power to surpass our desires is noted in Ephesians 3:20.

Prayer over the Offerings

We ask God to receive our oblation by which he brings about a glorious exchange, making us worthy to receive his very self. This same prayer is used on several weekdays of the Christmas season because of its reference to the "glorious exchange"—God becoming like us, so that we may become like God. It first appeared among the Verona Sacramentary's prayers for April. It was newly added to the post-Vatican II missal.

Preface

Any preface from Ordinary Time may be used. *See pp. 92–93.*

Communion Antiphon

Mercy and redemption come from the Lord. We sing as we receive the sacrament provided by God. From the Gospels, Jesus says he is the living bread come down from heaven, and he promises eternal life to those who eat of this bread. The text comes from the Gospel of Year B, and it is part of the series of Communion antiphons citing the "I AM" statements of Jesus. Both antiphons were new to the post-Vatican II missal.

Prayer after Communion

Sharing in this sacrament, and conformed to God's image on earth, we pray to be coheirs with Christ. The prayer makes an allusion to the creation of humans in Genesis 1:27. The text comes from the Paris Missal. It was brought into *The Roman Missal* after the Second Vatican Council.

LECTIONARY

In all the Eucharistic Prayers, the priest states that Jesus refers to "the blood of the new and eternal covenant." In Matthew 26:28 and Mark 14:24, Jesus just calls it the blood "of the covenant," and in Luke 22:20 and 1 Corinthians 11:25, he calls it the blood "of the new covenant." But in a verse from Year B's Gospel, John 6:54, he says that those who eat his flesh and drink his blood have "eternal" life; hence this word is included in the institution narrative at every Mass. The alternative Communion antiphon comes from this passage.

Blessing

Any solemn blessing from Ordinary Time may be used, or even a prayer over the people. *See pp. 94–96.*

PRAYER OF THE FAITHFUL

Year A

The gifts and the call of God can never be taken back. Aware of God's wondrous love, we present our needs in hope.

— Intercessions —

O God,
whose Son responded to all
who possessed great faith,
increase our faith and grant these prayers.
Through Christ our Lord.

Year B

Whoever eats the flesh and drinks the blood of Christ has eternal life. To the God who does not withhold any good gift, we present our prayers.

— Intercessions —

O God,
who bestow life on those who eat and drink
  in faith,
grant the prayers that will bring us
to live with you forever.
Through Christ our Lord.

Year C

Whenever we feel afflicted and poor, the Lord thinks of us. Let us ask God to come to our aid.

— Intercessions —

O God,
whose Son set the earth ablaze with faith,
turn to those who trust in you
and grant these prayers.
Through Christ our Lord.

Twenty-first Sunday in Ordinary Time

Overview

The *Book of Blessings* contains an Order for the Blessing of Students and Teachers within Mass (526–529). The first intercession includes an option to be used when this is celebrated at the beginning of a new school year. You may choose this or another appropriate weekend.

Entrance Antiphon

The psalmist prays for safety and mercy. Mass today opens with a petition that God will turn an ear to our prayers. This antiphon opened the Fifteenth Sunday after Pentecost from at least the eighth century until the pre-Vatican II missal.

Collect

We ask to love what God commands and to desire what he promises, so that our hearts may be fixed where true gladness is found. The text appeared in the Gelasian Sacramentary for the Third Sunday after the Octave of Easter. The post-Vatican II missal also assigned this prayer to Monday of the Fifth Week of Easter, but that collect was replaced with another one in 2002, so this is the only appearance of this prayer in the revised *Roman Missal*. The theme relates to Matthew 6:20–21, where Jesus encourages the disciples to store up treasures in heaven, for the heart follows where one's treasures are. Longing for the things of God is found in Psalm 42:1 and in Psalm 119:20 and 131.

Prayer over the Offerings

We ask God for the gifts of unity and peace. The prayer recalls Christ's single sacrifice in Hebrews 10:14. This was a newly composed prayer in the post-Vatican II missal.

Preface

Any preface from Ordinary Time may be used. *See pp. 92–93.* The eighth option calls the Church the Body of Christ, and the second reading of Year B makes the same point.

Communion Antiphon

The earth is replete with God's fruits that we may eat bread and be cheered with wine. This line from the psalms serves as a prophecy for the Eucharist, which brings us satisfaction and joy. It was formerly attached to the Twelfth Sunday after Pentecost from the eighth century to the pre-Vatican II missal.

From John's Gospel, Jesus promises that those who eat his flesh and brink his blood will have eternal life. Although this does not directly quote the Gospel in Year B for this Sunday, it is the line that provoked the reaction of unbelievers. We sing it at Communion in faith. It was new to the post-Vatican II missal.

Prayer after Communion

We pray for the complete healing work of God's mercy, so that we may please him. The text comes from the prayer for ordaining a bishop in the Gelasian Sacramentary.

LECTIONARY

Eucharistic Prayer IV (Order of Mass, 116) opens by addressing God as "living," the adjective that Simon Peter uses in Year A's Gospel when he addresses Christ as the "Son of the living God."

Year B's second reading is the last in the series from Paul's Letter to the Ephesians.

Blessing

Any solemn blessing from Ordinary Time may be used, or even a prayer over the people. *See pp. 94–96.*

PRAYER OF THE FAITHFUL

Year A

God's judgments are inscrutable. God's ways are unsearchable. We trust in God's wisdom to hear these prayers.

— *Intercessions* —

O God,
who share the keys of the kingdom
with your loyal servants,
hear our profession of faith in your Son
and grant the prayers we offer.
Through Christ our Lord.

Year B

Christ Jesus has the words of eternal life. Convinced that he is the Holy One of God, we present our prayers through him.

— *Intercessions* —

O God,
who reveal the mystery of the Eucharist
through the teaching of your Son,
hear the prayers of your faithful ones
who gather at his table.
Through Christ our Lord.

Year C

Like servants at the door of the master's house, we present our needs to the Lord.

— *Intercessions* —

O God,
who welcome to your table
people from east and west,
   north and south,
look kindly upon those gathered here
and grant our prayers.
Through Christ our Lord.

Twenty-second Sunday in Ordinary Time

Overview

Plan to include workers and the unemployed in the Prayer of the Faithful on Labor Day weekend.

Entrance Antiphon

With the psalmist we ask God's mercy upon those at prayer. Mass opens with an appeal for divine help. This was the antiphon for the Sixteenth Sunday after Pentecost from at least the eighth century to the pre-Vatican II missal.

Collect

We ask for a love of God's name that God will nurture in us what is good. The prayer comes from the collection of texts for Sunday Eucharist in the Gelasian Sacramentary. Other sources used it on the Sixth Sunday after Pentecost or even as a prayer after Mass. The phrase "giver of every good gift" probably alludes to James 1:17. God's "watchful care" is reminiscent of the Lord who guards the city in Psalm 127:1. In the New Testament, God's might and triumph over other powers is proclaimed in 1 Peter 3:22 and Ephesians 1:20–21.

Prayer over the Offerings

We pray for the blessing of salvation through this sacred offering. The prayer originated in the Gelasian Sacramentary for the Sunday after the Octave of Easter.

Preface

Any preface from Ordinary Time may be used. *See pp. 92–93.*

Communion Antiphon

God has reserved much goodness for those who fear him. We celebrate that special gift in this Communion. From the Sermon on the Mount we hear another of the Beatitudes as the alternative antiphon, promising the righteous a place in the kingdom. Both antiphons were new to the post-Vatican II missal.

Prayer after Communion

We pray that this food of charity may confirm our hearts for service. This was a new composition for the post-Vatican II missal.

Blessing

Any solemn blessing from Ordinary Time may be used, or even a prayer over the people. *See pp. 94–96.* The fifth solemn blessing mentions "citizens of heaven," which may allude to the second reading in Year C.

LECTIONARY

The language of Eucharistic Prayer I (Order of Mass, 88), asking God to make the sacrifice "spiritual and acceptable," is related to the first line of Year A's second reading, in which Paul urges the faithful to offer their bodies as a living, holy, and pleasing sacrifice. Eucharistic Prayer III asks God to look on "this holy and living sacrifice" (Order of Mass, 113), and Eucharistic Prayer IV asks that those who partake of the one bread and one chalice "may truly become a living sacrifice in Christ" (Order of Mass, 122). All these excerpts rely on this passage from Romans.

Year B's second reading is the first in the series from the Letter of James.

Year C's second reading is the last in this year's series from the Letter to the Hebrews.

PRAYER OF THE FAITHFUL

Year A

We do not ask to gain the world, but to deny ourselves and follow Christ. As faithful disciples, we present our prayers.

— Intercessions —

O God,
who transform your people by the renewal
of our minds,
help us to discern your will
and to do what is good
and pleasing to you.
Through Christ our Lord.

Year B

Let us honor God's commandments as we present our prayers in faith.

— Intercessions —

O God,
who reveal your teachings
through the Gospel of your Son,
keep our hearts close to you
and grant these prayers.
Through Christ our Lord.

Year C

In this church we approach the city of the living God, and Jesus, the mediator of a new covenant. In humility we present our needs.

— Intercessions —

O God,
who invite to your banquet
the poor, the crippled, the blind,
and the lame,
look with compassion upon our prayers.
Through Christ our Lord.

Twenty-third Sunday in Ordinary Time

Overview

Plan to include workers and the unemployed in the Prayer of the Faithful on Labor Day weekend.

Entrance Antiphon

We acknowledge that God is just, and ask him to show us mercy. The Mass begins with a plea for God to be attentive to what we are about to do. It opened the Seventeenth Sunday after Pentecost from the eighth century to the pre-Vatican II missal.

Collect

We ask God to look upon us, and to grant us true freedom and an everlasting inheritance. The prayer originated among those for Easter evening prayers in the Gelasian Sacramentary. After the Council it was assigned to this Sunday as well as to the Fifth Sunday of Easter, and again on Saturday of the Second Week of Easter. In 2002 other prayers replaced those earlier ones, and this is now the only day when this prayer is offered each year. It was lightly reworked to fit Ordinary Time. The promised inheritance to Abraham is mentioned in Galatians 3:14 and 29, and referred to in Galatians 5:21 and Ephesians 1:13–14. The themes of true freedom can be traced to Galatians 5:13, but also Romans 5:21 and 8:2 and Galatians 3:13 and 5:22. The adoption of God's children is in Romans 8:14–17, Galatians 4:4–7, and Ephesians 1:5.

Prayer over the Offerings

We pray to offer God fitting homage so that we can be faithfully united in mind and heart.

This prayer appears several times in the missal during the Christmas season.

Preface

Any preface from Ordinary Time may be used. *See pp. 92–93.*

Communion Antiphon

Like a deer for running streams, so our soul yearns for God. We sing this during Communion as we eat and drink the Body and Blood of Christ. From the Gospels we hear Jesus say that he is the light of the world. We pray that this Communion will bring us the light of Christ. This is one of the series of Communion antiphons citing the "I AM" statements of Jesus. Both antiphons were new to the post-Vatican II missal.

Prayer after Communion

We pray to be so nourished by this Communion that we may share the life of Christ forever. This prayer comes from the Paris Missal and was added to *The Roman Missal* after the Second Vatican Council.

Blessing

Any solemn blessing from Ordinary Time may be used, or even a prayer over the people. *See pp. 94–96.*

LECTIONARY

The alternative refrain for Year B's responsorial psalm, "Alleluia," is found in the full text of this psalm. The Gospel acclamation (Order of Mass, 13) uses this word for its biblical roots.

Year C's second reading is the only appearance of Paul's Letter to Philemon in the entire three-year cycle of Sunday readings.

PRAYER OF THE FAITHFUL

Year A

Wherever two or three are gathered in the name of Christ, he is present. With Christ and in confidence, we present our needs to the Father.

— Intercessions —

O God,
who reconcile us through the ministry
   of your Son,
grant the prayers
   that will help us follow him.
Who lives and reigns for ever and ever.

Year B

In his ministry, Jesus made the deaf hear and the mute speak. Let us ask God to work new wonders through the intercession of Christ.

— Intercessions —

O God,
who open our ears to hear your word,
open also our lips
   to proclaim your goodness
as you hear and answer these prayers.
Through Christ our Lord.

Year C

Who can know what God intends? Our own plans are timid and unsure. Trusting in God's wisdom, we announce our needs.

— Intercessions —

O God,
whose Son asked us to renounce all things,
make us faithful disciples
and grant these prayers.
Through Christ our Lord.

Twenty-fourth Sunday in Ordinary Time

Entrance Antiphon

We ask God to hear the prayers of his servants and to give peace. Mass begins with a petition that God will be attentive to our gathering this day. It opened the Eighteenth Sunday after Pentecost from at least the eighth century to the pre-Vatican II missal.

Collect

We ask God to lead us into wholehearted service, that we may feel the working of his mercy. The earliest version of this prayer comes from the Verona Sacramentary texts for the ordination of a bishop or for more generic occasions in September. It may have been composed after the siege of Rome was lifted in the early sixth century. Today the meaning has more to do with God's mercy for sinners, experienced in this service of worship.

Prayer over the Offerings

Each person brings an offering to this Eucharist. We ask God to accept each offering that it may serve the salvation of all. The prayer comes from the Gelasian Sacramentary's texts for Ordinary Time Sundays.

Preface

Any preface from Ordinary Time may be used. *See pp. 92–93.*

Communion Antiphon

We seek shelter in the shadow of God's wings for mercy. In the context of Communion, this antiphon shows our union with God and the protection we can expect. The alternative antiphon comes from First Corinthians instead of the Gospels. It proclaims that the chalice of blessing is the blood of Christ and the bread we break is a sharing in his body. The sequence of cup-bread is unusual, but it has parallels in Jewish rites, in Luke 22:17–20, and even in the first-century *Didache*. It may reveal an early and short-lived liturgical tradition. Both antiphons were new to the post-Vatican II missal.

Prayer after Communion

We pray that this Communion will take possession of our minds and bodies, over the strength of our own desires. The prayer comes from the Gelasian Sacramentary's texts for Ordinary Time Sundays.

Blessing

Any solemn blessing from Ordinary Time may be used, or even a prayer over the people. *See pp. 94–96.*

LECTIONARY

Year A's second reading is the last in the series from Paul's Letter to the Romans.

The priest quotes Psalm 51:4 when he washes his hands at every Mass. It is found in Year C's responsorial psalm. The second reading begins the short series from Paul's First Letter to Timothy.

PRAYER OF THE FAITHFUL

Year A

As the heavens are high above the earth, so is God's kindness to us. Trusting in God's goodness, we present our needs.

— Intercessions —

O God,
who command us to forgive
   from our heart,
look upon these contrite prayers
and show us your mercy.
Through Christ our Lord.

Year B

Saint James says that if faith does not have works, it is dead. Filled with faith, and practicing charity, we present our prayers in confidence.

— Intercessions —

O God,
who sent us your Christ and gave us faith
   in him,
help us follow him
by granting us what we truly need.
Through Christ our Lord.

Year C

Heaven rejoices over the return of sinners who repent. Mindful of our faults, we express our faith and hope in God through these prayers.

— Intercessions —

O God,
who show mercy to the contrite of heart,
grant these prayers
and open our lips
that our mouth may proclaim your praise.
Through Christ our Lord.

Twenty-fifth Sunday in Ordinary Time

Entrance Antiphon

We hear the voice of the Lord promising to hear those who cry out to him in any distress. The antiphon sounds like scripture, but it is not found there exactly in this form. It resembles a line from Solomon's prayer at the dedication of the Temple in Jerusalem (1 Kings 8:38). It still serves as the entrance antiphon for Thursday of the Third Week of Lent, where the traditional stational Mass in Rome is at the Church of Saints Cosmas and Damian. Inside that building, one line of an inscription in the apse resembles the opening of this introit. The feast of Cosmas and Damian is observed in late September, near the date when this Sunday falls each year. This antiphon opened the nineteenth Sunday after Pentecost from at least the eighth century to the pre-Vatican II missal.

Collect

All the commands of the law are founded on love of God and neighbor. We ask to be brought to eternal life as we keep these precepts. The prayer was created for the post-Vatican II missal from one for daily usage in the Verona Sacramentary in July, and another in the Mozarabic Sacramentary. The first part may have been composed for Mass on September 6, 537, during the siege of Rome by the Visigoths. It relies on the great commandments in Deuteronomy 6:4–6, Leviticus 19:17–19 and 34, and on the teaching of Jesus in Matthew 22:37–40, Mark 12:29–31, and Luke 10:27–28.

Prayer over the Offerings

Through God's acceptance of this offering we ask to possess in these mysteries what we profess in faith. This prayer also occurs several times on weekdays in the Christmas season. It originated among the October prayers in time of drought from the Verona Sacramentary.

Preface

Any preface from Ordinary Time may be used. *See pp. 92–93.*

Communion Antiphon

God commands the keeping of the divine precepts. We pray that our paths may be directed to keeping God's statutes. This brief excerpt from the Bible's longest psalm shows our love for God's law; singing it at Communion links our way of life with God's gift. This antiphon was coupled with the entrance antiphon on both occasions when it appeared in the pre-Vatican II liturgy.

From the Gospels, Jesus says he is the good shepherd who knows his sheep, and whose sheep know him. We are one with our shepherd in this Communion. This was the antiphon for the Second Sunday after Easter from at least the eighth century to the pre-Vatican II

LECTIONARY

Year A's second reading is the first in the series from Paul's Letter to the Philippians.

Year B's second reading inspired a couple of passages in the missal. In Appendix V, the first sample Prayer of the Faithful refers to 1 Timothy 2:4 when it addresses God, "who desires everyone to be saved and to come to the knowledge of the truth." Eucharistic Prayer IV opens with an address to "one God" (Order of Mass, 116), a teaching that is affirmed in the same passage.

Year C's responsorial is one of the psalms that uses the word "Alleluia," which is used so often as the Gospel acclamation (Order of Mass, 13). The second verse of this psalm is part of the dialogue that precedes a blessing given by a bishop (Order of Mass, 143).

missal. It is one of the series of Ordinary Time Communion antiphons that cite the "I AM" statements of Jesus.

Prayer after Communion

Renewed with this sacrament, we ask God to raise us up that we may possess redemption even in our manner of life. This comes from the Gelasian Sacramentary's prayers at Mass, perhaps at the ordination of a deacon.

Blessing

Any solemn blessing from Ordinary Time may be used, or even a prayer over the people. *See pp. 94–96.*

PRAYER OF THE FAITHFUL

Year A

We do not understand the generosity of God. In hope of salvation, we present our prayers.

— *Intercessions* —

O God,
ever near to those who call upon you,
be compassionate to us
    in our times of need.
Through Christ our Lord.

Year B

Saint James criticizes those who ask but do not receive because they wrongly ask to spend God's gifts on their own passions. We ask God for pure hearts and good gifts.

— *Intercessions* —

O God,
who uphold the life of your people, sustain us
that we may offer you sacrifice
and praise your name.
Through Christ our Lord.

Year C

No servant can serve two masters. Let us set our hearts on the One who made us, and bring forth our prayers in faith.

— *Intercessions* —

O God,
who lift up the lowly
and seat the poor among princes,
look favorably upon us in our time of need.
Through Christ our Lord.

Twenty-sixth Sunday in Ordinary Time

Entrance Antiphon

From the fiery furnace Azariah confesses that the people have sinned and are suffering justly at the hand of the Lord; still, he begs mercy for the glory of God's name. This antiphon comes from the same section of Daniel that supplies one of the private prayers of the priest during the preparation of the gifts. It was the entrance antiphon for the Twentieth Sunday after Pentecost from at least the eighth century to the pre-Vatican II missal.

Collect

God's almighty power is manifest above all in pardon and mercy. As we hasten toward his promises, we ask to be heirs of heaven. The Gelasian Sacramentary included this among its prayers for Ordinary Time Sundays. In some traditions it was used on the Tenth Sunday after Pentecost. In the Ambrosian Rite it was the third of the prayers for the Pentecost rogation days. Ephesians 2:4–6 explores the richness of God's mercy; Wisdom 11:27 tells of God's pardon. The manifestation of God's glory appears in the wedding at Cana (John 2:11) and in the Incarnation itself (1 John 1:1–2). Christians run toward God's promises, and this calls to mind Paul's image of an athlete competing for a prize (1 Corinthians 9:24). The image of sharing in the good things of heaven relates to the promise in 2 Peter 1:2–4.

Prayer over the Offerings

We pray that, in accepting this offering, God will open the wellspring of all blessing for us. The text was newly composed for the post-Vatican II missal from propers in the City of Rome. Its vocabulary relates to paragraphs 88 and 94 of the first Eucharistic Prayer.

Preface

Any preface from Ordinary Time may be used. *See pp. 92–93.* Both the second and the seventh options share thematic material with the second reading in Year A.

Communion Antiphon

The psalmist asks the Lord to remember his word, which gives hope. Taken again from the longest psalm in the Bible, these verses unite our Communion with the guidance we receive from the divine word. This antiphon served the Twentieth Sunday after Pentecost from at least the eighth century to the pre-Vatican II missal.

The First Letter of John, not a Gospel, provides today's alternative antiphon. We came to know the love of God when Christ laid down his life for us. We ought to love our brothers and sisters in the same way. We reflect on these demands as we share our Communion. This antiphon was new to the post-Vatican II missal.

LECTIONARY

The Kyrie (Order of Mass, 7) uses the word "Lord" for Jesus Christ. That title is affirmed at the conclusion of the longer form of Year A's second reading.

Year B's second reading is the last in the series from the Letter of James.

Year C's responsorial is one of the psalms that includes the word "Alleluia" in the full text. That word may be sung as an alternative refrain today. The same word, of course, is used in the Gospel acclamation (Order of Mass, 13). The second reading concludes the series from Paul's First Letter to Timothy. Eucharistic Prayer IV praises God "dwelling in unapproachable light," which refers to 1 Timothy 6:16.

Prayer after Communion

We pray that this Communion may restore us in mind and body, making us coheirs in glory with Christ. The prayer is based on one from the Verona Sacramentary, intended for daily usage in July. It has been amplified with a reference to 2 Peter 1:2–4, a passage that may have inspired today's collect. It was thus added to *The Roman Missal* after the Second Vatican Council.

Blessing

Any solemn blessing from Ordinary Time may be used, or even a prayer over the people. *See pp. 94–96.*

PRAYER OF THE FAITHFUL

Year A

Those who do God's will receive a favorable response to their prayers. Let us ask for the grace to love God's command as we present our needs.

— Intercessions —

O God,
who make known your ways
and teach us your paths,
remember your mercies,
hear our prayers,
and guide us in your truth.
Through Christ our Lord.

Year B

Whoever is not against Christ is for Christ. As we speak well of our Redeemer, let us request mighty deeds.

— Intercessions —

O God,
whose precepts give joy to the heart,
keep us blameless and innocent
and grant these prayers.
Through Christ our Lord.

Year C

The poor man Lazarus received little in this life, but rested at peace at the side of Abraham. Let us pray for those in need of God's unfailing help.

— Intercessions —

O God,
who give sight to the blind,
food to the hungry,
and justice for the oppressed,
turn your compassionate gaze
on those for whom we pray this day.
Through Christ our Lord.

Twenty-seventh Sunday in Ordinary Time

Overview

The *Book of Blessings* includes an Order for the Blessing of Animals (942–965). Many parishes offer this on October 4, or on some Sunday near that date.

Entrance Antiphon

In great distress Mordecai acknowledges that no one can resist God's will. He trusts that the God who made heaven and earth will come to the aid of his people. This antiphon opened the Mass for the Twenty-first Sunday after Pentecost from at least the eighth century to the pre-Vatican II missal.

Collect

God has kindness in abundance. We ask for mercy, pardon, and anything else we dare not request. This prayer comes from those for Ordinary Time Sundays in the Gelasian Sacramentary. In some traditions it was used on the Eleventh Sunday after Pentecost. God's compassion is revealed in the coming of Christ in 1 Timothy 3:16. God's abilities to do more than we can ask or imagine are affirmed in Romans 8:26 and Ephesians 3:20. The Lord's Prayer requests God's pardon for our sins (Matthew 6:12). The role of conscience in the spiritual life appears in 1 Timothy 1:5.

Prayer over the Offerings

We ask God to complete the sanctifying work of our redemption by accepting these sacrifices. The same prayer appears on Wednesday of the Seventh Week of Easter. This short prayer was newly composed for the post-Vatican II missal, taking lines from three prayers in the Verona Sacramentary for April, July, and August.

Preface

Any preface from Ordinary Time may be used. *See pp. 92–93.* The fifth says that God formed man and woman in the divine image, a theme that appears in the first reading and Gospel in Year B.

Communion Antiphon

The book of Lamentations supplies the first option for the Communion antiphon: God is good to those hoping in him. The goodness of God is revealed in this Communion. From Paul's letters, the second antiphon says we are one bread and one body, and we share in the one cup. The same verse is referred to in paragraph 122 of Eucharistic Prayer IV. Both antiphons were new to the post-Vatican II missal.

Prayer after Communion

We ask that we may be transformed into what we consume, through our refreshment in this sacrament. The prayer was newly composed for the post-Vatican II missal. It quotes the end of Leo the Great's Sermon 63, where he says that we pass into the Communion we take, carrying the risen Christ with us.

LECTIONARY

Year B's second reading is the first in this year's series from the Letter to the Hebrews. The letter concludes in Year C.

Year C's second reading is the first in the series from Paul's Second Letter to Timothy.

Blessing

Any solemn blessing from Ordinary Time may be used, or even a prayer over the people. *See pp. 94–96*. The second solemn blessing is based on the second reading in Year A.

PRAYER OF THE FAITHFUL

Year A

The kingdom of God is given to people who will produce its fruit. As workers in God's vineyard, let us present our prayers.

— Intercessions —

O God,
who send us into your vineyard
to spread the news of your love,
give us new life as we call upon your name.
Through Christ our Lord.

Year B

God made man and woman to be partners with each other. Believing that God still provides for our needs, we present our prayers.

— Intercessions —

O God,
who bless us all the days of our lives,
and manifest yourself
in the love of husband and wife,
grant these prayers from those
    who hope in you.
Through Christ our Lord.

Year C

When our faith is the size of a mustard seed, God can work wonders. In confidence we present our needs.

— Intercessions —

O God,
who promise life to those who are just,
make us pleasing in your sight
and favorably receive our prayers.
Through Christ our Lord.

Twenty-eighth Sunday in Ordinary Time

Entrance Antiphon

The psalmist praises the mercy of God, who does not mark our iniquities. With confidence in God's mercy, we begin our prayer. From at least the eighth century to the pre-Vatican II missal, this antiphon was used on the Twenty-second Sunday after Pentecost.

Collect

We pray that God's grace may accompany us, making us determined to do good. It is one of the evening and morning prayers collected in the Hadrian Sacramentary. It was used on the Sixteenth Sunday after Pentecost in some early traditions. The Latin word for the "determined" in this prayer is *intentos*, which inspired a custom in Lancashire for serving roast goose on Saint Michael's Day because of the old English word *tentaas*, meaning "on foot." The words were not related, but they sounded alike.

Prayer over the Offerings

We ask that our acts of devotedness will help us pass over to the glory of heaven. This same prayer is used on Palm Sunday and on Tuesday of Holy Week. It first appeared in the Hadrian Sacramentary on the Tuesday after Easter.

Preface

Any preface from Ordinary Time may be used. *See pp. 92–93.*

Communion Antiphon

The rich may suffer want and hunger, but those who seek the Lord lack no blessing. Sharing Holy Communion especially proves the point, for it satisfies our every need. From the First Letter of John, we hear that we will be like the Lord when he appears, for we shall see him as he is. In this Communion we see and touch our redeemer. Both antiphons were new to the post-Vatican II missal.

Prayer after Communion

As we are fed with this most holy Body and Blood, we ask to be sharers of the divine nature. This prayer was also used on Saturday of the Fifth Week of Lent. It comes from the July daily prayers of the Verona Sacramentary.

Blessing

Any solemn blessing from Ordinary Time may be used, or even a prayer over the people. *See pp. 94–96.*

LECTIONARY

Year A's second reading is the last in the series from Paul's Letter to the Philippians.

PRAYER OF THE FAITHFUL

Year A

God invites to this banquet the bad and the good alike. May our lives be pleasing, that God will answer these prayers.

— Intercessions —

O God, shepherd of your people,
who spread a table before us
and anoint us with the oil of gladness,
supply our needs
and make us worthy of your many gifts.
Through Christ our Lord.

Year B

For us, our salvation is impossible, but all things are possible for God. With humble trust, we present our prayers.

— Intercessions —

O God,
who fill us with your love,
help us to follow your commands,
as you grant what you know is best.
Through Christ our Lord.

Year C

Jesus the Master had pity on those who approached him with their needs. We humbly ask God to hear these prayers through his intercession.

— Intercessions —

O God,
who reveal your saving power
    to the nations,
let us see your salvation
as you receive these prayers.
Through Christ our Lord.

Twenty-ninth Sunday in Ordinary Time

Entrance Antiphon

God will heed the call of the psalmist, who now asks for protection. Mass begins with a simple prayer, acknowledging God's attention in the past and requesting it now. It comes from Tuesday of the Third Week of Lent in sources from at least the eighth century up to the pre-Vatican II missal.

Collect

We ask God's help to make our will obedient, and to serve him sincerely. The prayer opened the Mass for the Sixth Sunday after the Octave of Easter in the Gelasian Sacramentary. It also appeared there as a generic collect and even as a prayer after Communion. In some traditions it was used on the Fifteenth Sunday after Pentecost.

Prayer over the Offerings

We pray for a sincere respect for God's gifts so that we may be cleansed by these mysteries. The prayer comes from the collection for April in the Verona Sacramentary. It was newly added to *The Roman Missal* after the Second Vatican Council.

Preface

Any preface from Ordinary Time may be used. *See pp. 92–93.* The seventh option says that Jesus was like us "in all things but sin," a belief that comes from today's second reading in Year B.

Communion Antiphon

People hope in God's merciful love to be rescued from death and kept alive in famine—just as this Communion nourishes our deepest hungers. The text was used as the entrance antiphon for the feast of the martyrs Nereus and Achilles in eighth-century sources.

Explaining things to the apostles who were angry at James and John, Jesus says he came to give his life as redemption for many. In the bliss of this Communion, we recall the kind of love it demands. The alternative antiphon quotes the Gospel of Year B. It was new to the post-Vatican II missal.

Prayer after Communion

Having participated in this Communion, we ask that the gifts God gives us now will prepare us for those that are eternal. The prayer is based on one from the Verona Sacramentary for the consecration of a bishop in September.

Blessing

Any solemn blessing from Ordinary Time may be used, or even a prayer over the people. *See pp. 94–96.* The fourth solemn blessing mentions hope, faith, and love, which are also part of the second reading in Year A.

LECTIONARY

Year A's second reading is the first in the series from Paul's First Letter to the Thessalonians.

In all the Eucharistic Prayers, the institution narrative quotes Jesus saying he poured out his blood for "many," as he himself said at the Last Supper in Matthew 26:28 and Mark 14:24. He was probably expressing that he fulfilled the prophecy in Year B's first reading, Isaiah 53:11, that God's servant would justify "many." Eucharistic Prayer IV says that Christ "shared our human nature in all things but sin" (Order of Mass, 117), citing a verse from the second reading, Hebrews 4:15. The alternative Communion antiphon comes from Year B's Gospel.

PRAYER OF THE FAITHFUL

Year A

Jesus had little tolerance for religious hypo-
crites. Let us pray with sincerity for the
needs of our community.

— Intercessions —

O God,
who govern your people with equity,
hear the prayers of those
who gather today to give you glory.
Through Christ our Lord.

Year B

In Jesus Christ we have a high priest who
can sympathize with our weakness. Let
us approach the throne of grace with our
prayers, that we may receive mercy and
grace for timely help.

— Intercessions —

O God,
who desire our service,
let your mercy be on us
as we place our trust in you.
Through Christ our Lord.

Year C

Our help is from the Lord, who made heaven
and earth. To him we present our needs.

— Intercessions —

O God,
who care for the widow, the orphan,
    and the downcast,
render a just decision for us
and grant these prayers.
Through Christ our Lord.

Thirtieth Sunday in Ordinary Time

Overview

If the date of your parish church's dedication is unknown, this may be an appropriate day to commemorate it. Many dioceses set aside the Sunday before All Saints Day as the time for this observance. If so, you use the commons for the anniversary of the dedication of a church, and this Mass may be celebrated instead of the regular texts for a Sunday in Ordinary Time.

If the holy day All Saints Day falls this week, be sure to announce times for Masses.

Entrance Antiphon

The psalmist encourages the community to seek the face of the Lord. We do that as we gather for this Eucharist. This antiphon was new to this position in the post-Vatican II missal. In eighth-century sources it was used for Thursday of the Fourth Week of Lent, where it still appears today, and for the Saturday ember day in September. This latter usage probably influenced its choice for a Sunday late in the church year.

Collect

We ask for an increase in faith, hope, and charity, and to love what God commands, in order to obtain what he promises. The original comes from the morning and evening prayers in July from the Verona Sacramentary. In some traditions it was used on the Fourteenth Sunday after Pentecost. The three theological virtues are mentioned in 1 Corinthians 13:13 and 1 Thessalonians 1:3 and 5:8. They were mentioned in a different order in the collect for the Sixteenth Sunday in Ordinary Time. Psalm 119:97a says, "Lord, I love your commands."

Prayer over the Offerings

We pray that our acts of service may be directed to God's glory. This prayer is based on one from the Verona Sacramentary's daily prayers in the month of July. The second half of it was edited to make it more suitable for today. It appeared in *The Roman Missal* tradition for the first time after the Second Vatican Council.

Preface

Any preface from Ordinary Time may be used. *See pp. 92–93.*

Communion Antiphon

With the psalmist we rejoice at God's saving help and exult in God's name. This Communion fills us with joy and inspires us to give thanks. The Letter to the Ephesians supplies the alternative antiphon: Christ loved us and

LECTIONARY

Year A's first reading is part of the Sinai covenant God established with Moses. It is implied in the phrase "Time and again you offered them covenants" in Eucharistic Prayer IV (Order of Mass, 117).

Eucharistic Prayer III asks God to "gather to yourself all your children scattered throughout the earth" (Order of Mass, 113), and Eucharistic Prayer IV prays for those "gathered into one body by the Holy Spirit" (Order of Mass, 122). The theme of gathering the scattered is established in Year B's first reading from Jeremiah.

Year C's second reading is the last in the series from Paul's Second Letter to Timothy.

handed himself over for us as an offering to God. In gratitude for the sacrifice of Christ we share this Communion. Both antiphons were new to the post-Vatican II missal.

Prayer after Communion

We ask for these sacraments to perfect in us what lies within them that we may one day possess what they signify. The prayer comes from a special autumn Mass in the Gelasian Sacramentary. It has long been part of the Roman tradition.

Blessing

Any solemn blessing from Ordinary Time may be used, or even a prayer over the people. *See pp. 94–96.*

PRAYER OF THE FAITHFUL

Year A

Jesus taught his disciples to love God and their neighbor. Let us approach God in love with the concerns we hold for our neighbors.

— *Intercessions* —

O God,
our strength, our rock, our fortress,
    our deliverer,
look with love on the people who love you
and grant these prayers.
Through Christ our Lord.

Year B

Jesus asked the blind man, "What do you want me to do for you?" Let us address the Son of David, and ask him to have pity on us in our times of need.

— *Intercessions* —

O God,
who have done great things for us
and filled us with joy,
restore our fortunes and grant our prayers.
Through Christ our Lord.

Year C

The prayer of the lowly pierces the clouds and does not rest until it reaches its goal. Let us lift up our needs to God in hope.

— *Intercessions* —

O God,
who are merciful to the sinner,
hear the prayers of those
    who humbly cry to you.
Through Christ our Lord.

Thirty-first Sunday in Ordinary Time

Overview

Eucharistic Prayer I was handed down to us through a variety of sources, and the Gelasian Sacramentary preserved it in among the texts of one particular Mass near the end of the book. Today's prayer after Communion is taken from that same Mass in the Gelasian. It might be a good day to use the first Eucharistic Prayer.

If the holy day All Saints Day falls this week, be sure to announce times for Masses.

Entrance Antiphon

The psalmist in distress asks the Lord God for help and salvation. We too ask God not to forsake us, but to be present during this Eucharist. This antiphon was newly placed here for the post-Vatican II missal, but it appeared in eighth-century sources on Wednesday of the Second Week of Lent, where it also recurs today.

Collect

The service we offer is God's gift. We ask for help to hasten without stumbling toward what God has promised. The prayer is lifted directly from the Verona Sacramentary's collection of daily prayers for the month of July. It was used in some traditions on the Twelfth Sunday after Pentecost. It may have been composed by Pope Vigilius for Mass on November 22, 537, during the siege of Rome by the Arian Ostrogoths. In the post-Vatican II missal it was assigned to a Sunday not far from that date. Offering a sacrifice of praise is mentioned in Psalm 107:22 and Psalm 116:7. To run without stumbling is more literally "without offense," which calls to mind 1 Corinthians 10:31–33 and Philippians 1:9–11. The image is not far from Paul's athlete competing for the prize in 1 Corinthians 9:24.

Prayer over the Offerings

We pray that this sacrifice may be a pure oblation for God and an outpouring of mercy for us. This prayer was newly composed for the post-Vatican II missal, based on the concluding section of Sermon 91 by Pope Leo the Great.

Preface

Any preface from Ordinary Time may be used. *See pp. 92–93.* The third option says that God came to our aid, a theme that appears at the end of the Gospel in Year C.

Communion Antiphon

The Lord fills us with joy and shows us the path of life. We are filled with this Communion and all that it implies. It was new here to the post-Vatican II missal, though eighth-century sources used it on Wednesday of the Third Week of Lent, where it also appears today. From the Gospels, Jesus says that those who

---

LECTIONARY

The opening of Eucharistic Prayer IV addresses "the one God" (Order of Mass, 116). From the first reading in Year B, Deuteronomy 6:4 affirms that the Lord alone is God. In the third form of the penitential act, the final invocation addresses the Lord who sits at the right hand of the Father "to intercede for us" (Order of Mass, 6). This alludes to a verse from the second reading, Hebrews 7:25, which says that Jesus lives forever to make intercession.

Year C's second reading begins the short series from Paul's Second Letter to the Thessalonians.

feed on him will have life. We do, and we pray that we might. This antiphon was new to the post-Vatican II missal.

Prayer after Communion

We pray that God's power will help us receive what this Communion promises. A version of this prayer appears in the Gelasian Sacramentary among the Masses for Ordinary Sundays. This is the prayer after Communion included in the Gelasian's only Mass giving the complete text of the Roman Canon.

Blessing

Any solemn blessing from Ordinary Time may be used, or even a prayer over the people. *See pp. 94–96.*

PRAYER OF THE FAITHFUL

Year A

The word of God is now at work in us who believe. In confidence, we present our prayers.

— Intercessions —

O God,
in whom we find our peace,
be merciful to those who place their hope
    in you.
Through Christ our Lord.

Year B

Jesus Christ is always able to save those who approach God through him because he lives forever to make intercession for them. We ask Christ to intercede, as we make our prayers to the Father.

— Intercessions —

O God,
who teach us the commandment of love,
show us your loving care
and grant these petitions.
Through Christ our Lord.

Year C

The Son of Man came to seek and save what was lost. Let us ask his help for all who are in need.

— Intercessions —

O God,
gracious and merciful,
slow to anger and of great kindness,
show us your goodness
    by granting these prayers.
Through Christ our Lord.

Thirty-second Sunday in Ordinary Time

Entrance Antiphon

With the psalmist we ask that our prayer might enter God's presence. As we start this Mass, we call upon God to incline an ear toward us. This antiphon appeared in eighth-century sources on Saturday of the ember days in Lent, and on the Second Sunday of Lent. It was new to this position in the post-Vatican II missal.

Collect

We ask God to keep all adversity from us that we may pursue divine things. This comes from the Gelasian Sacramentary's prayers for Ordinary Time Sundays. It was often used on the Nineteenth Sunday after Pentecost. Various New Testament letters mention *adversaria*—the things that would harm the spiritual life: the desires of the flesh (Galatians 5:17), sinful be-haviors contrary to sound teaching (1 Timothy 1:9–10), those who oppose Christians (1 Thes-salonians 2:15), and even the devil himself (1 Peter 5:8). The value of true freedom is told in Galatians 5:13, but also in Romans 5:21 and 8:2 and Galatians 3:13 and 5:22.

Prayer over the Offerings

We pray to honor the mystery of the pas-sion of Christ with loving devotion, as God looks with favor upon these gifts. The prayer enjoys long usage in the history of *The Roman Missal*.

Preface

Any preface from Ordinary Time may be used. *See pp. 92–93.*

Communion Antiphon

From the most popular of the psalms, we proclaim that the Lord shepherds us and gives us repose near refreshing water. As we enjoy this spiritual food and drink, we praise God. Eighth-century sources placed this on Saturday of the Fourth Week of Lent; it appeared here for the first time in the post-Vatican II missal. From Luke's Gospel, the disciples at Emmaus recognize Jesus in the breaking of the bread. We who have recognized him here among us share this broken bread and cup outpoured. This antiphon was new to the post-Vatican II missal.

Prayer after Communion

We give thanks and beseech God's mercy that the grace of integrity may endure. The prayer is based on one that appears twice in the Gelasian Sacramentary, once among the general prayers for Sundays, and again on the occasion of dedicating as a Christian church a place that had once been a synagogue. Al-though this particular prayer never showed any prejudice against Jews, the collect for that Mass did. That collect is no longer in use. This prayer has been reworked anyway: only the first half of it shares these seventh-century origins. The rest was rewritten for more common usage over the years.

Blessing

Any solemn blessing from Ordinary Time may be used, or even a prayer over the people. *See pp. 94–96.*

LECTIONARY

Year B's responsorial is one of the psalms that incorporate the word "Alleluia" in its full text in the Bible, and as an alternative refrain here in the liturgy. The Gospel acclamation (Order of Mass, 13) borrows this word.

PRAYER OF THE FAITHFUL

Year A

Let us stay awake so that the Lord will recognize us when we ask him to open the doors of his bountiful care.

— Intercessions —

O God,
fill with joy those who are thirsting for you,
and grant the prayers of those
who meditate on you day and night.
Through Christ our Lord.

Year B

Jesus admired the woman who contributed all she had. Let us devote our thoughts completely to the needs of others.

— Intercessions —

O God,
who secure justice for the oppressed,
raise up those who are bowed down,
and grant these prayers.
Through Christ our Lord.

Year C

Saint Paul invited prayers so that the word of the Lord would speed forward and be glorified. Let us pray to the Lord, who is faithful.

— Intercessions —

O God, our living God,
make our joy full
through the appearance of your glory,
and grant what we ask.
Through Christ our Lord.

Thirty-third Sunday in Ordinary Time

Overview

This is the last Sunday you can use Eucharistic Prayer IV for a while. It may be a good occasion to offer it.

The *Book of Blessings* includes an Order for a Blessing on the Occasion of Thanksgiving for the Harvest (1007–1023). It could be used some Sunday near Thanksgiving.

Entrance Antiphon

From Jeremiah we hear the Lord say that he answers those who call upon him and leads them back from captivity. Confident that God hears and answers the prayers of the neediest, we begin the celebration. From the eighth century, this was used to open the Mass on the Twenty-third Sunday after Pentecost. It also served traditions with a longer Advent on the Fifth Sunday before Christmas, which would be next week, but that day is taken over by the Solemnity of Our Lord Jesus Christ, King of the Universe.

Collect

We ask for the constant gladness of being devoted to God because happiness is full if we serve the author of all that is good. The text is taken word for word from the Verona Sacramentary's daily prayers for July. It was added to *The Roman Missal* after the Second Vatican Council, perhaps in the spirit of joy that the council evoked. The prayer may have been written by Pope Vigilius for August of 537

when Rome was under siege by the Arian Ostrogoths. The Romans had just survived famine and pestilence, and victory in battle seemed close. When our fortunes are good, we should remember the source of our blessings. In the New Testament, Paul encouraged his readers to rejoice always (Philippians 4:4, 1 Thessalonians 5:16). He himself rejoices in the midst of hardships (Philippians 1:18).

Prayer over the Offerings

We pray for the gift of devotion and the happiness that lasts forever. This prayer comes from the Hadrian Sacramentary's prayers for Palm Sunday. It has enjoyed a long tradition in the Roman Rite, and was moved here from Palm Sunday with the post-Vatican II missal.

Preface

Any preface from Ordinary Time may be used. *See pp. 92–93.*

Communion Antiphon

With the psalmist we assert how happy we are to be near God and to place our hope in

---

LECTIONARY

Year A's second reading is the last in the series from Paul's First Letter to the Thessalonians.

Year B's second reading is the last in this year's series from the Letter to the Hebrews. The series will start again on the Nineteenth Sunday in Ordinary Time of Year C. When Eucharistic Prayer IV says, "we offer you his Body and Blood, the sacrifice acceptable to you which brings salvation to the whole world" (Order of Mass, 122), it implies the teaching of Hebrews 10:14, that there is one offering, that of Jesus Christ, and by it he has made perfect forever those who are being consecrated.

Year C's second reading is the last in the series from Paul's Second Letter to the Thessalonians.

God. We are closest to God in this Communion. This antiphon was new to the post-Vatican II missal. From Mark's Gospel, Jesus says that whatever we ask for in prayer will be given to us. We believe as we receive this gift that God will not withhold any other good. This second antiphon always accompanied today's entrance antiphon on the same two occasions of its usage ever since the eighth century.

Prayer after Communion

We have received this Communion imploring that what God's Son commanded us to do will bring us our growth in charity. The prayer is unusually declarative, even in the original Latin. It announces what we have done more than it makes a petition. The same prayer is used on quite a few weekdays in the Easter season. It comes from an evening Mass in July in the Verona Sacramentary, though it has been lightly reworked. It has been part of *The Roman Missal* for a long time. It recalls Jesus' words at the Last Supper in Luke 22:19 and 1 Corinthians 11:24. As we near the end of the liturgical year, it puts us back in touch with the paschal events that led to this celebration.

Blessing

Any solemn blessing from Ordinary Time may be used, or even a prayer over the people. *See pp. 94–96.*

PRAYER OF THE FAITHFUL

Year A

Saint Paul says the day of the Lord will come like a thief in the night. Let us pray that all the world may remain alert for his coming.

— *Intercessions* —

O God,
who bestow talents and gifts
upon your people,
grant also the prayers we ask this day.
Through Christ our Lord.

Year B

Heaven and earth will pass away, but the words of Jesus Christ will not pass away. Trusting in his promise, we make our needs known to God.

— *Intercessions* —

O God,
our allotted portion and cup,
grant our prayers;
show us the path to life
and the fullness of joys in your presence.
Through Christ our Lord.

Year C

Jesus says we will preserve our lives through perseverance. Let us pray for the grace of fidelity.

— *Intercessions* —

O God,
who come to rule the earth,
act with justice
and hear our prayers.
Through Christ our Lord.

The Most Holy Trinity

Overview

After the close of the Easter season, we enter Ordinary Time on weekdays. On Sunday, though, we first observe a solemnity that summarizes much of what we have experienced throughout the Church Year so far: the mystery of the Most Holy Trinity.

The presidential prayers for this Mass are notoriously difficult to locate. You've been flipping through the Lent and Easter seasons page by page, but now you have to find Trinity Sunday, which does not come after Pentecost in the missal. Look ahead—way after Ordinary Time. You'll find it. Mark it with the ribbon before Mass.

The first of the votive Masses in the back of the missal is for the Holy Trinity. It repeats all the texts found here.

Entrance Antiphon

The Trinity is blest for showing us merciful love. This is similar to the antiphon from the pre-Vatican II missal, inspired by Tobit 12:6.

Collect

We pray to God, who sent the Son and the Spirit into the world, to acknowledge the Trinity and to adore its Unity. This prayer is based on an older Roman prayer, but was new to the post-Vatican II missal on this day.

Prayer over the Offerings

We ask God to sanctify the oblation and to make us an eternal offering as well. This is the same prayer for this day in the pre-Vatican II missal.

Preface

The Father, Son, and Spirit are one God and Lord, not in the unity of a single Person, but in the Trinity of one substance. We confess the uniqueness of each Person, their oneness in substance and equality in majesty. The language of this preface is especially dense, but it is dealing with a very precise theological issue—a description of the Holy Trinity. This preface originated in the Gelasian Sacramentary for the Sunday after Pentecost. It was carried over from the pre-Vatican II missal to the one after the Council.

Communion Antiphon

God has sent the Holy Spirit into the hearts of his children. This passage from Galatians replaces the antiphon in the pre-Vatican II missal.

LECTIONARY

The conclusion of Year A's second reading is the source of one of the greetings used at the beginning of Mass (Order of Mass, 2). This is the only place in the New Testament where the formula appears exactly this way. The opening verse of the Gospel inspired a statement in Eucharistic Prayer IV: "And you so loved the world, . . . [that] you sent your Only Begotten Son" (Order of Mass, 117).

Eucharistic Prayer IV prays for entry "into a heavenly inheritance" (Order of Mass, 122). From the second reading of Year B, Romans 8:17 says we are heirs of God, joint heirs with Christ. The Communion antiphon comes from this section of Paul's letter. The references to the names of the Trinity can be traced to the Gospel of Year B. They appear in the sign of the cross (Order of Mass, 1) and in one of the formulas for the greeting (Order of Mass, 2).

Prayer after Communion

The community prays for health of body and soul, while confessing the Trinity and unity of God. This prayer evolved through the Roman tradition and took its place on this day in the post-Vatican II missal.

Blessing

There is no special solemn blessing or prayer over the people for this day, partly because the feast developed somewhat late in liturgical history. You could use the blessing from Pentecost Sunday, which is more precisely a blessing concerning the Holy Spirit. Or choose another from the options for Ordinary Time. *See pp. 88, 94–96.*

PRAYER OF THE FAITHFUL

Year A

God is merciful and gracious, slow to anger, and rich in kindness. Let us bring our petitions to the One who is faithful.

— *Intercessions* —

O God,
who gave us your only Son,
show the world your love again
and hear our prayers.
Through Christ our Lord.

Year B

We are children of God and joint-heirs with Christ. In the Spirit, we bring our prayers to the Father.

— *Intercessions* —

O God,
whose Son promised to be with us
until the end of the age,
hear your faithful ones,
show us your Christ,
and let us rejoice in your presence.
Through Christ our Lord.

Year C

Affliction produces endurance, and hope does not disappoint. Mindful of the needs of all the world, we bring our prayers in hope.

— *Intercessions* —

O God,
who pour love into our hearts
through the Holy Spirit,
show us also your mercy
and grant these prayers.
Through Christ our Lord.

The Most Holy Body and Blood of Christ

Overview

Although the calendar has moved firmly into Ordinary Time, the spirit of celebration lingers after the fifty days of Easter. On this day we pause to meditate on one of the greatest mysteries in Christianity: the Most Holy Body and Blood of Christ.

In some countries this is a holy day of obligation. There it is celebrated on the Thursday after Trinity Sunday. Where it is not—as in the United States—the solemnity transfers to the following Sunday. The Church wants everyone to celebrate this day.

There is an optional Sequence for today, *Lauda Sion*, which can be found in the *Lectionary for Mass*. As is customary, it follows the second reading. It is long. It may be abbreviated—and it may be omitted; this Sequence is not obligatory.

This may be a good day to sing the Eucharistic Prayer. Do something to draw attention to the Eucharist today.

Mass may conclude with a procession of the Blessed Sacrament. In this case, a host is placed in the monstrance after the prayer after Communion, and the greeting, blessing, and dismissal are omitted. Turn to *Holy Communion and Worship of the Eucharist Outside Mass*, where paragraphs 101–108 describe a Eucharistic procession. The priest wears the vestments for Mass or he may change into a white cope. Candles and incense may lead the way, and people may hold a canopy over the monstrance, though this is not required. At the end of the procession—whether in another church or the original one—the priest gives a blessing with the monstrance. Then he reposes the Blessed Sacrament in the tabernacle. Music should accompany the procession and would fittingly close the celebration. See also the *Ceremonial of Bishops*, 387–394.

Although Ordinary Time has already returned to weekdays, it will return to Sundays after today. Think about ways to simplify the music, the environment, and the vesture to make the transition more apparent.

The missal includes prayers of preparation for Mass and of thanksgiving after Mass. Some are by Saint Thomas Aquinas, who also composed many of the texts for this liturgy.

Entrance Antiphon

God fed the Israelites with manna in the desert and satisfied their thirst with water from the rock. Remembering this divinely-provided food and drink as the finest wheat and miraculous honey, we celebrate a solemnity of the Body and Blood of Christ. This antiphon appeared in the missal before the Second Vatican Council as well. It quotes a prophecy from one of the psalms.

Collect

The community prays to know constantly the fruits of redemption, as the members revere these sacred mysteries. This is the only Sunday collect addressed to Jesus Christ. It is clear from the words "your Passion" and "your Body and Blood." The prayer evolved through the tradition of the Roman missals, and it was carried over into the post-Vatican II missal from its predecessor.

Prayer over the Offerings

The community prays for the gifts of unity and peace, represented in the offerings. As with the collect, this prayer came down through the Roman tradition and was carried over from the previous missal to the present one without change.

Preface

At the Last Supper, Christ offered himself and established the saving memorial of the cross. Through celebrating this mystery, we who share one world are united in charity. We pray to pass over to heavenly realities. The preface for this day is the second one dedicated to the Most Holy Eucharist. It was a new composition for the 2002 missal, though based on earlier themes. Scriptural references include Exodus 12:5 and Leviticus 9:3 (the lamb without blemish), and 1 Corinthians 15:47–49 for the image of the heavenly Man.

Communion Antiphon

Jesus promises to remain with those who eat his flesh and drink his blood. This antiphon replaces the one from the pre-Vatican II missal. It is drawn from the Gospel of Year A.

Prayer after Communion

We ask to delight for all eternity in divine life. This prayer is also taken from the pre-Vatican II missal, completing the principal body of texts that went unchanged for this Mass after the Second Vatican Council.

Blessing

No special solemn blessing or prayer over the people is recommended for this Mass. You may choose any of the options from Ordinary Time. *See pp. 94–96.*

LECTIONARY

Eucharistic Prayer IV prays for "all who partake of this one Bread and one Chalice" (Order of Mass, 122). This refers to a passage from First Corinthians, found in the second reading of Year A. This is one passage that inspired the action of breaking bread at the Mass (Order of Mass, 129–130). In Year A's Gospel, Jesus promises eternal life to those who eat his flesh and drink his blood. The insertion of the word "eternal" into the institution narrative at every Mass is justified by this statement. The Communion antiphon comes from this section of John's Gospel.

In Year B, the first reading tells of the covenant between God and Moses. It is one of those implied in Eucharistic Prayer IV, which refers to the "covenants" God established time and again (Order of Mass, 117). The institution narratives of all the Eucharistic Prayers cite part of Year B's Gospel, including the phrase "poured out for many." The passage concludes by saying that the participants at the Last Supper sang a hymn, as is the practice throughout the celebration of the Eucharist today.

Melchizedek, who appears in the first reading of Year C, is mentioned in Eucharistic Prayer I (Order of Mass, 93). His name appears again in the responsorial psalm. Eucharistic Prayer III says we celebrate these mysteries at the "command" of Jesus Christ (Order of Mass, 109). The second reading in Year C records that command, and that Paul is passing on the tradition he has received. The institution narrative of all the Eucharistic Prayers relies on the testimony of the Gospels, but also on this passage from Paul. This one is probably the earliest of them all, written within twenty years after Jesus died. The second memorial acclamation comes from this reading. The first memorial acclamation was inspired by it.

PRAYER OF THE FAITHFUL

Year A

God grants peace and fills us with the best of wheat. Faithful to the command of Christ, let us make known our needs.

— Intercessions —

O God,
who revealed the mystery of the Eucharist
in the teaching of your only Son,
make us ready to sing your praises
and grant our prayers.
Through Christ our Lord.

Year B

Before we take up the cup of salvation, let us call upon the name of the Lord on behalf of all who are in need.

— Intercessions —

O God,
whose Son commanded us to eat and drink
his body and blood,
prepare us to experience
    your wondrous meal
and mercifully hear our prayers.
Through Christ our Lord.

Year C

Those who listened to Jesus received all the food they could eat. Having listened to his word, let us pray for the needs of all who hunger for a better life.

— Intercessions —

O God,
whose Son provided food in the wilderness,
supply an answer to all our wants.
Through Christ our Lord.

Our Lord Jesus Christ, King of the Universe (Last Sunday in Ordinary Time)

Overview

This feast now falls on the last Sunday of the liturgical year, where it sums up the role of Christ, whose ministry has unfolded throughout this time. The texts are not easy to find. Even though this Sunday follows the Thirty-third Sunday in Ordinary Time on the calendar, it is elsewhere in the missal. It is joined with Trinity Sunday and the Body and Blood of Christ as solemnities that fall during Ordinary Time.

The missal includes prayers of thanksgiving after Mass, including a universal one by Clement XI.

Entrance Antiphon

With myriads and myriads and thousands and thousands we sing that the Lamb who was slain is worthy to receive power and divinity and wisdom and strength and honor. The kingdom of Christ lasts for ever. This was the antiphon from the pre-Vatican II missal as well.

Collect

God willed to restore all things in Christ the King of the universe. We pray that all creation may be freed from slavery and praise God without ceasing. This is a new prayer based on the one from the pre-Vatican II missal, which asked that all nations would come under God's reign. The text is inspired by Ephesians 1:10, which Pope Pius X adopted as his papal motto: To restore all things in Christ. Pius XI instituted this feast. The liberation of creation from its bondage is found in Romans 8:21.

Prayer over the Offerings

We pray that Jesus Christ will bestow on all nations the gifts of unity and peace. This is a lightly edited version of the same prayer from the pre-Vatican II missal.

Preface

Jesus Christ was anointed as eternal Priest and King of all creation. He accomplished our redemption on the cross. When all things are subject to him, he will present to the Father an eternal and universal kingdom. This was a new composition for the post-Vatican II missal. Anointing with the oil of gladness is noted in Psalm 44:8. The eternal priesthood appears in Psalm 109:4 and Hebrews 5:5–6 and 6:20. Jesus discusses his kingship with Pilate in John 18:33–38. Paul says Jesus will hand the kingdom to God in 1 Corinthians 15:24. He says Christ offered himself to God in Ephesians 5:2;

LECTIONARY

Year A's second reading is cited in the preface.

The word "Amen" that appears so frequently in the Mass and in Christian prayer appears in a verse from Year B's second reading, Revelation 1:6, where it concludes a prayer formula very familiar to contemporary worshipers. The Gospel may have influenced the composition of the preface.

Through the Nicene Creed we express our belief in the God who made things "visible and invisible" (Order of Mass, 18), which is affirmed in a verse from Year C's second reading, Colossians 1:16.

a similar theme appears in Hebrews 7:26 and 9:14. First Timothy 6:13–16 calls him King of kings, and Revelation 15:3 calls Christ the King of the ages.

Communion Antiphon

The psalmist says the eternal king, the Lord, will bless his people in peace. In this Communion we experience that very blessing.

Prayer after Communion

We glory in obeying the commands of Christ the King, and we ask to live with him eternally in heaven. This was a new composition based on the prayer from the pre-Vatican II missal, rendered less militaristic.

Blessing

Any solemn blessing or prayer over the people from Ordinary Time may be used. *See pp. 94–96.*

PRAYER OF THE FAITHFUL

Year A

The Good Shepherd seeks out the stray and binds up the injured. Let us pray for all who need a God of compassion.

— Intercessions —

O God,
whose Son at the end of time
will hand over his kingdom to you,
help us to rejoice in your saving mercy
by granting these prayers.
Through Christ our Lord.

Year B

Because we belong to the truth, we have listened to the voice of Jesus Christ. Let us ask God to hear our prayers through him.

— Intercessions —

O God,
whose Son is coming amid the clouds,
help our eyes to see him
by granting these petitions.
Through Christ our Lord.

Year C

We have come rejoicing into the house of the Lord. Let us present our needs, as well as those of the whole world.

— Intercessions —

O God,
whose Son reigned as king
even from the cross,
hear the prayers of those who hope
to be with him in paradise.
Through Christ our Lord.

Our Lord Jesus Christ, King of the Universe | **169**

SOLEMNITIES AND FEASTS

The Presentation of the Lord (February 2)

Overview

Forty days after Christmas, we remember the day that Joseph and Mary brought Jesus to the Temple in Jerusalem. The Mass is a postscript to the Christmas season. It includes a charming blessing of candles because Simeon proclaims the forty-day-old Jesus a light to the nations.

The missal offers two possible forms for the blessing of candles at the start of this Mass. One involves a gathering of the faithful outside the church, and the other presumes that they are already at their places. When this feast falls on a Sunday, it should be observed with the appropriate blessing of candles. You may invite people to bring from their homes any candles that they wish to have blessed for devotional purposes. Or you may provide them with blessed candles to bring home after Mass. Many churches put into view their whole storage of altar candles. Once blessed, these candles will be lighted throughout the coming year.

In the first form, the faithful gather someplace outside the main church holding unlighted candles. The priest wears a white chasuble, or he may begin with a cope and switch to the chasuble when he reaches the chair at the conclusion of the entrance procession. The first antiphon is sung as the candles are lighted. Another song may be used. However, these texts have been part of this liturgy since at least the eighth century. The priest makes the sign of the cross and greets the people.

The priest explains the meaning of the celebration. The missal provides a catechetical text, but the priest is free to choose other words that make the same points: Forty days ago was Christmas. Today we commemorate the presentation of Jesus in the Temple. As an infant, Jesus fulfilled the law and met those who already believed in him. In the Holy Spirit, elders recognized him as the Christ. We process in the same Spirit to meet Christ in the breaking of the bread.

The priest says one of two prayers. The first blesses the candles. It was a new composition for the post-Vatican II missal, inspired by Luke 2:32, which calls Jesus the light of revelation to the nations, and Sirach 24:6, which mentions the light that never fails. The alternative prayer is based on an older text from the Missal of Tours. Both these choices were new to the post-Vatican II missal. They simplified the complex prayers that formerly accompanied this part of the ritual.

After the prayer, the priest sprinkles the candles with holy water. He adds incense to the thurible. He takes up a lighted candle, and the deacon or he invites everyone to process in peace to meet the Lord. Musical notes appear in the missal for these parts. It would be good for people to learn the chants. A selection of texts is provided for the procession, all of which are best sung rather than recited. But another fitting song may be sung.

LECTIONARY

The first reading's prophecy concerning the Temple is interpreted in the preface. The Gospel inspired most of the other texts for this day.

When the procession arrives in the sanctuary, the music may change again to the entrance antiphon. The priest kisses the altar, and he may incense it. When he reaches his chair he removes the cope if he was wearing one, and puts on the chasuble. All sing or recite the Gloria, and after the collect, Mass continues as usual.

The rubrics never say when people should extinguish their candles, but a logical time would be when all are seated for the readings.

The second form for the entrance has the faithful gathered in the church with their candles. The priest should stand at the door or inside the church where some of the faithful can participate with him. The texts and actions are the same as in the first form. The main difference is that people are already in place, and the priest and ministers are the only ones who process.

As you can tell, this Mass will take a little longer. When February 2 falls on a Sunday, it would be kind to let people know ahead of time what to expect.

Entrance Antiphon

We have received God's merciful love in the midst of his temple. We sing with the psalmist a prophecy of what this day signifies: God's merciful love was revealed in the Temple when Mary and Joseph presented Jesus there, and we experience it today—and every day—when we gather in this holy place. This antiphon has appeared on this day ever since eighth-century sources.

Collect

As Jesus was presented in the Temple in flesh like ours, we pray that we may be presented to God with minds made pure. This prayer comes from the Hadrian Sacramentary and remains unchanged in today's missal. The text relies on the Gospel account.

PRAYER OF THE FAITHFUL

Years A, B, C

The Holy Spirit revealed to Simeon that he should not see death before seeing Christ the Lord. Let us ask God to be faithful to the promises of the covenant.

— *Intercessions* —

O God,
whose Son is a light for the nations
and the glory of your people,
shine your face upon us
    and grant these prayers.
Through Christ our Lord.

Prayer over the Offerings

As Jesus offered himself as the Lamb without blemish, we ask God to be pleased with the offering of the Church today. This was a newly composed prayer for the post-Vatican II missal.

Preface

We praise God, whose coeternal Son was presented on this day in the Temple, and was revealed by the Spirit as the glory of Israel and the light of the nations. The text was a new composition for the post-Vatican II missal, based on the general thought of some other prefaces in the history of this liturgy. The Temple is mentioned in Psalm 47:10 and Malachi 3:1. The "glory of Israel" is prophesied in Micah 1:15. The Gospel account for the day provides the main inspiration.

Communion Antiphon

Quoting Simeon in the Gospel, we proclaim that our eyes have seen God's salvation. We see Jesus here in the temple of our church as we share this Communion. This antiphon was new to the post-Vatican II missal.

Prayer after Communion

We ask God to bring his grace to perfection within us, that we may obtain eternal life when we go forth to meet the Lord. The prayer comes from the Paris Missal and was added to *The Roman Missal* after the Second Vatican Council. It is based on Luke 2:26.

Blessing

No solemn blessing or prayer over the people is recommended for this day, but see the blessings for the Christmas season in the missal and in the *Collection of Masses of the Blessed Virgin Mary*, pp. 81–82.

The Nativity of Saint John the Baptist, at the Vigil Mass

Overview

The Church observes the birth of John the Baptist on June 24 each year. When it falls on a Sunday, these are the texts for the Saturday evening Mass.

Entrance Antiphon

An angel predicts that the child born to Elizabeth will be great in the sight of the Lord, that he will be filled with the Holy Spirit, and that many will rejoice at his birth. We come in joy to celebrate the birth of John the Baptist. This antiphon first appeared in eighth-century sources.

Collect

We ask to walk in the way of salvation and come to Jesus Christ, the one whom John the Baptist foretold. The prayer is based on one in the Verona Sacramentary for this feast. It relies on the *Benedictus*, the canticle sung by Zechariah upon the birth of his son, John, in Luke 1:76–77.

Prayer over the Offerings

With deeds of devoted service, we ask to follow what we celebrate in mystery. We want to perform our duty in this holy place in the same way that Zechariah did in the Temple (Luke 1:8). This prayer alludes to the one in the Verona Sacramentary for this day, but it was a new composition for the post-Vatican II missal.

Preface

God consecrated John the Baptist for a singular honor among those born of women.

His birth brought rejoicing at the coming of our salvation. He pointed out the Lamb of God, baptized the author of baptism, and bore supreme witness by shedding his blood. This was a new composition for the post-Vatican II missal, though it relies on themes of several ancient prefaces for the same day. Jesus said there was none born among women greater than John the Baptist (Matthew 11:11 and Luke 7:28). John's leap in the womb of his mother is told in Luke 1:41. The baptism of Jesus appears in Matthew 3:13–16, Mark 1:9–11, Luke 3:21–22, John 1:32–34, and Acts 10:37–38. John pointed out Jesus as the Lamb of God in John 1:29 and 35. The death of John is related in Matthew 14:10–12 and Mark 6:27–29.

Communion Antiphon

Quoting Zechariah's hymn of praise upon the birth of his son, John, we proclaim that God has visited and redeemed his people. This is fully realized in the coming of Christ, whom we share in this Communion. This antiphon was new to the post-Vatican II missal.

Prayer after Communion

John proclaimed that Jesus is the Lamb who takes away sin. We ask for John to implore God's favor for us. A version of this prayer appeared in the Roman and Ambrosian traditions.

LECTIONARY

The Vigil's Gospel prophesying John's birth and tomorrow's Gospel relating his birth lie behind most of the presidential prayers for this day.

Blessing

No solemn blessing or prayer over the people is recommended for this day. However, the blessings for Advent or Christmas in the missal and in the *Collection of Masses of the Blessed Virgin Mary* are worth a look.

PRAYER OF THE FAITHFUL

Years A, B, C

God has been our strength since our mother's womb. To the Lord of every generation, we present our needs.

— *Intercessions* —

O God,
our rock of refuge,
on whom we depend from birth,
protect and sustain us
    by hearing these prayers.
Through Christ our Lord.

The Nativity of Saint John the Baptist (June 24), at the Mass during the Day

Overview

When June 24 falls on a Sunday, these texts for Mass replace the ones for Ordinary Time. This date is chosen because Gabriel announced to Mary that she would become a mother six months after Elizabeth conceived; the assumption is that the births of John and Jesus were six months apart (Luke 1:26 and 36). As the days of the Northern Hemisphere grow shorter, we can imagine John decreasing so that Christ may increase (John 3:30).

Entrance Antiphon

From two different Gospels we hear the news that John was sent by God to testify to the light and to prepare a people for the Lord. This biographical detail sets the stage for the Eucharist. The antiphon was new to the post-Vatican II missal.

Collect

We ask for the grace of spiritual joys and direction into the way to salvation. This prayer was newly composed for the post-Vatican II missal, though it is based on one from the Verona Sacramentary for this day. The text relies on several passages from Luke: the prophecy that John would prepare people for the Lord (1:17), the spiritual joys that come from the nearness of salvation (1:44), and the way of salvation and peace (1:76–77 and 79).

Prayer over the Offerings

Presenting our gifts, we celebrate with fitting honor the birth of the one who foretold and pointed out the coming of our Savior. The text is taken from the Mass for this day in the Verona Sacramentary. It is inspired by more passages from the Gospels: Zechariah's dutiful service at the altar (Luke 1:8), John proclaiming the coming of Christ (Matthew 3:11, Mark 1:7, Luke 3:16, John 1:26), and John pointing out Jesus to his disciples (John 1:29 and 35).

Preface

The same preface is offered on the Vigil and on the day. For comments, *see p. 176.*

Communion Antiphon

Quoting Zechariah's hymn of praise upon the birth of his son, John, we proclaim the mercy of God and the dawn from on high visiting us. That Dawn is Jesus Christ. The antiphon was new to the post-Vatican II missal.

Prayer after Communion

On the anniversary of John's birth, we pray to know Christ who is the author of our rebirth. This was a new composition for the post-Vatican II missal.

Blessing

No special blessing is recommended, but see the comments for the Vigil, *p. 177.*

LECTIONARY

The Gospel account lies behind the texts of this Mass.

PRAYER OF THE FAITHFUL

Years A, B, C

God mercifully granted the infant John the Baptist to parents who were thought too old to conceive. Aware of God's mercy, we present our needs in hope.

— *Intercessions* —

O God,
whose servant John
proclaimed a baptism of repentance,
hear these prayers from those
    who seek your mercy.
Through Christ our Lord.

Saints Peter and Paul, Apostles, at the Vigil Mass

Overview

Tradition has it that on this day, on the Via Ostiense in Rome, Peter and Paul met each other and embraced on the way to their executions. It is likely that they actually died some years apart, but this day has been preserved as a reminder of their meeting and their martyrdom in Rome. Both are mentioned in Eucharistic Prayer I, also known as the Roman Canon because of its origins. It would be appropriate to use that prayer today.

When June 29 falls on a Sunday, this Mass is celebrated on Saturday night, replacing the Ordinary Time texts in the missal and the Lectionary.

Entrance Antiphon

We profess that Peter the apostle and Paul the teacher taught us the law of the Lord. The text does not come from any biblical source, but states the reason we praise God today. It was new to the post-Vatican II missal.

Collect

God provided the foundations of the Church in the ministry of Peter and Paul. We pray that they may help us toward eternal salvation. This prayer originated in the Veronese Sacramentary for the feast of Saint Andrew the Apostle. His name was replaced with those of Peter and Paul. Note the careful use of the word "intercession" here. We ask God to sustain us "by" the intercession of the saints; we are not telling God how to help us "through" the intercession of the saints.

Prayer over the Offerings

Fearful of our meager merit, we rejoice in God's loving kindness. The prayer is derived from one in the Verona Sacramentary for the celebration on this day at the church where Paul's remains are buried outside the walls of Rome.

Preface

Peter was foremost in confessing the faith, Paul in preaching. Peter established the church from the remnant of Israel; Paul taught the Gentiles. They shared a martyr's crown as they gathered together the family of Christ. This preface was newly composed for the post-Vatican II missal, though it borrows some thoughts from one in the Verona Sacramentary for this day. In Matthew 16:16–19 Peter confesses his faith in Christ and Jesus proclaims him the foundation of the church. Paul's mission to the Gentiles is noted in Acts 9:15, Galatians 1:15–16 and 2:7–8, 1 Timothy 2:7, and 2 Timothy 1:10–11. He calls himself an apostle in Romans 1:1, 1 Timothy 2:7, and 2 Timothy 1:10–11. Paul refers to the crown that awaits him in 2 Timothy 4:8.

Communion Antiphon

From the Gospel we recall the conversation between Jesus and Simon: "Do you love me?" As we share this Communion, we make the same profession of faith: "You know that I love you." In eighth-century sources, this antiphon was used for the Mass on the day, rather than the Vigil.

LECTIONARY

The second reading is reflected in the preface. The Communion antiphon comes from today's Gospel.

Prayer after Communion

Enlightened by the apostles, we ask for strength through this Eucharist. This prayer is based on one from the Paris Missal. It was added to *The Roman Missal* after the Second Vatican Council.

Blessing

The solemn blessing for this day reflects on the ministry and martyrdom of these two great apostles. This threefold blessing is based on one from the Hadrian Supplement.

PRAYER OF THE FAITHFUL

Years A, B, C

Jesus invited Simon to love him and to follow him. As faithful disciples, we present our prayers.

— *Intercessions* —

O God,
whose message resounds
to the ends of the world,
hear the prayers of this community
as we proclaim the glory of your name.
Through Christ our Lord.

Saints Peter and Paul, Apostles (June 29), at the Mass during the Day

Overview

When June 29 falls on a Sunday, this Mass replaces the Ordinary Time texts in the missal and the Lectionary.

Entrance Antiphon

Peter and Paul planted the church with their blood, drank the chalice of the Lord's suffering, and became the friends of God. The antiphon asserts why we celebrate this day. It relies on 1 Corinthians 3:6, the planting and watering of the church and the cup of suffering the disciples are asked to drink in Matthew 20:22 and Mark 10:39. This antiphon was new to the post-Vatican II missal.

Collect

We ask to follow the teachings of those who gave us the beginnings of our religion. The prayer is based on one from the Verona Sacramentary for the feast of Saint John the Evangelist, though the name and the ending were changed to fit today's feast.

Prayer over the Offerings

We pray that our gift may make us devoted to God. We also pray that the prayers of the apostles will accompany our request. This prayer was newly composed for the post-Vatican II missal.

Preface

See comments on *p. 180.*

Communion Antiphon

Drawing a text from today's Gospel, the antiphon reports the dialogue between Jesus and Peter, which proclaimed Jesus as the Christ and Peter as the rock of the church. In this Communion we proclaim Christ among us, and we build upon the foundation set by Peter and Paul. In eighth-century sources, this antiphon was used for the Vigil Mass, rather than this one.

Prayer after Communion

We pray for unity in heart and soul, as we persevere in breaking bread and in the teaching of the apostles. This prayer is based on one from the Paris Missal. It was inspired by the description of the apostolic community in Acts 2:42.

Blessing

See comments on *p. 181.*

PRAYER OF THE FAITHFUL

Years A, B, C

The angel of the Lord will rescue those who fear him. Let us reflect on God's great power as we present our prayers.

— *Intercessions* —

O God,
who built your church
    on the rock of Saint Peter,
hear the prayers of your chosen ones
who gather here in faith.
Through Christ our Lord.

LECTIONARY

The crown of glory that Paul awaits in the second reading is mentioned in the preface. The Communion antiphon comes from the Gospel.

The Transfiguration of the Lord (August 6)

Overview

Jesus took Peter, James, and John up a mountain where he was transfigured before them, giving them a glimpse of the glory to come. We celebrate the Transfiguration of the Lord every year on August 6. When that day falls on a Sunday, this Mass replaces the one for Ordinary Time because of the significance of this event in the life of Christ. It affects the readings in the Lectionary and the prayers in the missal.

Entrance Antiphon

We hear the Father's voice from a resplendent cloud, asking us to listen to his Son. Ears attentive, we begin this Eucharist. This antiphon was new to the post-Vatican II missal.

Collect

We ask that we may be coheirs with Jesus, the beloved Son, whose voice we hear and heed. This collect was used on this day in the pre-Vatican II missal. It makes several references to the Gospel of the day. The word "sonship" sounds gender-exclusive, but in this context it is thought to retain Christological meaning—servants share in the sonship of Christ.

Prayer over the Offerings

We ask to be cleansed of the stains of sin by the radiant splendor of the transfigured Son. This is essentially the same prayer from the pre-Vatican II missal. It first appeared in the eighth-century Gellone Sacramentary.

Preface

Christ revealed his glory, filling his human form with splendor. He removed the scandal of the cross and showed that his body, the church, would shine with the glory of the Head. This preface was a new composition for the post-Vatican II missal based on Sermon 51:3 of Pope Leo the Great. Before the council, the priest used the Christmas preface on this day. The new one relies on the Gospel accounts of the event (Matthew 17:1–9, Mark 9:2–10, and Luke 9:28–36). Paul speaks of looking on the glory of the Lord in 2 Corinthians 3:18. God has given us light in the face of Jesus Christ (2 Corinthians 4:6). The scandal of the cross is handled in Galatians 5:11. Philippians 2:5–7 says Jesus shared our human form, and Philippians 3:21 says we will be conformed to Christ's body in glory. The glory of Christ is noted in Ephesians 3:16 and Hebrews 1:3. The revelation of Christ is told in 2 Timothy 1:10 and 1 Peter 1:5, 4:13, and 5:10. First John 3:2 says that we will see Christ as he is.

Communion Antiphon

When Christ appears we shall be like him because we shall see him as he is. Christ has come in this Communion. We see, taste, and experience his glory among us. This antiphon was new to the post-Vatican II missal.

Prayer after Communion

We pray to be transformed into the likeness of Christ through this Communion. This prayer originated in the Paris Missal and was brought into *The Roman Missal* after the Second Vatican Council.

LECTIONARY

The Gospel story of each year tells of the event that inspired all the texts for this Mass.

Blessing

No solemn blessing or prayer over the people is recommended. You may choose one from the list for Ordinary Time. *See pp. 94–96.*

PRAYER OF THE FAITHFUL

Years A, B, C

We have been attentive to the prophetic message, as to a lamp shining in a dark place. Let us ask God to listen kindly to the prayers we offer through Christ.

— *Intercessions* —

O God,
the Most High over all the earth,
hear these prayers
and let justice and judgment extend
    to all the earth.
Through Christ our Lord.

The Assumption of the Blessed Virgin Mary, at the Vigil Mass

Overview

As we believe that Mary was conceived without original sin, so we believe that she was preserved from its adverse effects: sin and death. At the end of her life, Mary, God's special daughter, was assumed body and soul into heaven. We observe this mystery each year on August 15. These Mass texts are for the evening of August 14. When August 15 falls on a Sunday, this Mass is prayed on Saturday night.

The missal includes prayers for preparation for Mass, including one to the Blessed Virgin Mary.

Entrance Antiphon

Glorious things are said of Mary, exalted above the choirs of angels to eternal triumph with Christ. The text is inspired by Psalm 87:3, which announces that glorious things are said of the City of God. Just as Jerusalem is the place of God's presence in the Temple, so Mary was the place of God's presence in her womb. In her assumption, she takes a place higher than the angels, a teaching from scholasticism that Pope Pius XII repeated in his apostolic constitution *Munificentissimus Deus* (25). This antiphon was new to the post-Vatican II missal.

Collect

God looked on the lowliness of the Virgin Mary and raised her to grace. She became the mother of his only Son, and she was crowned with surpassing glory. We pray that we may be saved by the mystery of redemption and exalted on high. This prayer comes from the Cluny Missal of 1733. It was brought into *The Roman Missal* for the first time after the Second Vatican Council. The prayer is complex in Latin and in the revised English translation. The text refers to Mary's self-proclaimed lowliness in Luke 1:48. Paul says Jesus was born according to the flesh in Romans 1:3.

Prayer over the Offerings

We ask that this sacrifice may lead us to pardon and confirm us in perpetual thanksgiving. The original prayer comes from Ambrosian sources.

Preface

Mary's assumption marks the beginning and image of the Church's coming to perfection. She offers us a sign of hope and comfort. She did not experience the corruption of the tomb because her own body brought forth God's Son, the author of life. This preface was newly composed for the post-Vatican II missal, drawing many of its ideas from the Constitution on the Church (*Lumen gentium*) #68. Christ is called the author of life in Acts of the Apostles 3:15. The contrast between corruption and life is in Psalm 16:10–11 and in Acts 2:27–28.

Communion Antiphon

With a woman from the crowd hearing Jesus preach, we proclaim that Mary's womb is blessed, for she carried the Son of the eternal Father. Christ is present to us now in this Communion, and we carry him forth from this Mass. This antiphon was retained from the pre-Vatican II missal.

LECTIONARY

The Gospel provides the text for the Communion antiphon.

Prayer after Communion

Having partaken at this table, we pray to be freed from every threat of harm. This prayer from the Roman tradition was added to the missal after the Second Vatican Council.

Blessing

The solemn blessing for Masses of the Blessed Virgin Mary may be used. God willed to redeem the human race. We pray that God will protect us through Mary as we carry the gifts of spiritual joys and heavenly rewards. This threefold blessing comes from the Hadrian supplement.

PRAYER OF THE FAITHFUL

Years A, B, C

Those who hear the word of God and keep it are blessed indeed. Having listened with faith, let us pray in hope.

— *Intercessions* —

O God,
who give us the victory
through our Lord Jesus Christ,
as you bestowed grace on Mary,
grant us what we need
to enjoy your presence forever.
Through Christ our Lord.

The Assumption of the Blessed Virgin Mary (August 15), at the Mass during Day

Entrance Antiphon

In the book of Revelation, John sees a great sign in the heavens, a woman clothed with the sun. She is an image of Mary, crowned with glory in heaven. This antiphon was retained from the pre-Vatican II missal. In the alternate entrance antiphon we rejoice with the angels at the assumption of Mary. This was a new antiphon for the post-Vatican II missal.

Collect

God assumed Mary body and soul into heaven. We pray that we may be attentive to the things that are above, so that we may share her glory. This is the prayer from the pre-Vatican II missal. It refers to the teachings of *Munificentissimus Deus*. The phrase "always attentive to the things that are above" may allude to Colossians 3:2 or to Mary pondering the events of Jesus' young life in Luke 2:19 and 51.

Prayer over the Offerings

We ask that our hearts may constantly long for God. This is the same prayer from the pre-Vatican II missal.

Preface

See *p. 186.*

Communion Antiphon

Mary sings in her *Magnificat* that all generations will call her blessed because God has done great things for her. We too are blessed as we share this Communion because of the marvels God works in our lives, in this Mass. This antiphon appeared in the pre-Vatican II missal.

Prayer after Communion

We ask to be brought to the glory of the resurrection. This prayer also comes from the pre-Vatican II missal, but the request to grant prayers through the "merits" of the Blessed Virgin Mary was eliminated for the post-Vatican Ii missal. Here the words "through the intercession" are retained because they pertain more to "brought" than to "grant." We are not asking God to grant a prayer through Mary, but that we may be brought to glory through her. It's a subtle difference, but the point is that we do not tell God how to grant our prayers even as we rely on the help of the saints.

Blessing

See *p. 187.*

LECTIONARY

The first reading supplies the first option for the entrance antiphon. The Communion antiphon is drawn from the Gospel.

PRAYER OF THE FAITHFUL

Years A, B, C

Mary proclaimed the greatness of the Lord because he showed the strength of his arm and remembered his promise of mercy. Let us ask God to come to our aid.

— *Intercessions* —

O God,
who raised Christ from the dead
and bring to your side
    all who belong to him,
destroy every adverse power
and grant our prayers.
Through Christ our Lord.

The Exaltation of the Holy Cross (September 14)

Overview

Today's feast commemorates the day when the newly discovered relics of the true cross were first put on display for public veneration. It provides us an opportunity outside the season of Lent to reflect on the saving mystery of the cross of Christ.

You may want to draw attention to the crucifixes in your church. Decorate the processional cross for the liturgy.

The missal includes prayers of thanksgiving after Mass. One of them is addressed to Jesus Christ crucified.

Entrance Antiphon

With Saint Paul, we must glory in the cross of our Lord Christ, in whom is our salvation, life, and resurrection. This is the same antiphon that opens the Thursday of the Lord's Supper. It has been sung at this Mass since at least the eighth century.

Collect

As we have known the mystery of Christ on earth, we pray to receive the grace of his redemption in heaven. This is a slightly emended version of the prayer that appeared in the pre-Vatican II missal. This one explains the place of the cross in the mystery of salvation. Jesus accepted the Father's will in his prayer at Gethsemane (Matthew 26:42).

Prayer over the Offerings

Upon the altar of the cross, Jesus canceled the offense of the world. We pray that this sacrifice will cleanse us of our sins. Jesus' mission to take away sins is announced in John 1:29. The text is inspired by one from the Hadrian Sacramentary for the Third Sunday of Lent.

Preface

God placed our salvation on the wood of the cross. Where death arose, life would spring forth again. The evil one, who conquered Adam by means of a tree, was conquered through the tree of the cross of Christ. This preface comes from the pre-Vatican II missal. The story of the tree of Adam's sin is told in Genesis 3:1–7.

As an alternative, you may use the first preface of the Passion. *See pp. 48–49.*

Communion Antiphon

Jesus says that when he is lifted up, he will draw everyone to himself. We draw especially close to him in this Communion. This antiphon was new to the post-Vatican II missal.

Prayer after Communion

We ask God to bring to the resurrection those who are redeemed by the Cross. This prayer has been handed down in the tradition of *The Roman Missal*.

Blessing

No special blessing is recommended, but see the missal's solemn blessing for the Passion of the Lord.

LECTIONARY

The Gospel's message of salvation is echoed in the preface.

PRAYER OF THE FAITHFUL

Years A, B, C

God sent the Son into the world not for condemnation, but for salvation. Let us pray for help through the cross of Christ.

— Intercessions —

O God,
who heal the sick and forgive the sinner,
be merciful to us who remember your works
and grant our prayers.
Through Christ our Lord.

All Saints (November 1)

Overview

As the Church year enters its final month, the community turns its gaze toward the saints who live triumphantly in heaven. This Mass honors all the citizens of heaven, even those whose feasts are not on the universal calendar. When this day falls on a Sunday, the readings and prayers for All Saints replace the ones for Ordinary Time.

Which saints are depicted in your church in statuary and paintings? Is this an occasion to draw attention to them?

The missal includes some prayers of thanksgiving after Mass, including the famous *Anima Christi*. Its final petition asks for union with the saints.

Entrance Antiphon

We rejoice in God, celebrating a feast of all the saints. Even the angels rejoice and praise the Son of God with us. This is the traditional antiphon for this day, summoning all of creation to praise God for the saints. It is based on one from eighth-century sources for the feast of Saint Agatha on February 5.

Collect

We venerate all the saints in a single celebration. We ask for an abundance of God's reconciliation at the intercession of the saints. This is the same prayer that was in use in the pre-Vatican II missal. John sees a great multitude of saints in Revelation 7:9.

Prayer over the Offerings

We ask to experience the concern that the saints have for our salvation. After all, they have already been assured of their own. This prayer came from the Paris Missal and was

brought into *The Roman Missal* after the Second Vatican Council.

Preface

We celebrate the festival of the new Jerusalem, where many of our brothers and sisters already give God eternal praise. We pilgrims hasten eagerly to the same eternal city, rejoicing in the glory of the saints. Their glory gives us strength and good example. This preface was newly composed for the post-Vatican II missal. Galatians 4:26 calls Jerusalem our mother. Hebrews 11:13 calls us pilgrims. Our ascent to the heavenly Jerusalem is imagined in Hebrews 12:22. The everlasting city appears in Hebrews 13:14 and Revelation 21:10.

Communion Antiphon

Jesus promises that the blessed will see God, be called children of God, and possess the kingdom of heaven. In this Communion we pray to be numbered among them. This antiphon appeared in the pre-Vatican II missal.

LECTIONARY

The multitude of saints from the first reading is mentioned in the collect. The Communion antiphon comes from the Gospel.

192 | All Saints (November 1)

Prayer after Communion

We adore the Holy One, who is wonderful in all the holy ones. We ask for the holiness that will help us pass from this pilgrim's table to the heavenly banquet. This prayer was adopted from the Paris Missal for the post-Vatican II missal.

Blessing

We pray for God's unending blessing, devotion to our service, and entrance into the joys of our peaceful homeland. This solemn blessing was newly composed for the post-Vatican II missal.

PRAYER OF THE FAITHFUL

Years A, B, C

We are God's children now, and we shall see him as he is. Our hope is strong, and we offer these prayers in purity of heart.

— Intercessions —

O God,
look kindly upon the people
who long to see your face,
and grant these petitions.
Through Christ our Lord.

The Commemoration of All the Faithful Departed (All Souls Day)(November 2)

Overview

On the day after we commemorate all the saints, we pray for all the others who have died but are still awaiting their redemption. The Church's traditional belief in purgatory (*Catechism of the Catholic Church,* 1030–1032) lies behind today's observance. When November 2 falls on a Sunday, these Masses replace the ones for Ordinary Time. The Gloria is omitted, but the Creed is recited.

Traditionally a priest may celebrate three Masses today. Many of the faithful participate in three Masses as well.

Regarding music, this may be a good day to sing pieces you'd like people to know at funerals. Music for the final commendation and the *In paradisum* merit a place in local repertoire. But instruments should be used only to support the singing, and flowers should not adorn the altar (*Ceremonial of Bishops,* 397).

Appendix V offers several sample formularies for the Prayer of the Faithful. The last one is for Masses for the Dead, and it would be appropriate—or an appropriate model—today.

If there is a procession to the cemetery after Mass, see the Order for Visiting a Cemetery on All Souls Day (November 2), Memorial Day, or on the Anniversary of Death or Burial in the *Book of Blessings* (1734–1754). Mass may be celebrated at the cemetery. Wherever the Mass takes place, it may conclude with the sprinkling and incensing of the graves of the faithful departed (*Ceremonial of Bishops,* 399–403).

Entrance Antiphon

The death and resurrection of Jesus foreshadow our own. This message is stated from two of Paul's letters, forming the antiphon for this Mass. This was new to the post-Vatican II missal.

Collect

As our faith in the risen Christ is deepened, we seek new strength for our hope in the resurrection of our departed brothers and sisters. This is the plural version of one of the prayers for funerals during the Easter season. It was newly composed for the post-Vatican II missal. The Nicene Creed includes the expression "look forward to the resurrection."

Prayer over the Offerings

We ask God to look favorably on our offerings, that the faithful departed may be taken up into glory. This is the plural version of one of the prayers for funerals during the Easter season. It was newly composed for the post-Vatican II missal.

LECTIONARY

The readings from Masses for the Dead may be proclaimed. Many of the scriptures there inspired the texts of this Mass.

Preface

Any of the five prefaces for Masses for the Dead may be used. The first concerns the hope of resurrection in Christ. That hope consoles our sadness concerning death. Life is changed, not ended. Our earthly dwelling is dust compared with the eternal dwelling that awaits us in heaven. This is the preface from the pre-Vatican missal for Masses of the Dead. The hope of salvation is announced in Romans 8:24 and repeated in Titus 1:1–2, 2:13, and 3:6–7. Paul compares our body to an earthly dwelling place in 2 Corinthians 5:1–7. Philippians 3:20 says our dwelling place is in heaven.

The second preface announces that Christ died that we all might live. Christ is the One who accepted death that we might escape from dying, who chose to die that all might live. The preface was newly composed for the post-Vatican II missal, though it shares some thought with one for Thursday of the Easter Octave in the Ambrosian tradition. In John 11:50 Caiaphas unknowingly prophesies that one would die for the sake of the people. The thought is repeated in Romans 5:12 and again in 2 Corinthians 5:14.

The third preface is called "Christ, the salvation and the life." It proclaims Christ to be the salvation of the world, the life of the human race, and the resurrection of the dead. It was newly composed for the post-Vatican II missal, though it shares some vocabulary with a preface for the salvation of the living in the Gelasian Sacramentary. Jesus' name means "savior" (Matthew 1:21), and he is called the author of salvation in Hebrews 2:10. Jesus is called the life in John 1:4. He calls himself the resurrection and the life at the raising of Lazarus in John 11:25; and the way, the truth, and the life in John 14:6.

The fourth preface is called "From earthly life to heavenly glory." We come to birth when God summons us. We are governed by God's will. After we die, God shall raise us up to the glory of the resurrection. The text was newly composed for the post-Vatican II missal, but it was inspired by an early Ambrosian preface for the third, seventh, or thirtieth day after burial. Genesis 2:7 says that God formed Adam from the earth. The word for "governed" is the same word in Psalm 23 for the way God shepherds and leads us. Paul writes of the freedom from the law of sin in Romans 8:2 and 1 Corinthians 15:55–56.

The fifth preface concerns our resurrection through the victory of Christ. We deserve to perish, but when we die because of sin, we are called back to life with Christ. This was also newly composed for the post-Vatican II missal, but inspired by another early Ambrosian preface for the third, seventh or thirtieth day after burial. Paul writes of the salvation that is ours through Christ in Romans 5:12–17. The victory of death is proclaimed in 1 Corinthians 15:54–57 and in 1 John 5:4.

Communion Antiphon

Jesus is the resurrection and the life. Those who believe in him will never die. Our faith in the Resurrection leads to our faith in the presence of the risen Christ in this Communion. This antiphon was new to the post-Vatican II missal.

PRAYER OF THE FAITHFUL

Years A, B, C

Jesus went up the mountain to teach his disciples how to live. As we strive toward the mountain of God, let us present our needs.

— Intercessions —

O God,
whose Son proclaimed
that those who suffered persecution
   were blessed,
hear our prayers
and make us rejoice and be glad
   in our heavenly reward.
Through Christ our Lord.

Prayer after Communion

We pray that the faithful departed may pass over into a dwelling place of light and peace. This prayer was newly composed for the post-Vatican II missal. In the singular, it may be used for a funeral Mass in the Easter season.

Blessing

God created us and gave us the hope of rising again. We pray for pardon for ourselves and a place of light and peace for the dead. We ask that we may all live happily with Christ. This was a new composition for the post-Vatican II missal. The opening title of the God of all consolation is based on 2 Corinthians 1:3.

All Souls 2 (November 2)

Overview

This is the second suite of Mass texts that may be used among the three Masses for All Souls Day.

Entrance Antiphon

"Eternal rest grant unto them, O Lord, and let perpetual light shine upon them." This is the antiphon that gave the Requiem Mass its name: the first word is the Latin word for "rest." It also forms a couplet well known by faithful Catholics. The citation calls its source the Fourth Book of Esdras, which is known as the Second Book of Esdras in some Bibles. It is an apocryphal book, one that is regarded as holy, but not as holy as scripture. After Ezra appealed to Israel, they rejected him and refused the Lord's command. He prophesies to the nations that do hear and understand that perpetual light will shine on them for ever. This was the entrance antiphon for all three All Souls Day Masses in the pre-Vatican II missal.

Collect

God is the glory of the faithful and the life of the just. We have been redeemed by the death and resurrection of God's Son. We pray that the faithful departed may receive the joys of eternal happiness. It is based on a prayer following a reading from Deuteronomy in the Gelasian Sacramentary's Mass for the Pentecost Vigil. The newer Latin prayer is complex, as is the revised English translation.

Prayer over the Offerings

We pray that God will wash away the sins of the faithful departed in the blood of Christ, to purify those who were cleansed in baptism.

This prayer was newly composed for the post-Vatican II missal, but it is based on one from the Mozarabic Rite. It is based on Revelation 7:14 and 22:14.

Preface

Any of the five prefaces for Masses for the Dead may be used. *See p. 195.*

Communion Antiphon

We pray that perpetual light may shine on the faithful departed, who will dwell with the saints because of God's mercy for them. This is based on the same passage as the entrance antiphon, and is the traditional Communion antiphon for funeral Masses. It was used at all three Masses on All Souls Day in the pre-Vatican II missal.

Prayer after Communion

We pray that the faithful departed, cleansed by the paschal mysteries, may glory in the Resurrection. This prayer was newly composed for the post-Vatican II missal, but also based on one from the Mozarabic Rite.

Blessing

The solemn blessing for Masses for the Dead may be used. *See p. 196.*

LECTIONARY

The readings from Masses for the Dead may be proclaimed. Many of the scriptures there inspired the texts of this Mass.

PRAYER OF THE FAITHFUL

Years A, B, C

Jesus invited those who labor and are burdened to come to him. Let us approach him in faith, that God will listen favorably to our prayers.

— Intercessions —

O God,
who hide your mysteries from the wise
and reveal them to children,
show us your wisdom and grant our prayers.
Through Christ our Lord.

All Souls 3 (November 2)

Overview

This is the third set of texts for commemorating the faithful departed.

Entrance Antiphon

God, who raised Jesus from the dead, will bring life to us because of the Holy Spirit within us. This Mass begins with confident faith. The antiphon was new to the post-Vatican II missal.

Collect

Conquering death, the Son of God passed over to the realm of heaven. We pray that the faithful departed may gaze eternally on their Creator and Redeemer. This was newly composed for the post-Vatican II missal, based on Mozarabic sources.

Prayer over the Offerings

We pray that the faithful departed may merit eternal life, set free from death by this sacrifice. This was newly composed for the post-Vatican II missal.

Preface

Any of the five prefaces for Masses for the Dead may be used. *See p. 195.*

Communion Antiphon

We await our savior, Jesus Christ, who will change our earthly body and conform it to his. We reflect on his eternal presence as we consume the Body and Blood of Christ. This antiphon was new to the post-Vatican II missal.

Prayer after Communion

We ask God to bestow mercy upon the faithful departed, that those who received baptism may have the fullness of eternal joy. The prayer is based on one from the Gelasian Sacramentary's prayers for Mass at cemeteries.

Blessing

The solemn blessing for Masses for the Dead may be offered. *See p. 196.*

PRAYER OF THE FAITHFUL

Years A, B, C

Jesus promised a place in the kingdom for those who cared for the hungry. Let us pray for all who are in need.

— Intercessions —

O God,
who are present in the hungry,
grant these prayers
and help us to see your face.
Through Christ our Lord.

LECTIONARY

The readings from Masses for the Dead may be proclaimed. Many of the scriptures there inspired the texts of this Mass.

The Dedication of the Lateran Basilica (November 9)

Overview

Today marks the anniversary of the dedication of the cathedral of the city of Rome. It is named Saint John after the Baptist and the Evangelist. It is called "Lateran" because the Lateran family originally owned the property. After the Edict of Constantine, churches began to spread, and this is regarded as the first church ever built, the mother church of all Christianity. When this feast falls on a Sunday, it is observed in Catholic churches throughout the world, replacing the texts for Ordinary Time. This would be an appropriate day to use the Roman Canon—Eucharistic Prayer I.

Entrance Antiphon

Two options are given for the entrance antiphon, both from Revelation 21. In the first, John sees the new Jerusalem coming down from heaven. The second proclaims that it is the dwelling place of God, and that we are his people. As we celebrate the anniversary of the dedication of the world's cathedral church, we look for the day when we will dwell together in the place it represents. Both were new to the post-Vatican II missal.

Collect

Two options for the collect are given, the same ones offered in the Commons for the anniversary of the dedication of a church outside the church actually being remembered; for example, each parish should use these texts for the anniversary of the dedication of the cathedral church in its diocese. All the texts of this Mass are also found in those Commons.

God's eternal dwelling place is made from living and chosen stones. We pray for the growth that will build up the heavenly Jerusalem. The text is based on one from the Gellone Sacramentary and on 1 Peter 2:5. The heavenly Jerusalem is found in Revelation 21:2–3.

The alternative prayer recalls that God named the Church as his bride. We pray to revere, love, and follow God, attaining the promises of heaven. The image is based on Revelation 21:2 and on a prayer from the Gellone Sacramentary.

Prayer over the Offerings

We pray that those who seek God's favor in this place may receive an answer to their prayers. This oration is based on a text in the Hadrian Sacramentary for the dedication of a church.

Preface

God dwells in a house of prayer to perfect us as the temple of the Holy Spirit. Each year God sanctifies the Church in visible buildings, so that the Church may be given heavenly glory. This preface was newly composed for the post-Vatican II missal. The concept of a house of prayer is found in Isaiah 56:7. Jesus quotes this when cleansing the Temple (Matthew 21:13, Mark 11:17, and Luke 19:46). Paul calls us the temple of the Holy Spirit in 1 Corinthians 6:19. The assistance that Christ gives is noted in Ephesians 5:25–26. The new Jerusalem is called the bride of Christ in Revelation 21:2.

LECTIONARY

Any of the texts from the Mass of Dedication of a Church may be used, many of which inspired the prayers for this day.

Communion Antiphon

We are built up as living stones into a spiritual house and a holy priesthood. We are the body of Christ, sharing the Body of Christ. This antiphon was new to the post-Vatican II missal.

Prayer after Communion

The Church on earth foreshadows the Jerusalem above. We ask to be made the temple of God's grace and enter the dwelling place of glory. This prayer is based on one from the Paris Missal.

Blessing

The solemn blessing for a church dedication may be used. God has gathered us to commemorate the dedication of this church, and has willed that all his scattered children be gathered. We pray to become his temple, the dwelling of the Holy Spirit, and that God may dwell in us. The blessing comes from a Frankish Gelasian Sacramentary, and it relies on 1 Corinthians 6:19 and Romans 8:32.

PRAYER OF THE FAITHFUL

Years A, B, C

The disciples believed the scripture and the word that Jesus had spoken. Gathered in this holy place, hearing God's own word, we present our prayers.

— Intercessions —

O God,
whose holy City rejoice in the waters
of baptism,
hear the prayers of your faithful ones.
Through Christ our Lord.

The Immaculate Conception of the Blessed Virgin Mary (December 8)
Patronal Feastday of the United States of America

Overview

The Church believes that Mary was conceived without original sin, and that she lived her entire life free of sin. Gabriel calls her "full of grace," and this is the logical conclusion.

When December 8 falls on a Sunday, the observance is transferred to Monday, December 9 because the Second Sunday of Advent ranks higher in the liturgical calendar. The observance transfers, but not the obligation. The liturgy is observed, but not the holy day.

Among the prayers of thanksgiving after Mass the missal includes two to the Blessed Virgin Mary.

Entrance Antiphon

Jerusalem sings with joy that God has clothed the city in salvation, surrounded it with justice, and adorned it like a bejeweled bride. We sing this as the Church, and we can imagine Mary singing it, too. From before her birth, God clothed her in the mystery of salvation.

Collect

God preserved Mary from every stain to make her a worthy dwelling place for his Son. As she was immaculate, we pray that we may also be cleansed and admitted into God's presence. The prayer is the same one from the pre-Vatican II missal, which was inspired by the Apostolic Constitution of Pope Pius IX on the Immaculate Conception.

Prayer over the Offerings

We believe that Mary was untouched by any stain of sin through God's prevenient grace.

We ask that with her intercession we may be delivered from all our faults. The prayer acknowledges that we sin, though Mary did not. This is basically the same prayer from the pre-Vatican II missal. It deals with the doctrine of prevenient grace—that God loves us first.

Preface

God preserved Mary from original sin, preparing a worthy mother for his Son. Mary signifies the beginning of the church, God's spotless bride. She would bring forth the innocent Lamb who would wipe away our offenses. She is our advocate and model. This was a new composition for the post-Vatican II missal, based on the Dogmatic Constitution of the Church, *Lumen gentium*, 59 and 65. The spotless lamb appears in Exodus 12:5. The beauty of the bride recalls the Song of Songs 1:4. The angel Gabriel calls the Virgin Mary full of grace in Luke 1:28. Ephesians 5:27 says the church has no stain or wrinkle. Hebrews 7:26 calls Jesus innocent.

LECTIONARY

From the Gospel, Mary's title "full of grace" lies behind many of the prayers of this day.

Communion Antiphon

We sing to Mary that glorious things are spoken about her, for the sun of justice was born from her. This antiphon is inspired by Psalm 87:3. The same verse lies behind the entrance antiphon for the Vigil Mass for the Assumption of Mary *(p. 186)*.

Prayer after Communion

We pray that God will heal in us the wounds of original sin, from which Mary as the Immaculate Conception was preserved. This prayer is the same one from the pre-Vatican II missal.

Blessing

The solemn blessing for Masses of the Blessed Virgin Mary may be used. *See p. 187.*

PRAYER OF THE FAITHFUL

Years A, B, C

Through the power of the Holy Spirit, God worked marvels for the Virgin Mary. With trust in God's amazing power, we make known our needs.

— *Intercessions* —

O God,
who have done wondrous deeds
and won victory by your strong right hand,
show us your power
and grant these prayers.
Through Christ our Lord.

Timeline

1st c: The New Testament

2nd c.:   The *Didache* and the *Apologies* of Justin Martyr

3rd–4th c.: The Apostolic Tradition and the Apostolic Constitutions

4th c.:   Earliest known form of Roman Canon, in Ambrose of Milan

5th– 6th c.: The Rotulus of Ravenna

6th c.:   The Verona Sacramentary

7th c.:   The Gelasian Sacramentary

7th–8th c.: The Gothic Missal

8th c.:   The Hadrian Sacramentary

8th c.:   The Gellone Sacramentary

9th c.:   The Hadrian Sacramentary Supplement

9th c.:   The Sacramentary of Bergamo

14th c.:   The Paris Missal

1474:   First edition of the *Missale Romanum*

1570:   Publication of the *Missale Romanum* after the Council of Trent

1962:   Last publication of Trent's *Missale Romanum*

1970:   Publication of the *Missale Romanum* after the Second Vatican Council

1974:   Publication of the first edition of the Sacramentary in English

1975:   Publication of the second edition of the *Missale Romanum* after the Second Vatican Council

1985:   Publication of the second edition of the Sacramentary in English

2001:   Publication of new rules for translation in *Liturgiam authenticam*

2002:   Publication of the third edition of the *Missale Romanum* after the Second Vatican Council

2008:   Reprint of the 2002 *Missale Romanum* with a few corrections and additions

2011:   Publication of the third edition of *The Roman Missal* (formerly the Sacramentary) in English

Glossary

Bergamo Sacramentary. A ninth-century collection of prayers from the Ambrosian Rite, a non-Roman Rite centered in Milan, Italy.

Gelasian Sacramentary. A book of prayers said by the presider at Mass, copied c. 750, but containing texts dating to the seventh century or earlier.

Gellone Sacramentary. An edition of the Gelasian Sacramentary dating to about the eighth century.

General Instruction of the Roman Missal. The official explanation of how the Mass is celebrated and how *The Roman Missal* is used.

Gothic Missal. A collection of prayers from the non-Roman West, dating to the seventh to eighth centuries.

Hadrian Sacramentary. A papal sacramentary containing earlier material, sent by Hadrian I to Charlemagne in the eighth century to spread the collected texts of the Roman Rite.

Order of Mass. The "script" of dialogues, prayers, and rubrics followed by all ministers at every Mass.

Paris Missal. A book for the Mass from the late fourteenth century, including some prayers not found in the 1474 edition of *The Roman Missal*.

Post-Vatican II Missal. The *Missale Romanum* published in 1970 from which the English Sacramentary was translated.

Presidential prayers. The prayers that the priest says aloud on behalf of the gathered assembly. These include the collect (formerly the opening prayer), the prayer over the offerings, the preface, and the prayer after Communion. Eucharistic Prayers are also presidential prayers, but they are usually considered in a category of their own.

The Roman Missal. The official book of prayers for the Roman Catholic Mass. The present edition replaces the book formerly known as the Sacramentary.

Rotulus of Ravenna. A fifth- to sixth-century collection of prayers rediscovered in the nineteenth century. Some of its contents were included in the post-Vatican II missal.

Sacramentary. The English translation of *The Roman Missal* that was in use from 1970 to 2011. The present *Roman Missal* is another edition of the Sacramentary, with a new English title.

Verona Sacramentary. A collection of papal Mass prayers adapted for use by priests in the churches of Rome, dating to about the sixth century.

Bibliography

Antiphonale Missarum Sextuplex. Ed. Dom René-Jean Hesbert, Freiburg-im-Breisgau: Herder, 1985.

Appreciating the Collect: An Irenic Methodology. Ed. James G. Leachman and Daniel P. McCarthy. *Liturgiam Æstimare*: Appreciating the Liturgy. Farnborough, Hampshire: Saint Michael's Abbey Press, 2008.

Johnson, Cuthbert. "The Sources of *The Roman Missal* (1975): *Proprium de tempore, proprium de sanctis.*" *Notitiae* 32:354/355/356 (Jan–Feb–Mar 1996 – 1/3):3–180.

Johnson, Cuthbert, and Ward, Anthony. "The Sources of *The Roman Missal* (1975): Advent, Christmas." *Notitiae* 22:240–241–242 (July–August–September 1986 – 7–8–9):441–747.

McCarthy, Daniel. *Listen to the Word: Commentaries on Selected Opening Prayers of Sundays and Feasts with Sample Homilies.* London: The Tablet Publishing Company Limited, 2009.

Moore, Gerard. *A Study of the Relationship of the Christian People to God as Expressed in the Collects for the Sundays in Ordinary Time in* The Roman Missal *as Published by Authority of Paul VI (1975).* Catholic University of America: Washington DC, 1996.

Ward, Anthony. "The Palm Sunday Mass Formulary in the 2000 'Missale Romanum.' " *Notitiae* 515–516/7–8 (August 2009):392–428.

Ward, Anthony, and Johnson, Cuthbert. *The Prefaces of The Roman Missal: A Source Compendium with Concordance and Indices.* Congregation for Divine Worship. Rome: Tipografia Poliglotta Vaticana, 1989.